W9-CAL-408

BIOMES OF THE EARTH

# GRASSLANDS

Michael Allaby

Illustrations by
Richard Garratt

CHELSEA HOUSE
PUBLISHERS
An imprint of Infobase Publishing

# Grasslands

Chelsea House
An imprint of Infobase Publishing
132 West 31st Street
New York NY 10001

**Library of Congress Cataloging-in-Publication Data**
Allaby, Michael.
  Grasslands / author, Michael Allaby ; illustrations by Richard Garratt.
    p. cm.—(Biomes of the Earth)
  Includes bibliographical references and index.
  ISBN 0-8160-5323-5
  1. Grassland ecology—Juvenile literature. 2. Grasslands—Juvenile literature. I. Garratt, Richard, ill. II. Title. III. Series.
  QH541.5.P7A38 2006
  577.4—dc22                                    2005005615

Text design by David Strelecky
Cover design by Cathy Rincon
Illustrations by Richard Garratt
Photo research by Elizabeth H. Oakes

Printed in China

CP FOF 10 9 8 7 6 5 4 3 2 1

This book is printed on acid-free paper.

*From Richard Garratt:*
*To Chantal, who has lightened my darkness.*

# CONTENTS

## CHAPTER 4
# HISTORY OF GRASSLANDS

## CHAPTER 5
# LIFE ON THE GRASSLANDS

# PREFACE

Earth is a remarkable planet. There is nowhere else in our solar system where life can survive in such a great diversity of forms. As far as we can currently tell, our planet is unique. Isolated in the barren emptiness of space, here on Earth we are surrounded by a remarkable range of living things, from the bacteria that inhabit the soil to the great whales that migrate through the oceans, from the giant redwood trees of the Pacific forests to the mosses that grow on urban side-walks. In a desolate universe, Earth teems with life in a bewildering variety of forms.

One of the most exciting things about the Earth is the rich pattern of plant and animal communities that exists over its surface. The hot, wet conditions of the equatorial regions support dense rain forests with tall canopies occupied by a wealth of animals, some of which may never touch the ground. The cold, bleak conditions of the polar regions, on the other hand, sustain a much lower variety of species of plants and animals, but those that do survive under such harsh conditions have remarkable adaptations to their test-ing environment. Between these two extremes lie many other types of complex communities, each well suited to the particular conditions of climate prevailing in its region. Scientists call these communities *biomes*.

The different biomes of the world have much in common with one another. Each has a plant component, which is responsible for trapping the energy of the Sun and making it available to the other members of the community. Each has grazing animals, both large and small, that take advantage of the store of energy found within the bodies of plants. Then come the predators, ranging from tiny spiders that feed upon even smaller insects to tigers, eagles, and polar bears that sur-vive by preying upon large animals. All of these living things form a complicated network of feeding interactions, and, at the base of the system, microbes in the soil are ready to consume the energy-rich plant litter or dead animal flesh that remains. The biome, then, is an integrated unit within which each species plays its particular role.

This set of books aims to outline the main features of each of the Earth's major biomes. The biomes covered include the tundra habitats of polar regions and high mountains, the taiga (boreal forest) and temperate forests of somewhat warmer lands, the grasslands of the prairies and the tropical savanna, the deserts of the world's most arid locations, and the tropical forests of the equatorial regions. The wetlands of the world, together with river and lake habitats, do not lie neatly in climatic zones over the surface of the Earth but are scattered over the land. And the oceans are an exception to every rule. Massive in their extent, they form an interconnecting body of water extending down into unexplored depths, gently moved by global currents.

Humans have had an immense impact on the environment of the Earth over the past 10,000 years since the last Ice Age. There is no biome that remains unaffected by the presence of the human species. Indeed, we have created our own biome in the form of agricultural and urban lands, where people dwell in greatest densities. The farms and cities of the Earth have their own distinctive climates and natural history, so they can be regarded as a kind of artificial biome that people have created, and they are considered as a separate biome in this set.

Each biome is the subject of a separate volume. Each richly illustrated book describes the global distribution, the climate, the rocks and soils, the plants and animals, the history, and the environmental problems found within each biome. Together, the set provides students with a sound basis for understanding the wealth of the Earth's biodiversity, the factors that influence it, and the future dangers that face the planet and our species.

Is there any practical value in studying the biomes of the Earth? Perhaps the most compelling reason to understand the way in which biomes function is to enable us to conserve their rich biological resources. The world's productivity is the basis of the human food supply. The world's biodiversity holds a wealth of unknown treasures, sources of drugs and medicines that will help to improve the quality of life. Above all, the world's biomes are a constant source of wonder, excitement, recreation, and inspiration that feed not only our bodies but also our minds and spirits. These books aim to provide the information about biomes that readers need in order to understand their function, draw upon their resources, and, most of all, enjoy their diversity.

# ACKNOWLEDGMENTS

Richard Garratt drew all of the diagrams and maps that appear in this book. Richard and I have been working together for many years in a collaboration that succeeds because Richard has a genius for translating the weird electronic squiggles I send him into clear, simple artwork of the highest quality. As always, I am grateful to him for all his hard work. I also wish to thank Elizabeth Oakes for her fine work as a photo researcher.

I must thank Frank K. Darmstadt, Executive Editor, at Chelsea House. Frank shaped this series of books and guided them through all the stages of their development. His encouragement, patience, and good humor have been immensely valuable.

I am especially grateful to Dorothy Cummings, project editor. Her close attention to detail sharpened explanations that had been vague, corrected my mistakes and inconsistencies, and identified places where I repeated myself. And occasionally Dorothy was able to perform the most important service of all: She intervened in time to stop me making a fool of myself. No author could ask for more. This is a much better book than it would have been without her hard work and dedication.

Michael Allaby
Tighnabruaich
Argyll
Scotland
www.michaelallaby.com

# INTRODUCTION

## What are grasslands?

A wave moves over the landscape as the rustling grass bows before the wind and then rises again. Another wave follows the first, and then another, and the eye follows the rippling motion across the plain until each wave disappears in the haze that obscures the distant horizon. Overhead the cloudless sky is the palest blue, and immensely large. On a moonless night the sky blazes with the light from countless millions of stars.

Grass is the predominant vegetation, but it is mixed with a bewildering variety of other herbs. Scattered shrubs and small belts of trees lining the river courses relieve what might otherwise be a monotonous scene. Birds fly overhead, foraging for insects or seeds, and high above them the hawks circle slowly, alert to the tiniest flicker of movement that betrays the presence of a small animal. Mice and ground squirrels live on and below the ground, feeding on the vegetation and ever watchful for snakes as well as birds of prey. Herds of bigger animals graze the pasture and browse the leaves of shrubs and the lower branches of the trees.

This is one of the world's great grasslands, which lie between the temperate forests and the semiarid lands bordering the desert, where meager seasonal rains allow a sparse, coarse pasture to survive. Grasslands once covered more than 1 million square miles (2.59 million km²) in North America, extending from Illinois to Colorado and from Alberta to Texas.

It is a place of changing colors. In winter the northern grasslands are white, hidden beneath a covering of snow. Southern grasslands see little or no snow, and there the land remains brown through the winter. In spring both are green, as the returning warmth and moisture from the rain or melting snow stimulate new plant growth. As the hot, dry summer progresses, the plants wilt and then turn yellow and brown.

Grasslands occur in the deep interior of continents, far from the ocean, where rainfall is generally low. Temperate grasslands receive an average 12–40 inches (305–1,016 mm) of rain a year and tropical grasslands 25–60 inches (635–1,524 mm). Rainfall is not distributed evenly through the year, however. In temperate regions there is a dry season that begins in the late summer, fall, or winter and continues until spring. In the Tropics the dry season begins in early summer and most of the rain falls in the winter.

Although grasses are the most abundant plants in all grassland, there are many types of grasses, and grasslands are not all the same. Tropical grasslands lie between the edge of the subtropical deserts and the tropical forests. They are often called *savanna* (or *savannah*) grasslands, a name that seems to have originated in the Caribbean region and to have entered English from *zavana*, which was the Spanish form of the original name. Savanna grasslands extend across Africa as two belts, one on each side of the equator. Grasslands of this type also occur in South America, southern Asia, and Australia. They are usually dominated by grasses five to six feet (1.5–1.8 m) tall, interspersed with thorn trees that are mostly less than 33 feet (10 m) tall and have distinctive flat tops.

Savanna grasslands have regional names. They are called *llanos* in Venezuela and Colombia, and *campo cerrado* and *campo sujo* are two different varieties of savanna found in Brazil. The Australian grasslands are identified not by their grasses, but by the species of acacia trees that grow among the grasses: *brigalow scrub* and *mulga scrub.*

Temperate grasslands occur between the subtropical deserts and the temperate forests or the coniferous forest known as *taiga.* Where rainfall is relatively high, the grasses are about five feet (1.5 m) tall. These are the typical grasses of North American *prairie* and they occur on the eastern side of the continent. Shorter grasses—less than 18 inches (45 cm) tall—grow on the drier western side, in the *plains,* although nowadays the two types of grassland are usually called tallgrass and short-grass prairie. *Palouse prairie,* also called *bunchgrass prairie,* grows in Washington State and British Columbia.

In South America the temperate grassland is called *pampa.* The Eurasian grasslands stretch from Hungary in the west, across Russia, and as far as Mongolia and China. They are called *puszta* in Hungary and *steppe* in Russia. There are two main types of steppe. *Meadow steppe* occurs in the north, where the climate is relatively moist, allowing many flowering herbs to flourish. *Dry steppe* occurs in the south and supports fewer herbs. Southern African grasslands are called *veld* or *grassveld.*

Climate determines the growing season for plants anywhere in the world, and grasslands are no exception. In temperate regions plants are able to grow when the temperature is above freezing. The growing season in the prairie lasts from about 150 days in the palouse prairie to 270 days in Texas. In the Tropics, where the temperature is warm enough for plant growth throughout the year, rainfall is the crucial factor.

A type of vegetation that covers a very large area in continents around the world is called a *biome,* and geographers divide the entire world into a series of biomes. The species of plants vary from one part of a biome to another; what matters is that the predominant plants are all similar. They might be temperate trees, for example, or tropical trees, or grasses, but regardless of the species, North American grassland is much more similar to South American, Eurasian, African, or Australian grassland than any of these is to forest.

All biomes are important to us, but the grassland biome is especially important. Most of our staple foods, including wheat, rice, barley, rye, corn (maize), and sugarcane, are grasses, and wheat, barley, and rye were first cultivated on the grasslands of what are now Turkey and Iraq. Our cereal and livestock farms are like artificial grassland and in many places the lands they occupy were natural grasslands until farmers cleared away the wild grasses to grow cultivated grasses.

Some areas of natural grassland are not suitable for farming, usually because they experience severe and prolonged drought from time to time, but many make good farmland. This means they are valuable, and over the centuries most of the natural grassland has been converted into farmland. When the grassland is plowed, the plants that grow among the grasses are destroyed along with the grasses themselves, and many of the animals that find food and shelter among the plants die or move away. If we wish the members of the natural grassland community to survive, we must preserve areas of the grassland itself.

## CHAPTER 1

# GEOGRAPHY
# OF GRASSLANDS

## Where grasslands occur

Grasslands once covered more than 40 percent of the Earth's land surface. Grasses are geographically more widespread than any other group of plants, and grasslands compose one of the most extensive types of vegetation on the planet. As the map shows, they are found on every continent except Antarctica.

Although the map shows the areas where grassland is the natural vegetation, in fact large areas of grassland have been converted to farmland. Where the rainfall is sufficient to support farming, the abundant sunshine, level plains, and fertile soils are ideal for growing wheat and corn. These crops are also grasses, so the conversion is from one type of grassland to another. *Agricultural grassland* may also consist of pasture grasses that have been sown to feed livestock.

Grasses thrive in climates that are too dry for most trees. They tolerate grazing by animals (see "How grasses work" on pages 85–90), but they cannot survive in deep shade. Consequently natural grasslands occupy those parts of the world that are neither desert, which is too dry, nor forest, which is too shady.

The map divides grasslands into two types—temperate grassland and tropical savanna grassland. Temperate grassland occurs in regions with a temperate climate and is most widespread in North America, eastern Europe, Turkey and northern Iran, central Asia, and part of southern China. There is much less land in the Southern Hemisphere to the south of the tropic of Capricorn, and that is why southern temperate grasslands are confined to part of Argentina and a small area of Peru and South Africa.

Savanna grassland covers a large part of Africa, extending from the southern edge of the Sahara to the southeastern tip

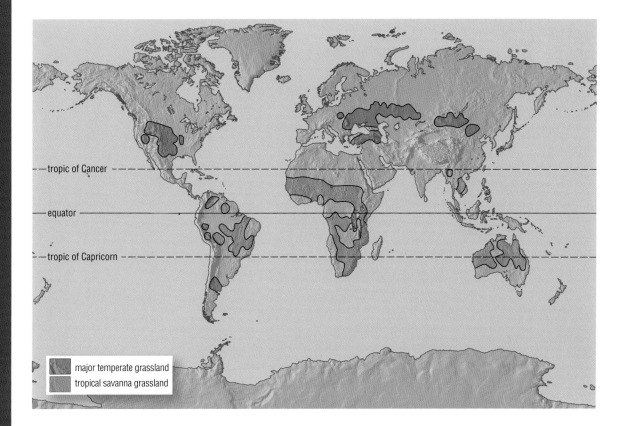

*Distribution of temperate and tropical grasslands. Grasslands tend to occupy the interior of continents, where the rainfall is sparse because of the distance from the ocean.*

of the continent, broken only by areas of tropical forest. There are also large areas of savanna in South America and Australia.

The climatic conditions that favor grasslands also occur in mountainous regions. Temperature decreases with altitude, and there is a level beyond which the mountain climate is too cold for trees. At this height—and it varies according to the latitude (see "Upland grasslands" on pages 22–25)—the growing season is so short that the needles of coniferous trees have insufficient time to mature before they are killed by frost. Trees cannot survive, but grasses and many flowering herbs are able to do so. Between the upper limit for tree growth, called the *tree line,* and the region of bare rock and permanent snow, there are mountain grasslands, more often known as *alpine meadows.* Their composition varies from place to place, and in the Tropics there are also *alpine savannas.* Alpine grasslands occur in mountain ranges throughout the world.

Grasses are quick to invade land that has been cleared of other types of vegetation. Ordinarily these grasses will disappear if taller plants, such as shrubs and trees, become established and shade the ground. There are places, however, where this has not been allowed to occur, resulting in *successional grasslands* that are maintained by burning or grazing, both of which destroy shrub and tree seedlings. Successional savanna grassland has replaced tropical forest in many areas. Farmers clear an area of forest, farm it for a few years, and then abandon it to allow the soil to recover fertility. If they return to the site before the forest has had time to reclaim it, over a number of these cycles grasses may replace the trees. Such farming has not only extended the boundary of the savanna grassland into what was formerly forest; it has also produced areas of grassland inside the forest.

## Temperate grasslands and tropical grasslands

Temperate and tropical grasslands are distinguished by their climate. They occur inland and are confined to particular latitudes, because climate characteristics largely depend on distance from the equator and from the ocean (see the sidebar "How climates are classified" on page 49).

Different climates suit different types of plant. Although grass is the most obvious and abundant vegetation in any grassland, there are many species of grass and those found in one type of grassland could not survive in another. All grasses share certain characteristics (see "What is grass?" on pages 82–84) that make them resemble each other more closely than they resemble any other type of plant, such as a tree. But the great variety among grasses gives each kind of grassland a distinctive appearance, and there is a great contrast between temperate and tropical grasslands.

Temperate grasslands consist of grasses and herbs that extend across vast plains with occasional low, rolling hills. Trees grow only beside rivers—and rivers are often many miles apart. Although there are also areas of tropical grassland that contain only grasses and herbs, woody plants—shrubs and trees—grow in most savanna grasslands. The number of woody plants varies from place to place, but because of them much of the savanna is open woodland or parkland, in which scattered shrubs and trees are surrounded by grass. Depending on the number of woody plants, tropical grasslands are divided into three categories: *savanna woodland, savanna parkland,* and *savanna grassland.* In savanna woodland the tree canopy covers more than 50 percent of the ground; in savanna parkland it covers between 20 percent and 50 percent; and in savanna grassland it covers less than 20 percent.

The weather is always warm everywhere in the savanna. The average temperature is higher than 64°F (18°C) throughout the year, although occasionally it can fall as low as 40°F (4°C). It rises to 80°–100°F (27°–38°C) in summer. The three to five months of winter are not cold; they are dry (see "Dry seasons and rainy seasons" on pages 51–55). During the rainy season the amount of rainfall ranges from about two inches (50 mm) near the desert edge to 60 inches (1,525 mm) close to the edge of the tropical rain forest. Where rainfall is heavy, it often causes flooding. Savanna woodland occurs in the wetter areas and savanna grassland prevails where the rainfall is low.

Temperate grassland also grows in a fairly dry climate where prolonged drought occurs from time to time. Droughts occasionally last for 10 years (see "The Dust Bowl" on pages 55–57). Annual rainfall on the North American grasslands averages about 40 inches (1,016 mm) in the east, decreasing to about 10 inches (250 mm) in the west, and it occurs mainly in winter. As well as being dry, summers are hot, with temperatures rising to 100°F (38°C). Winters are cold, with daytime temperatures falling to about 10°F (–12°C) or sometimes much lower. The lowest temperature ever recorded in Winnipeg, Manitoba, was –54°F (–48°C), and Saskatoon, Saskatchewan, has recorded –55°F (–48°C). High summer temperatures and the incessant wind mean that the rate of evaporation is high, making the soil very dry.

## Prairie

The first Europeans to gaze upon the grasslands of North America were French. They approached from the east and saw before them an ocean of waving grass extending across the level plain as far as the horizon. As they moved through it and the horizon receded, the grassland continued to stretch for as far as they could see. It seemed endless. The French called it *la prairie,* "the meadow."

Nowadays people often call the whole of the North American grassland "prairie," but as the map shows, there are several distinct types of grassland. Originally only the tall-grass grassland was called prairie. The short-grass grassland was known simply as "the plains," and the area of overlap

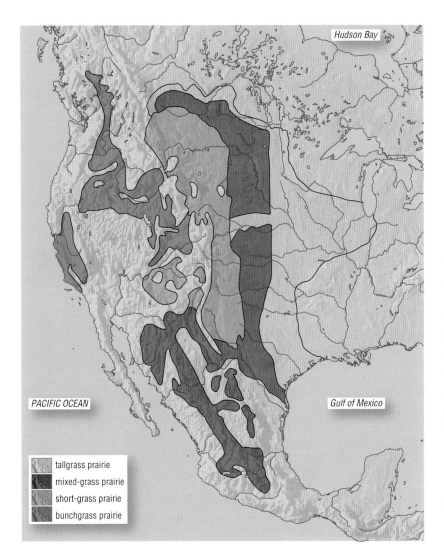

Hudson Bay

PACIFIC OCEAN

Gulf of Mexico

tallgrass prairie
mixed-grass prairie
short-grass prairie
bunchgrass prairie

*Prairie. There are several types of prairie. Tallgrass prairie occurs in the east, where the climate is moister than it is farther west, where short-grass prairie is found. Mixed-grass prairie forms a wide boundary between the two and contains both tall and short grasses. Bunchgrass and desert grassland are found to the west and south of the short-grass prairie.*

between the two was called "mixed prairie." Bunchgrass prairie, or *palouse prairie,* occurs to the west of the Rocky Mountains from Colorado to Oregon and northward to British Columbia, and in part of California. Tallgrass and short-grass areas are defined by the height of the grasses when they are in flower. All of the plants die down in winter, and although most of them are *perennial*—living for many years—growth above ground starts afresh each year.

Big bluestem (*Andropogon gerardii*) is the most typical grass of the tallgrass prairie. It flowers in late summer, when it reaches an average height of five feet (1.5 m). In some places big bluestem can reach a height of 10 feet (3 m). Other tall-grass species include sand bluestem (*A. halli*), Indian grass (*Sorghastrum nutans*), slough grass (*Spartina pectinata*), and switchgrass (*Panicum virgatum*). All of these grow 3.3–10 feet (1–3 m) tall. Growing among the grasses there is a wide range of herbs, called *forbs.*

Tallgrass prairie grows in the east, where the annual rain-fall averages about 34 inches (864 mm), with rather more falling in summer than in winter. Formerly, in spring, after the thin covering of snow had melted but before the temper-ature had risen high enough to evaporate water near the sur-face, the native prairie was very wet in some places. Nowadays the ground is much drier. The land has been drained and plowed, and today it grows wheat and corn. Most of the tallgrass prairie has disappeared.

Short-grass prairie—the plains grassland—grows to the west of longitude 100°W, where the climate is drier. Great Falls, Montana, for example, has an average annual rainfall of 15.3 inches (388 mm). Farmers can grow row crops only where they are able to irrigate their fields, and the area is mainly given over to cattle ranching. The low rainfall also means that native plants cannot grow very tall. Most of the grassland plants are less than eight inches (20 cm) high. These include buffalo grass (*Buchloe dactyloides*), galleta grass (*Hilaria jamesii*), needle-and-thread grass (*Stipa comata*), vari-ous grama grasses (*Bouteloua* species), and penn (or Pennsylvania) sedge (*Carex pensylvanica*). Grasses survive bet-ter than most other plants in this climate, so there are fewer forbs in short-grass prairie than there are in tallgrass prairie.

Between the tallgrass and short-grass grasslands, the mixed prairie consists of grasses of both types. Tall grasses grow in the wetter areas and short grasses in the drier places—although most of the area is now farmed, growing corn and soybeans. The natural grassland plants grow up to about three feet (90 cm) tall. They include little bluestem grass (*Schizachyrium scoparium*), needle grasses (*Stipa* species), dropseed grasses (*Sporobolus* species), June grass (*Koeleria pyramidata*), wheatgrass (*Elytrigia* species), and wild rye (*Elymus canadensis*). Wild rye is not related to cultivated rye.

Palouse prairie occurs around the Palouse River, in Washington State, extending eastward and northward from there. It is dominated by bunchgrasses. Most prairie grasses have roots that form a continuous mat below the surface and produce new shoots at intervals from stems that grow horizontally. Bunch or tussock grasses produce new shoots from the base of the main stem. Consequently they grow in dense, but separate, clumps or bunches. Bluebunch wheatgrass (*Elytrigia spicata*) is a typical grass of the palouse prairie. There are many forbs, and sagebrush (*Artemisia tridentata*) is widespread.

The bunchgrass prairie in California has long vanished. Travelers who saw it in the middle of the 19th century described an area 400 miles (640 km) long that in spring was a mass of yellow and purple flowers. Purple needlegrass (*Stipa pulchra*) was the predominant grass.

## Steppe

From the Danube in the west to Mongolia and China, 3,500 miles (9,000 km) to the east, and from the edge of the Sahara and the Arabian Desert in the south to the taiga in the north, the grasslands of Europe and Asia are the most extensive in the world. They are called *puszta* in Hungary. Farther east they are known by their more familiar Russian name—*steppe*. The map shows their original extent, but large areas have been converted to farming, including almost all of the puszta, and forests have been planted in the north.

The name *steppe* is sometimes used to describe temperate grasslands of all kinds, including the prairie, pampa, veld, and Australian grasslands. But there are differences among these types, and strictly speaking *steppe* refers to the Eurasian grasslands. These are open, grass-covered plains, which are treeless except where the steppe merges into the northern forests. The climate is dry, with 12–20 inches (300–500 mm) of rain a year in most places, and drought is common. All the steppe plants are able to survive drought. Taller plants grow in the wetter areas, and shorter plants grow where the ground is dry most of the time.

Many grasses thrive in this vast area, but feather grasses grow throughout the steppe and are the most typical grasses of the drier southern steppe. As their name suggests, they produce long, feathery flowers, and toward the end of May these dominate the landscape, swaying gracefully in the wind. The feather grasses belong to the genus *Stipa,* and this Latin name may be related to the word *steppe.* Oat grasses (*Avena* species), fescues (*Festuca* species), and sedges (*Carex* species) are also widespread. Viviparous bluegrass (*Poa bulbosa*), goose onions (*Gagea* species), and tulips (*Tulipa*

*Steppe. The steppe grasslands extend from eastern Europe all the way to western China, a distance of approximately 3,500 miles (9,000 km).*

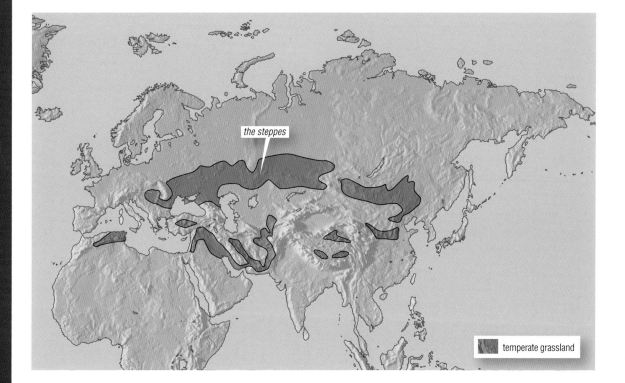

the steppes

temperate grassland

species) grow in the south of the region, near the Black Sea and in Kazakhstan, in places where the climate is warm and relatively moist. Wormwoods, also called sagebrushes (*Artemisia* species), grow in the Central Asian steppe. The steppe is rich in plants. There are up to 73 plant species in every square yard of the surface (80/m$^2$) in some parts of the northern steppe.

The steppe lie between latitudes 40°N and 50°N, and Russian scientists have divided them into four types of grassland. The most northerly steppe borders the taiga. It is called *forest steppe*. Trees grow scattered across the landscape, becoming more frequent in the north until the steppe merges into the coniferous forest.

Just south of the forest-steppe the *meadow steppe* has a relatively moist climate. Sedges (*Carex* species) and feather grasses (*Stipa* species) grow there, and parts of the meadow-steppe are used to graze livestock.

*Dry-steppe* lies to the south of the meadow-steppe. There the ground is dry most of the time because the annual rainfall is less than the amount of water that could evaporate in a year. Shorter feather grasses grow there, such as Ukrainian feather grass (*Stipa ucrainica*); *S. capillata,* known locally as *tyrsa;* and *S. pennata,* as well as fescues (*Festuca* species). Continuing southward, the climate becomes progressively drier as the steppe merges into the subtropical desert.

Although the climate is moister in the north, all four types of steppe have a generally similar climate. The winter is cold, with temperatures below freezing for at least four months and snow cover that is more than four inches (10 cm) deep. Irgiz, Kazakhstan, at latitude 48.37°N, experiences typical steppe temperatures. The average temperature remains below freezing from November through March. Summers are warm, with an average temperature of 73°F (23°C) from June through August. Irgiz is rather dry, however, with an average annual rainfall of only seven inches (180 mm). Rainfall is distributed evenly through the year, but on average occurs only 11 days between the beginning of May and the end of August. These are the months with the longest hours of sunshine, and the little rain that does fall evaporates quickly.

By August the grasses are brown and wilting everywhere, and the steppe remains brown and dry until the following spring. Droughts are common in late summer and autumn.

## Pampa

In Quechua, the Native American language spoken over much of western South America, a terrace or open space is called a *bamba*. Spanish settlers changed the word to *pampa* and used *la pampa* to describe a large plain. English speakers often use the plural form, calling the grassland pampas, but the singular, *pampa,* is more correct. The pampa covers a total area of about 290,000 square miles (751,000 km²), mostly in Argentina but extending into Uruguay. It is the home of the gaucho, the South American cowboy, and today most of the pampa area is used to ranch cattle and sheep. Very few areas of the original pampa remain.

The pampa extends from the Colorado River in the south to the forested depression called the Gran Chaco in the north, and from the Atlantic coast in the east to the foothills of the Andes in the west. Lying approximately between latitudes 27°S and 38°S, the pampa has a warm climate. Temperatures range between about 85°–90°F (29°–32°C) in summer and 57°–59°F (14°–15°C) in winter. Winter nights are cold, however, with temperatures often falling below freezing.

Highlands—*sierras*—in the northwest, including the large San Luis and Córdoba sierras, and some hills in the south break up what otherwise is fairly level plain that slopes gently from a little above sea level to an elevation of 2,320 feet (708 m) in the Andean foothills of Mendoza Province. The map shows the extent and location of the pampa.

There are two distinct types of pampa. On the western side the "sterile pampa" is a dry plain that in places gives way to sandy desert. There are rivers in this part of the pampa carrying water that is too salty to drink and areas where the soil is salty. The vegetation is sparse, with scattered thornbushes and small trees, including *chanal* or *chañar* (*Geoffroea decorticans*), a low, thorny shrub that is fed to livestock and produces edible fruit pods. Rainfall is also low in the southern pampa. Victorica, in San Luis Province in the west, has an

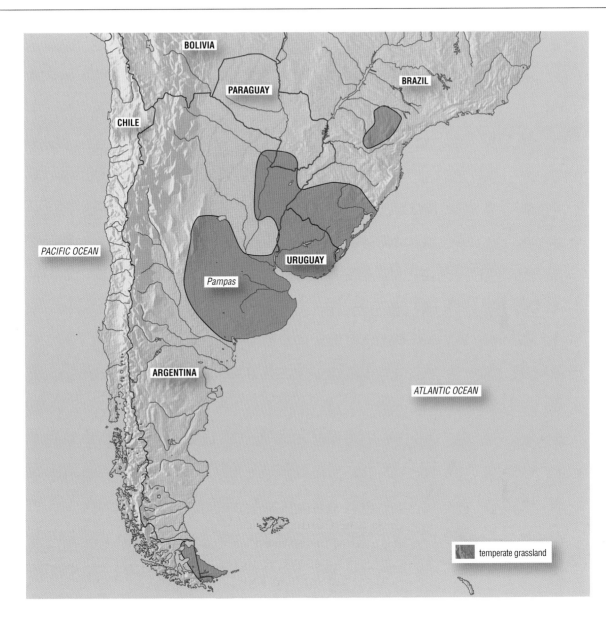

BOLIVIA

PARAGUAY

BRAZIL

CHILE

PACIFIC OCEAN

URUGUAY

Pampas

ARGENTINA

ATLANTIC OCEAN

temperate grassland

annual rainfall of about 22 inches (559 mm), and Bahía Blanca in the south receives an average of 20 inches (500 mm). Most of the rain falls in summer.

The eastern pampa receives an average 39 inches (1,000 mm) of rain a year and its soils are fertile. Buenos Aires has an average 37 inches (940 mm) of rain a year. This part of the pampa is the most productive agricultural land in Argentina.

*Pampas. Pampa grasslands occur in southern Argentina.*

Its most famous native grass is "pampas grass," which is grown ornamentally in many parts of the world but has become a very invasive weed in other regions, including California, Hawaii, and New Zealand. Also known as silver pampas grass and Uruguayan pampas grass (*Cortaderia selloana*), this grass grows in dense tussocks eight to 12 feet (2.4–3.7 m) tall and produces large, feathery flowers. Over large areas of the pampa, silver pampas grass crowds out all other plants, except for the herbs that grow between its tussocks. It is used to make paper, but it is of little use for pasture. More nutritious pasture grasses and herbs have been sown to replace most of it.

There are few trees in the eastern pampa, because they cannot tolerate the frequent winter fires that are fanned by the strong, perpetual winds. The grasses recover quickly from fire and benefit from the nutrients in the wood ash that the rain soon washes down to their roots.

The one woody plant that does withstand fire is called the ombu (*Phytolacca dioica*). It grows to a height of 40–60 feet (12–18 m) and its girth—the trunk circumference measured about four feet (1.2 m) above ground level—can reach 40–50 feet (12–15 m). The plant often produces many trunks growing side by side. Technically this structure makes it a shrub rather than a tree, despite its height. The ombu's trunk is spongy because it contains tissues that store water, making it fire-resistant. Its ability to store water also helps it survive drought.

Gauchos nicknamed these plants "lighthouses," because they are visible from afar and the umbrella-shaped top offers shade on a hot, sunny day. Ombus are planted as shade trees in places with a suitable climate, such as Southern California.

## Veld

Grasslands known as the *veld* or *grassveld* cover the high plateau that occupies the eastern side of South Africa. *Veld* is the Afrikaans word for "field." The elevation varies from approximately sea level to more than 9,000 feet (2,745 m). The veld extends over most of the Eastern Cape, Free State, and Eastern Transvaal, as well as parts of KwaZulu-Natal,

North West, and Northern Province. It covers all of Lesotho and part of Swaziland. The map shows the area and location of the South African veld. The largest area, called the *Highveld,* covers most of the Free State. To the north of the Highveld the land rises into the Witwatersrand—Afrikaans for "ridge of white waters"—and beyond that is the *Bushveld,* a region of dry savanna-type grassland. The *Cape middle veld* lies to the west of the Highveld.

The veld is also divided into "sweet" and "sour" types. Sweet veld occurs mainly on the western side of the country, where the annual rainfall is less than about 25 inches (635 mm). Grasses found there have a low fiber content and retain their nutrients through the winter, so they are palatable to livestock. The grasses of the sour veld grow on the wetter, eastern side of the region. They are fibrous and lose their nutrients when they die down in winter. Winter is the dry season, although there is some rain in every month of the year.

Red oat grass (*Themeda triandra*) is the most widespread species. It grows to a height of 12–36 inches (30–90 cm) and

*Veld. The veld grassland of southern Africa occurs on the eastern side of South Africa and covers Lesotho and the western half of Swaziland.*

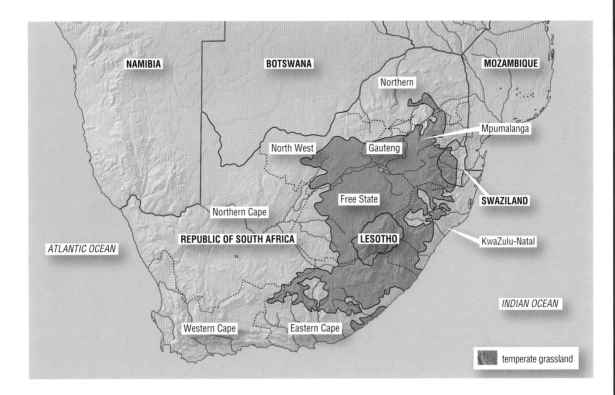

is of poor nutritional value and readily overgrazed. Where red oat grass has been overgrazed, love grass (*Eragrostis* species) often takes its place. Bristle grass, also called wire grass, Ngongoni three-awn grass, and Gongoni steekgras (*Aristida junciformis*), and Bermuda grass (*Cynodon dactylon*) are also widespread. Bristle grass grows to a height of 20–36 inches (50–90 cm) and Bermuda grass to four to 15 inches (10–40 cm). Bluegrass (*Festuca* species) grows on the higher ground, where the climate is cooler.

The veld has been farmed for many years. It supplies most of South Africa's dairy, beef, and wool products, and large areas have been converted to cropland. Corn (maize) is the most important crop, but sorghum, wheat, and sunflowers are also grown. Part of the veld is highly urbanized and industrial. The Witwatersrand is an important mining and industrial region, and the cities of Johannesburg and Pretoria are located there.

## Tropical grasslands of South America

Most of us think of tropical South America lying to the east of the Andes as a land of forests growing in a hot, wet climate. South America is the continent of rain forests. As the map shows, however, that picture is incomplete. Almost half of tropical South America is not forest at all, but open grassland.

The northern grasslands, covering about 125,000 square miles (323,750 km²) in Venezuela, are known as the *llanos,* and those occupying 100,000 square miles (260,000 km²) in Colombia are the *llanos orientales,* the "eastern llanos." The llanos grasslands cover plains that are bounded by the mountains of the Cordillera Mérida in the north and by the Orinoco and Guaviare Rivers in the south. Together the grasslands of the two countries compose the *llanos orinoquia,* the "Orinoco llanos." This is the home of the *llaneros,* the skilled horsemen who are the equivalent of the gauchos of the pampa, far to the south. In 1548 cattle were introduced to the llanos, and it is an important ranching and stockbreeding region.

The llanos lie in a large basin that formed millions of years ago between the Guiana Highlands in the east and the Andes

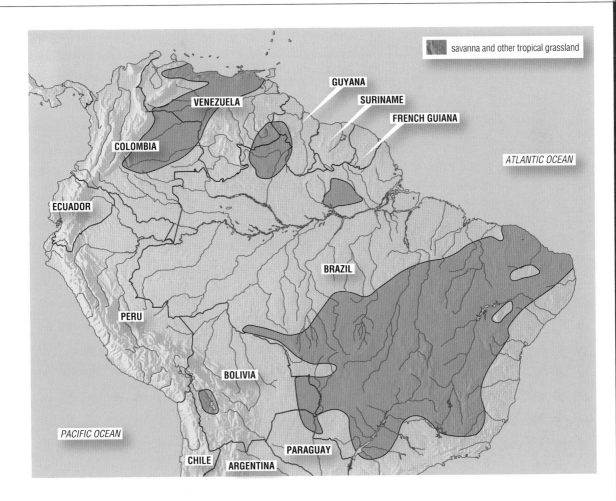

savanna and other tropical grassland

*Tropical grasslands of South America. The grasslands occupy the drier regions, beyond the edges of the forests. The largest area is in Brazil.*

in the west and then filled with sediment. Later the basin subsided in some places, creating the present landscape of almost completely level plains interrupted by flat-topped hills called *mesas*. The grasslands are probably no more than 10,000 years old. The llanos is a complex landscape, and scientists studying it divide it into seven regions.

Grasses are the predominant plants, and over large areas of the llanos *Trachypogon* is the most widespread grass genus. *Trachypogon* grasses grow in tussocks four to 12 inches (10–30 cm) apart to a height of more than six feet (1.8 m). Between the tussocks there are herbs up to about three feet (1 m) tall. Several other grasses grow on the llanos, and there are scattered trees. These include various palm trees; the manteco or golden spoon (*Byrsonima crassifolia*), which produces edible fruits; the chaparro or rough-leaf tree, with leaves that are used for polishing metal (*Curatella americana*); and the alcornoque or sucupira (*Bowdichia virgilioides*), the bark of which is used to treat tuberculosis and rheumatism. Dense forests grow beside the rivers.

There are two seasons on the llanos. Winters, lasting from December through April, are dry, with less than two inches (50 mm) of rain a month. Most of the rain falls during the rainy season, from April through November, and large areas are flooded between June and October. The total annual rainfall averages 30–47 inches (760–1,200 mm) in the northeast, 47–63 inches (1,200–1,600 mm) in the center, and 98 inches (2,500 mm) in the southwest. The average temperature is 80°F (27°C) throughout the region, with no more than about 3.6°F (2°C) difference between the warmest and coolest months.

South of the forests grasslands originally covered 580,000–770,000 square miles (1.5–2 million km²) of central Brazil. That area, approximately equal to the combined areas of France, Germany, Italy, Spain, and the United Kingdom, amounts to about one-fifth of the total area of Brazil. Today about 40 percent of the original area has been converted to agriculture and grows crops such as soybeans.

These grasslands, called *cerrado,* include varying numbers of trees and are intersected by forests along the river valleys. The cerrado also includes the world's largest area of continental wetlands, known as *pantanal.* The cerrado is divided into four distinct types. *Campo limpo* is open grassland with no trees. *Campo sujo,* literally "dirty field," is grassland with trees. *Cerrado sensu strictu* is grassland with trees and areas of woodland, and *cerradão* is woodland. This diversity of conditions supports an estimated 6,600 species of plants, including more than 1,000 species of trees, as well as 110 species of mammals—most of them rodents—and 400 species of birds. There are approximately 500 species of grasses and almost as many orchid species. The most common grasses are perennial tussock grasses, such as *Trachypogon spicatus,* which grows to about 24–36 inches (60–90 cm) tall.

The cerrado climate is tropical. It is hot throughout the year, with temperatures averaging 72°F (22°C) in the south of the region and 81°F (27°C) in the north. Annual rainfall averages 47–71 inches (1,200–1,800 mm), about 90 percent of which falls during the Southern Hemisphere summer, between October and March. Over two-thirds of the cerrado the summer dry season lasts for five or six months and in some months there is no rain at all.

## Savanna

The name *savanna* or *savannah* was first given to the tropical grasslands of the Caribbean islands and Central and South America (see "What are grasslands?" on pages xv–xviii). The term is now applied to any tropical grassland with a winter dry season lasting three to five months, a rainy season in summer, and temperatures that never fall below 64°F (18°C). But today the word *savanna* is especially associated with Africa—perhaps because animals of the African savanna have featured in so many nature programs on television. This savanna is home to such nature program favorites as lions, cheetahs, zebras, gazelles, elephants, wildebeests, and meerkats.

It is also vast. As the map shows, the northern boundary of the African savanna extends from the southern edge of the Sahara, along a line from Senegal and Guinea-Bissau, to the Nile River. Southward the grassland continues to the edge of the tropical rain forest in West Africa and to the Ubangi (or Oubangi) River and Lake Victoria in Central and East Africa. South of the equator the savanna covers the region bounded by the southern edge of the tropical forests, at about latitude 7°S, to latitude 32°S in South Africa, excluding the Namib and Kalahari deserts. In all, it occupies approximately 5 million square miles (13 million km²). That is almost half of the total area of Africa—and considerably more than the entire area of the United States (3.675 million square miles [9.52 million km²]).

Much of the area is classed as *derived savanna*. This means that it was once forest, but people cleared most of the trees long ago. Grasses invaded the cleared area, followed by herds of grazing animals that nibbled and trampled tree seedlings, preventing the return of the forest. Fires occur naturally dur-

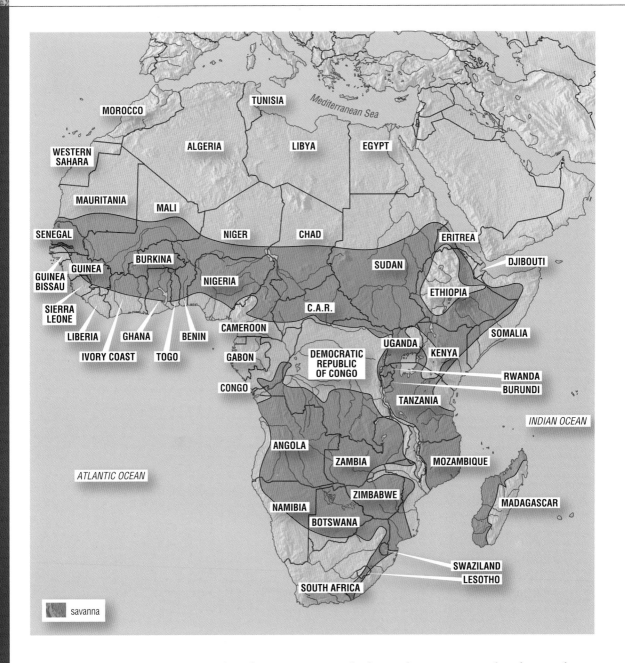

savanna

ing the dry season, and they also prevent the forest from returning. Instead there are grasses. The tall grasses grow in the moister areas, where the annual rainfall is 24–40 inches (600–1,000 mm), as it is along the edge of the tropical forests. Elephant grass (*Hyparrhenia* species) grows 10–13 feet (3–4 m) tall. One species, *H. filipendula,* is used to make paper, and it (opposite page) *African savanna. Africa has the world's largest area of tropical grassland. It occupies most of the continent between the Sahara in the north and the Kalahari and Namib Deserts in the south, except for the tropical forest on either side of the equator centered on the Congo Basin.*

is grown in some areas of savanna for this purpose. In drier areas, where the rainfall is eight to 24 inches (200–600 mm), several species of wire grass (*Aristida*) occur, especially *A. stipoides,* as does Indian sandburr (*Cenchrus biflorus*), an annual grass—one that lives for only one year—growing to six to 24 inches (15–60 cm) tall.

Trees grow among the grasses. Thorn trees (*Acacia* species) are the most characteristic woody plants, and *A. tortilis* is the most widespread. It grows to a height of 13–50 feet (4–15 m) and has the umbrella-shaped top that is typical of acacias. According to tradition, wood from this tree was used to make the biblical Ark of the Covenant. *A. senegal* is the principal source of gum arabic, a material used to make glues and pastes and a component of some medicines. *A. laeta,* another widespread savanna thorn tree, is also an important commercial source of gum arabic.

Possibly the most extraordinary savanna trees are the baobab (*Adansonia digitata*) and the candelabra tree (*Euphorbia candelabrum*). The baobab grows up to 40 feet (12 m) tall, but its lower trunk is as much as 30 feet (9 m) in diameter. Its peculiar appearance gave rise to a legend that the devil pulled the baobab tree from the ground and pushed it back upside down, leaving its branches below ground and its roots sticking up in the air. The baobab is very long lived. Specimens have been reliably dated at 2,000 years old, and less reliable methods suggest that some baobabs are very much older. The tree does not grow each year; sometimes it shrinks, probably because of the loss of fluid in times of drought. Every part of the tree is useful: Cloth is made from its outer bark and rope from its inner bark; its timber is used; its seeds are edible and rich in vitamin C; and its leaves are eaten as a vegetable. The candelabra tree, found on the East African savanna, is closely related to the spurges. Its many branches grow from the top of the trunk, all pointing upward.

## Australian grasslands

There was a time long ago when Australia was a land of rivers, lakes, and forests. Its climate turned drier about 10 million years ago. The lakes disappeared and as they shrank, so did the forests. Trees need a plentiful supply of water, but grasses can manage with less. Consequently, the retreat of the forests was accompanied by the expansion of grassland. Today much of the interior of Australia is desert. There is some tropical forest in the north and east, and eucalyptus forest is widespread in the east, but the natural vegetation over a large part of the continent is a mixture of grassland and scrub. *Mallee,* in the south of the country, composes dense thickets of dwarf eucalyptus. The Australian grassland forms a savanna landscape similar to the African savanna but composed of different species. The map shows the tropical grassland areas of Australia.

Mitchell grasses (*Astrebla* species) cover the northern part of the region, known as the *Mitchell Grass Downs.* These extend for about 930 miles (1,500 km) from the center of the Northern Territory to the middle of southern Queensland, as a belt of almost treeless grassland. Mitchell grasses grow 12–36 inches (30–90 cm) tall and occasionally to as much as 48 inches (1.2 m). They resist drought and provide nutritious pasture. Sheep and cattle graze the Downs. The annual rainfall averages 14–30 inches (350–750 mm). Temperatures often exceed 100°F (38°C) in summer, but sometimes frosts occur in winter.

---

(opposite page) *Australian grasslands. Grasslands of several types surround the central deserts. The Mitchell grass* (Astrebla pectinata) *resists drought and provides good pasture. It grows on rolling hills (downs) across the north of Australia. There is savanna grassland to the south. Between them are desert sand dunes that are stabilized with* Triodia *grass. The remaining areas of Australia are dominated by scrubland, where different* Acacia *species grow among the grasses.*

Mitchell grasses give way in the north to bluestem grasses (*Dichanthium* species). These grow only about six inches (15 cm) tall in the drier areas, but where there is more moisture they sometimes stand 6.5 feet (2 m) high. The Mitchell grass pastures separate areas of woodland dominated by thorn trees (*Acacia* species). Australia is home to more species of *Acacia* than any other continent, and the most common varieties found beside Mitchell grassland are gidgee (*A. cambagei*) and brigalow (*A. harpophylla*).

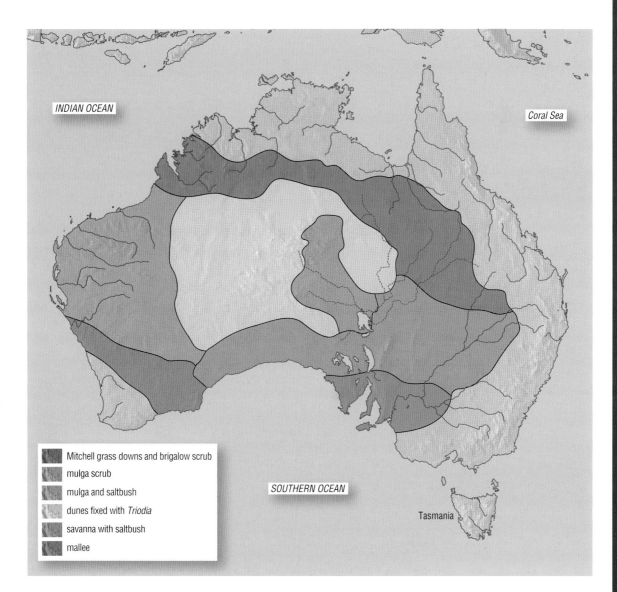

INDIAN OCEAN

Coral Sea

SOUTHERN OCEAN

Tasmania

Mitchell grass downs and brigalow scrub
mulga scrub
mulga and saltbush
dunes fixed with *Triodia*
savanna with saltbush
mallee

Savanna with brigalow extends down most of the eastern side of Australia. It covers 132,200 square miles (342,400 km²), approximately from Townsville, Queensland, at latitude 19.25°S, to the Queensland–New South Wales border, at 28.58°S. Here the rainfall ranges from more than 30 inches (750 mm) a year in the east to less than 20 inches (500 mm) in the west. Gidgee replaces brigalow in the drier areas, and in some places there are open grasslands, dominated by bluestem grasses (*Dichanthium*).

Brigalow scrub also includes some other trees. These are predominantly species of *Eucalyptus,* another characteristically Australian genus. There are ironbarks (*E. melanophloia* and *E. crebra*), poplar box (*E. populnea*), and Brown's box (*E. brownii*). Farther south there are also spotted gum (*Corymba maculata*) and red bloodwood (*C. gummifera*); *Corymba* species are types of eucalyptus. In places there are open woodlands of brigalow and belah (*Casuarina cristata*).

Mulga scrub, composed of the dwarf thornbush mulga (*Acacia aneura*) and *Spinifex* species of grasses, extends down the western side of Australia, and in the center of the country there is an area of mulga with saltbushes (*Atriplex* species, especially *A. vesicaria*). Savanna grassland with saltbushes extends across much of the continent on the southern side of the desert. As the name suggests, saltbushes can grow in places where the soil is salty. Mulga grows up to 20 feet (6 m) tall. Livestock feed on its leaves, and its wood has many uses. Boomerangs, for instance, are traditionally made from mulga wood. *Spinifex* grasses are 20–40 inches (50–100 cm) tall, and they grow from underground stems rather than in tussocks. This makes them very useful for stabilizing loose sand dunes. Porcupine grass (*Triodia* species), which is used for this purpose in the desert, grows in the same way, usually to a height of eight to 48 inches (20–120 cm) but sometimes to eight feet (2.4 m) tall.

## Upland grasslands

Few trees are able to grow anywhere the average summer temperature is lower than 50°F (10°C). Grasses, however, tolerate lower temperatures. Consequently, if the average summer temperature decreases over a distance, the line where it falls below 50°F (10°C) marks the limit for tree growth. Trees grow on one side of this line and grasses on the other side. The boundary is called the *tree line, timberline,* or *forest limit.*

The boundary between trees and grasses is not always quite so abrupt as this description makes it sound. Between the dense part of the forest and the forest limit, the plant composition of the forest changes gradually. If at first there are broad-leaved evergreen trees, these may give way to deciduous trees—trees that shed their leaves in winter—and then to coniferous trees, such as firs, pines, and spruces. The coniferous forest then becomes more open. Instead of being closely packed so that their shade makes the forest floor very dark, the trees are more widely spaced, and there are gaps and clearings where the sunshine reaches the forest floor, allowing grasses and herbs to grow. As the trees become even more widely scattered, they also become smaller and increasingly stunted. Finally there are no trees at all; this is the tree line. Rather than a clearly marked line, however, it is more like a belt in which the concentration of trees gradually decreases.

One type of tree line is latitudinal. Average temperatures decrease with increasing distance from the equator, and forests give way to temperate grasslands when the average summer temperature dips below 50°F (10°C). The term *tree line* is more usually applied to mountains, however. Because temperature decreases with altitude, there is a height beyond which trees cannot survive. The forests that blanket the lower slopes of a mountain gradually become sparser and finally disappear, and above this altitudinal tree line there are meadows forming *alpine savanna* in the Tropics and *alpine grassland* elsewhere.

The rate at which temperature decreases with height is known as the *environmental lapse rate* (ELR), and it varies from place to place and day to day. It is the average ELR that matters, however, because it is the average summer temperature that determines whether or not trees will survive. The average ELR is 3.6°F per 1,000 feet (6.5°C/km). If you know both the average summer temperature in a particular place and the height of that place above sea level, you can calculate the approximate altitude of the tree line. At El Paso, Texas, for example, the average temperature (counting both day and night) in the warmest month is 80°F (27°C). The temperature must decrease by 30°F (17°C) to reach the transition point of 50°F (10°C), and it will do so at a height of about 8,300 feet (2,500 m). El Paso is already 3,920 feet (1,196 m) above sea level, so the average summer temperature will be 50°F (10°C) at an elevation of 12,220 feet (3,700 m). Consequently, that will be the average height of the tree line in the mountains above the city. At Banff, Alberta, the average July temperature is 57.9°F (14.4°C), and Banff is about 4,583 feet (1,397 m) above sea level in the Canadian Rocky Mountains. Hence the tree line there will be at about 6,780 feet (2,070 m). The tree line descends with increasing distance from the equator, because with increasing distance the summers become progressively cooler. In northern Canada and Eurasia, where the summer temperature never reaches 50°F (10°C), the tree line is at sea level.

Calculating the height of the tree line on a real mountain is rather more complicated, however. Some parts of the mountain face the Sun and others face away from the Sun, and some areas will be in full sunshine, while other areas are shaded for much of the time. Consequently the average temperature will vary markedly from place to place on the mountainside. Cold air from higher on the mountain, perhaps from the region that is permanently covered with snow, will frequently subside down the mountainside, lowering the temperature—and therefore the tree line.

Above the tree line, whatever its height, there are alpine grasslands or savannas. The composition of the grasslands varies, but they are always rich in flowering herbs and, often, heathers that grow among the grasses. Fescue grasses (*Festuca* species) are common in most mountains. They grow in clumps and are known as bunchgrasses or tussock grasses.

Alpine meadows are valuable to the farmers living in the valleys. Traditionally they are cut to make hay to feed animals through the winter, and in many parts of the world sheep and, to a lesser extent, cattle graze them through the summer. In late spring herders drive the animals from the valleys and stay with them throughout the summer, living in tents or cabins high in the mountains. This type of farming is called *transhumance*. It is less common now than it used to be, but it has not died out, although the methods have changed in some places. In the European Alps, for example, the sheep now travel to and from the mountains in huge articulated trucks, rather than being driven on foot.

## CHAPTER 2

# GEOLOGY OF GRASSLANDS

## Movement of continents

Grasslands occupy the centers of continents, far from the ocean, where the climate is too dry for forests but not dry enough to produce deserts. They do not move, although clearing forest to provide pasture will produce new grassland, and abandoning the pasture may allow the forest to return, even centuries after it was originally cleared. Our planet has existed for a very long time, however, and these are short-term changes.

Although grasslands continue to occupy continental interiors, the continents themselves are moving. About 350 million years ago, for example, North America was pivoted about a quarter turn from its present position and the equator passed through it, from the eastern end of Hudson Bay to approximately where San Francisco sits today. At that time, however, the whole of what is now the Great Plains and all of the land to the west of it lay beneath a shallow sea, and the Rocky Mountains had not formed. The prairie could not have existed then, not only because sea covered the entire area, but also because grasses had not yet evolved. The earliest fossils of grasses—and grasslands—are found in North America, and they are about 45 million years old. The earliest clear record of African grasslands is about 14 million years old, although fossilized grass pollen that is older has been found.

Grasses probably appeared first in the Tropics, close to the edge of tropical forests. The first grasslands were of the savanna type, but as climates became cooler the grasslands changed. They continued to be grassland, but savanna was gradually transformed into prairie, pampa, and steppe. The tropical grasslands became temperate grasslands.

Climates change for several reasons; the changes that convert savanna to prairie result from the movement into higher latitudes of the continents carrying them. The process is called *continental drift.*

Conclusive evidence for continental drift was not discovered until the middle of the 20th century, but the idea was far from new. Some scholars were proposing something rather like it as early as the 16th century. With access to the first reasonably accurate maps of the world, they could see that the continents fit together rather more neatly than was likely to be due to chance. Evidence continued to accumulate over the centuries: The rocks forming the mountains of Scotland are very similar to those of the Appalachian Mountains; North American coal, made from plant remains, is very similar to the coal found in Europe; certain plants and animals are found only in particular places, and those places are separated by thousands of miles of ocean. Early in the 20th century the German meteorologist Alfred Wegener (see the sidebar) drew together these and other strands of evidence to propose that at one time all the continents had been joined to form a single "supercontinent," which he called Pangaea, surrounded by a vast ocean, Panthalassa.

One of Wegener's supporters was the South African geologist Alexander Logie Du Toit (1878–1948), who had found similarities in the rock formations of South Africa and South America. He renamed Wegener's "continental displacement," calling it *continental drift,* which is the name that survived. Then the American oceanographer Robert Sinclair Dietz (1914–95) proposed the theory of *seafloor spreading* to describe the way oceans grow wider from a central ridge. Finally in 1967 Dan McKenzie (born 1942) of Cambridge University synthesized all that was known at the time and proposed a new theory, *plate tectonics. Tectonics* refers to the deformation of the Earth's crust and structures resulting from it, and the theory proposes that the solid crust consists of discrete sections, called plates. A scientific theory is an explanation of a natural process, with solid evidence to support it.

There are two types of crustal plate: continental plate and oceanic plate. They differ in the rocks from which they are made and in their thickness. Oceanic plates are made from very dense rock and are three to nine miles (5–15 km) thick. Continental plates are less dense and 19–50 miles (30–80 km)

## Alfred Lothar Wegener and continental drift

Since the first realistic maps of the world were published in the 16th century, many geographers had puzzled over the fact that the continents on each side of the Atlantic Ocean looked as though they might fit together. Some thought it mere coincidence, but others suggested ways a single continent might have split into two parts that then moved apart.

The German meteorologist Alfred Lothar Wegener (1880–1930) went much further. Wegener compiled a mass of evidence to support what he called "continental displacement." This phenomenon came to be called *continental drift.* He studied the scientific literature for descriptions of rocks that were similar on each side of the Atlantic. He found plants with limited distribution that are separated by vast oceans and fossil organisms that are also distributed in this way.

Finally he proposed that about 280 million years ago, during the Upper Paleozoic subera, all the continents were joined, forming a single "supercontinent," which he called *Pangaea* (from the Greek *pan,* meaning all, and *ge,* meaning Earth), surrounded by an ocean called *Panthalassa* (*thalassa* means ocean). He theorized that Pangaea broke apart and the separate pieces drifted to their present locations; the continents are still drifting.

In 1912 Wegener published a short book outlining his theory, *Die Entstehung der Kontinente und Ozeane* (The Origin of the continents and oceans). He was drafted into the German army in 1914 at the start of World War I but was wounded almost at once. He developed his ideas further while recovering in a hospital, and in 1915 he published a much longer edition of his book (it was not translated into English until 1924).

His idea found little support. Geologists at the time believed the *mantle*—the material beneath the Earth's crust—to be solid, and they could not imagine any way that continents could move. They also found that some of Wegener's calculations of the rate of continental displacement were incorrect.

But support for Wegener's idea began to grow in the 1940s, when for the first time scientists were able to study the rocks on the ocean floor. These studies indicated that the oceans had grown wider by spreading outward from central ridges, where underwater volcanoes were erupting, laying down new rock. Wegener's theory was generally accepted by the late 1960s, but by then Alfred Wegener was dead. He had died in 1930 during his third expedition to study the climate over the Greenland ice sheet.

thick. Both types of crust rest upon the material of the *mantle,* but because it is less dense, continental crust projects higher than oceanic crust and oceans fill the basins between continents. There are seven major plates: the African, Eurasian, Pacific, North American, South American, Antarctic, and Australian plates. There are also several lesser plates: the Cocos, Caribbean, Nazca, Arabian, Indian, Philippine, and Scotia plates. In addition, there are minor plates such as the Juan de Fuca plate, microplates, and fragments of former plates that have broken apart. The map shows the present location of the major and lesser plates.

Plates fit tightly together and move in relation to one another in three basic ways: apart, causing oceans to widen; toward each other, causing oceans to grow narrower and continents to collide; or past one another, traveling in opposite directions. Some plates are no longer moving, and some have been permanently incorporated into other plates, but many are still on the move. The North American and Eurasian

*Tectonic plates. The map shows the major plates and larger minor ones into which the Earth's crust is broken. Continents move across the Earth's surface carried on the plates.*

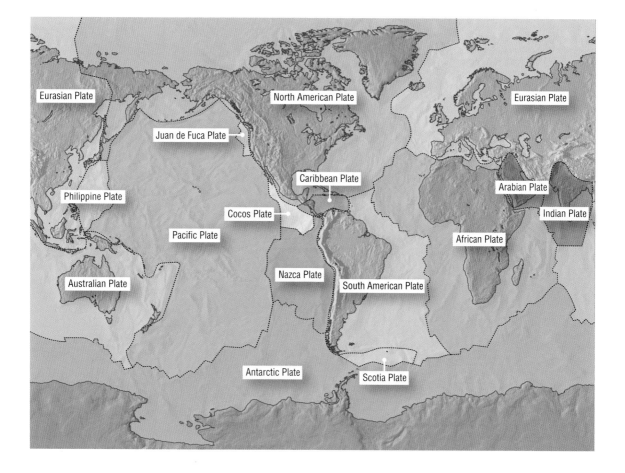

plates are moving apart, for example, at about 0.8 inch (2 cm) a year, and the Pacific and Nazca plates are moving away from each other at about six inches (15 cm) a year. The boundaries between moving plates are called *active margins,* and they are sites of earthquakes and volcanic eruptions.

Beneath the Earth's crust the rocks of the mantle are extremely hot and are compressed under tremendous pressure. They are very much denser than the crustal rocks, but the high temperature and pressure cause them to deform—they can be squeezed, bent, and stretched by the movement of material around them. They can also transmit heat by *convection.*

Convection is the process by which liquid heats up in a pan sitting on a stove. The pan is heated from below and the liquid at the bottom is first to warm. As it warms, the liquid expands. Expansion makes the liquid less dense because it occupies a bigger volume without gaining any more molecules. Cooler and therefore denser liquid sinks beneath the warmer liquid, pushing it upward. The warm liquid cools as it rises away from the source of heat, and the cool liquid, now at the bottom of the pan, heats up and rises in its turn. A vertical circulation develops, with warm liquid rising, cooling, moving to the sides at the surface as warmer liquid pushes upward through it, and sinking to be warmed and rise again. The liquid moves in *convection currents,* and a set of rising and sinking currents is known as a *convection cell.* There are usually several convection cells in a pan of liquid on the stove.

Rocks in the Earth's mantle are not liquid, but they are heated from below because the Earth's core is its hottest part, and they deform sufficiently for convection cells to develop in the material on which the crust rests. As the mantle material moves horizontally before sinking, very, very slowly it drags the continental and oceanic plates with it.

Scientists have been able to determine the movements of plates over hundreds of millions of years, and this capacity has allowed them to reconstruct maps of the world as it appeared at different times in the past. The illustration shows how the continents and oceans were arranged 135 million years ago and 65 million years ago compared with their present arrangement. Look further into the past and the map of the world becomes even more unrecognizable. Today plates

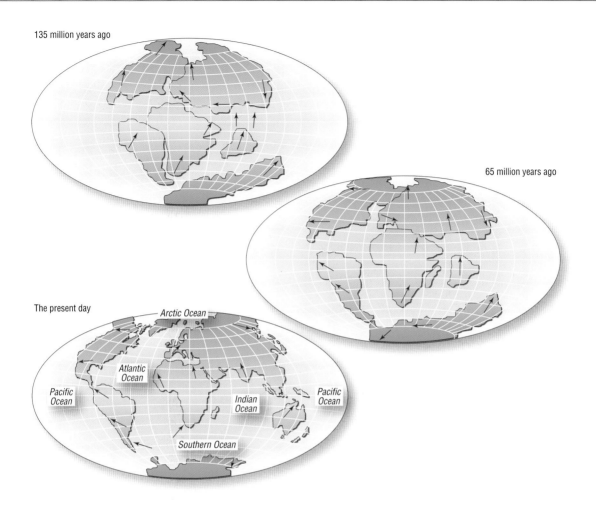

135 million years ago

65 million years ago

The present day

Arctic Ocean

Atlantic
Ocean

Pacific
Ocean

Indian
Ocean

Pacific
Ocean

Southern Ocean

are still moving, seafloors are spreading, and continents are drifting. Eventually North America will collide with Asia, and perhaps the prairie and steppe will join into a continuous belt of grassland. As Australia continues its journey northward it will one day enter the humid Tropics, and perhaps forests will blanket what are now its dry grasslands.

*Continental drift. The continents are constantly in motion. The map shows the way they were distributed 135 million and 65 million years ago, compared with their familiar arrangement today.*

## How mountains rise and wear away

When drifting plates collide, mountain ranges are born. There are two ways in which this can happen. Oceanic crust is denser than continental crust. If an oceanic plate and a continental plate collide, the denser oceanic crust will slide—

usually rather jerkily—beneath the continental crust. This process is called *subduction*. As it sinks deep into the mantle, the ocean crust melts and some of the material rises to the surface again some distance away in the direction of the continent, producing volcanoes.

The dense rock of the crust is covered by sediment. Fine rock particles are washed from the continents, are carried to

## Geologic time scale

| Eon/ Eonothem | Era/ Erathem | Subera | Period System | Epoch/ Series | Began Ma* |
|---|---|---|---|---|---|
| | | *Quaternary* | Pleistogene | Holocene | 0.11 |
| | | | | Pleistocene | 1.81 |
| Phanerozic | Cenozoic | *Tertiary* | Neogene | Pliocene | 5.3 |
| | | | | Miocene | 23.03 |
| | | | Paleogene | Oligocene | 33.9 |
| | | | | Eocene | 55.8 |
| | | | | Paleocene | 65.5 |
| | Mesozoic | | Cretaceous | Upper | 99.6 |
| | | | | Lower | 145.5 |
| | | | Jurassic | Upper | 161.2 |
| | | | | Middle | 175.6 |
| | | | | Lower | 199.6 |
| | | | Triassic | Upper | 228 |
| | | | | Middle | 245 |
| | | | | Lower | 251 |
| | Paleozoic | Upper | Permian | Lopingian | 260.4 |
| | | | | Guadalupian | 270.6 |
| | | | | Cisuralian | 299 |
| | | | Carboniferous | Pennsylvanian | 318.1 |
| | | | | Mississippian | 359.2 |
| | | | Devonian | Upper | 385.3 |
| | | | | Middle | 397.5 |
| | | | | Lower | 416 |
| | | Lower | Silurian | Pridoli | 422.9 |
| | | | | Ludlow | 443.7 |
| | | | | Wenlock | 428.2 |
| | | | | Llandovery | 443.7 |
| | | | Ordovician | Upper | 460.9 |
| | | | | Middle | 471.8 |

| Eon/ Eonothem | Era/ Erathem | Subera | Period System | Epoch/ Series | Began Ma* |
|---|---|---|---|---|---|
| | | | | Lower | 488.3 |
| | | | Cambrian | Furongian | 501 |
| | | | | Middle | 513 |
| | | | | Lower | 542 |
| Proterozoic | Neoproterozoic | | Ediacaran | | 600 |
| | | | Cryogenian | | 850 |
| | | | Tonian | | 1000 |
| | Mesoproterozoic | Stenian | | | 1200 |
| | | | Ectasian | | 1400 |
| | | | Calymmian | | 1600 |
| | Paleoproterozoic | Statherian | | | 1800 |
| | | | Orosirian | | 2050 |
| | | | Rhyacian | | 2300 |
| | | | Siderian | | 2500 |
| Archean | Neoarchean | | | | 2800 |
| | Mesoarchean | | | | 3200 |
| | Paleoarchean | | | | 3600 |
| | Eoarchean | | | | 3800 |
| Hadean | Swazian | | | | 3900 |
| | Basin Groups | | | | 4000 |
| | Cryptic | | | | 4567.17 |

Source: International Union of Geological Sciences, 2004.

Note: *Hadean* is an informal name. The Hadean, Archean, and Proterozoic eons cover the time formerly known as the Precambrian. *Quaternary* is now an informal name and *Tertiary* is likely to become informal in the future, although both continue to be widely used.

*Ma means millions of years ago.

the ocean by rivers, and then settle onto the ocean floor. Over the many millions of years of the ocean's existence, these sediments slide down the submerged sloping edges of the continents until they cover every part of the ocean floor. Gradually the weight of the upper layers of sediments compresses the lower layers until they form rock—called *sedimentary* rock. Sedimentary rock is less dense than the rock of the oceanic crust itself (called *igneous* rock, from the Latin *ignis*, meaning fire), which is formed directly from the hot material in the mantle. Where the plates collide, the continental plate scrapes sedimentary rock from the surface of the oceanic plate and crumples it upward to form a mountain range made from a mixture of continental rock and sedimentary rock from the ocean. A mountain range formed in this way is called a *cordillera*.

Where two continents collide, the rocks of both plates are equally dense, so one cannot sink beneath the other. Instead, the two crumple upward, in the way a tablecloth crumples upward if you place your hands some distance apart on it and push them together.

More than 100 million years ago, during the Cretaceous period (see the sidebar showing the geologic timescale), the Atlantic Ocean began to open and North and South America began to move westward against the Nazca and Pacific plates. These oceanic plates began to be subducted beneath the North American and South American plates, crumpling the rocks, and by about 50 million years ago the Andes and Western Cordillera had started to form. The Western Cordillera is the mountain chain down the western side of North and Central America, including the Rocky Mountains. The Nazca and Pacific plates are still disappearing beneath North and South America, at a rate of one to three inches (2–8 cm) a year. The Pacific plate is also being subducted on the western side of the ocean, and this motion produces the volcanoes and earthquakes that surround the Pacific Basin with what is often called a "ring of fire."

During the Silurian period the closure of two oceans produced a chain of mountains that extends from the southern Appalachians, across Ireland and Scotland, to Svalbard, the group of islands to the north of Norway. This was another example of a collision between continents and oceans, with oceanic crust sinking beneath continental crust.

Between 54 million and 49 million years ago, the Indian Plate, traveling northward, collided with the southern margin of the Eurasian plate. This was a collision of a different kind: Two continental plates had collided. This collision raised the Himalayas and the Tibetan plateau, causing a major change in the global climate (see "Evolution of grasslands" on pages 71–73). India is still moving northward, at 1.5–2 inches (4–5 cm) a year.

Since the collisions that have produced the Andes, Rocky Mountains, and Himalayas are still continuing, the processes that raise mountains also continue. This means that the mountains should continue to grow taller. In fact, though, two other processes check the growth of mountains: isostatic adjustment and erosion.

Together the rocks of the Earth's crust and the uppermost layer of the underlying mantle compose the *lithosphere* and the plates that form continents and ocean basins are sometimes called *lithospheric plates.* Immediately below the lithosphere there is a layer of the mantle called the *asthenosphere.* The lithosphere rests on top of the asthenosphere; individual lithospheric plates float on the asthenosphere as ice shelves and icebergs float on the ocean surface.

The thickness of the lithosphere varies from place to place. Ocean floors are about three miles (5 km) thick, continents are thicker, and lithosphere carrying mountain ranges can be nearly 40 miles (64 km) thick. Ocean crust is made from denser rock than continental crust, but the difference is not sufficient to compensate for so great a difference in thickness, and where the crust is very thick it is also heavier than adjacent crust and the heavy section of lithosphere sinks into the asthenosphere. The lithospheric plates are free to move up and down until their weight, pushing downward, balances their buoyancy, pushing upward. Ice floating on water behaves in the same way, with the result that most of an iceberg lies below the ocean surface. This situation is called *isostasy,* from the Greek words *isos,* "equal," and *stasis,* "station." When rocks are crumpled to build mountains, the mass of material increases, making that section of plate sink lower into the asthenosphere, as shown in the diagram. In this process, *isostatic adjustment,* as material is added to make the mountain higher, the mountain sinks down, making it lower. Isostatic adjustment consequently offsets part of the increase in height.

The moment rocks are thrust into the air they are exposed to the weather. Rain, made slightly acid by the carbon dioxide dissolved in it, reacts with some of the chemical compounds in the rock to produce soluble substances that are washed away by the rain, leaving tiny cracks, holes, and

mountain

sea level

ocean floor

asthenosphere

*Isostasy. The Earth's crust is thicker in mountainous regions than it is elsewhere, and the mass of the crust depresses the top of the asthenosphere. As wind and rain wear away the mountains and they grow smaller, the reduction in their mass causes them to float higher in the asthenosphere, so the mountains rise.*

weaknesses. Water seeps into cracks and freezes there, expanding as it does so, widening the cracks along lines of weakness and breaking off fragments of rock. When the ice melts, these fragments fall away. Rivers transport small rocks, rolling them against one another and knocking away the sharp corners and projections. Eventually the rock fragments are reduced to the size of sand grains, and in this form some of them are carried out to sea, where they settle to the bottom as sediment that one day may be raised above the surface once more in a new range of mountains.

Over millions of years this continual process of erosion wears away even the mightiest mountain chain. We may think of mountains as being eternal, but they are not. They appear and disappear. The processes seem slow to us, but compared with the age of the Earth—approximately 4.6 billion years—the few hundred million years required to raise and lower a mountain chain is not really a very long time at all.

# Grassland soils

Grasses and the herbs associated with them grow in soil, not on bare rock. Soil is a mixture of mineral particles derived from rock and the remains of plants and animals. Bare rock is exposed to the weather (see "How mountains rise and wear away" on pages 31–36), and erosion by wind and water breaks it down into small particles. This process is called *physical weathering*. Water moving between the particles reacts with some of their chemical ingredients to produce soluble compounds that enter the water, producing a *soil solution*. This is *chemical weathering,* and the compounds it releases include some that nourish plants.

Once plants become established, they begin to add organic material in the form of fallen leaves and dead plants. Animals that feed on the plants and on each other also add material. When plants and animals die, other animals, followed by fungi and bacteria, break down the organic material into simpler chemical substances, some of which are absorbed by plant roots. At this stage the physical, chemical, and biological processes have together produced a soil.

As time passes, the soil changes. Organic matter forms a layer on the surface. At the base of that layer, the organic material is being decomposed. Water, draining downward, carries some of the soluble substances resulting from decomposition into a lower layer, where they accumulate. Beneath that layer there is a layer consisting mainly of mineral material derived from the *bedrock* at the base. A trench cut through a soil reveals these layers as series of *horizons* that together form a *soil profile.* The illustration shows a complete soil profile, but many soils contain fewer horizons than this, because the soil is not fully developed.

Soil is alive with organisms, some big enough to be visible and countless billions more that are microscopically small, but the amount of life in the soil depends on the climate and the amount and type of plants that it supports. Climates vary greatly (see the sidebar "How climates are classified" on page 49), and plants have particular climatic requirements. Consequently there are many different types of soil. The soil beneath the Arctic tundra is very different from the soil of

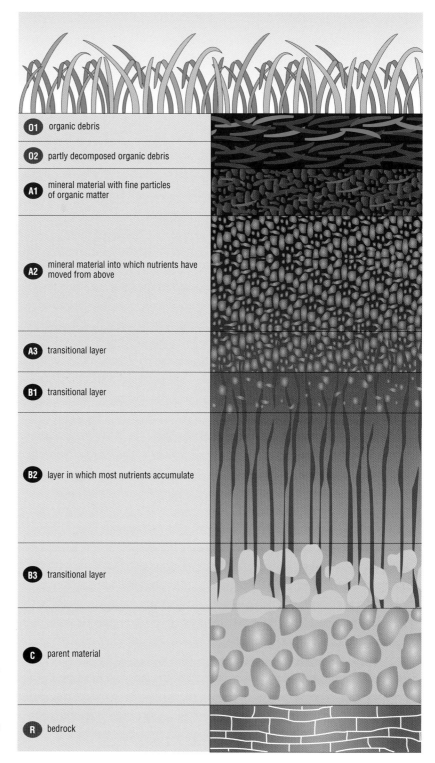

| | |
|---|---|
| **O1** | organic debris |
| **O2** | partly decomposed organic debris |
| **A1** | mineral material with fine particles of organic matter |
| **A2** | mineral material into which nutrients have moved from above |
| **A3** | transitional layer |
| **B1** | transitional layer |
| **B2** | layer in which most nutrients accumulate |
| **B3** | transitional layer |
| **C** | parent material |
| **R** | bedrock |

*Soil profile. An ideal soil forms a series of layers, or horizons. Few soils possess all of these layers.*

the Mojave Desert, and both are different from the soils of the tropical rain forests. Scientists have devised systems for classifying soils (see the sidebar).

## How soils are classified

Farmers have always known that soils vary. There are good soils and poor soils, heavy soils containing a large proportion of clay, sandy soils that dry out rapidly, and light, loamy soils that retain moisture and nutrients. Loam is a mixture of sand, silt, and clay—mineral particles of different sizes. In the latter part of the 19th century Russian scientists were the first to attempt to classify soils. They thought that the differences between soils were due to the nature of the parent material—the underlying rock—and the climate. They divided soils into three broad classes. *Zonal* soils were typical of the climate in which they occur, *intrazonal* soils were less dependent on climate for their characteristics, and *azonal* soils were not the result of climate. Azonal soils include windblown soils and those made from silt deposited by rivers on their floodplains. Individual soil types were placed in one or other of these broad groups. This system remained in use until the 1950s, and some of the Russian names for soils are still widely used, such as Chernozem, Rendzina, Solonchak, and Podzol.

American soil scientists were also working on the problem, and by the 1940s their work was more advanced than that of their Russian colleagues. By 1975 scientists at the United States Department of Agriculture had devised a classification they called "Soil Taxonomy." It divides soils into 10 main groups, called orders. The orders are divided into 47 suborders, and the suborders are divided into groups, subgroups, families, and soil series, with six "phases" in each series. The classification is based on the physical and chemical properties of the various levels, or *horizons,* that make up a vertical cross section, or *profile,* through a soil. These were called "diagnostic horizons."

National classifications are often very effective in describing the soils within their boundaries, but there was a need for an international classification. In 1961 representatives from the Food and Agriculture Organization (FAO) of the United Nations, the United Nations Educational, Scientific and Cultural Organization (UNESCO), and the International Society of Soil Science (ISS) met to discuss preparing one. The project was completed in 1974 and is known as the FAO-UNESCO Classification. Like the Soil Taxonomy, it was based on diagnostic horizons. It divided soils into 26 major groups, subdivided into 106 soil units. The classification was updated in 1988 and has been amended several times since. It now comprises 30 reference soil groups and 170 possible subunits. The FAO has also produced a World Reference Base (WRB), which allows scientists to interpret the national classification schemes.

The soils of the South American llanos and cerrado grasslands are predominantly old soils from which most of the plant nutrients have been lost. In many places there are layers of *laterite* (see the sidebar), which give them a red or yellow color. African savanna soils are much younger and more fertile. These shade into arid soils in the north and into wetter soils on high ground. On the southern side there are poor, exhausted, lateritic soils typical of tropical rain forest. The soils of temperate grasslands—the prairie, steppe, pampa, and veld—are deep and fertile, making them ideal agricultural soils in places where the climate is suitable for farming.

# *Laterite*

Tropical soils are often red or yellow, as a result of the presence of oxides and hydroxides, chiefly of iron and aluminum. These compounds sometimes form hard lumps or continuous layers of a rock called *laterite*. The name is from *later*, the Latin word for "brick."

Most laterite is porous and claylike in texture. The surface is dark brown or red, but if the laterite is broken, the interior is a lighter red, yellow, or brown. Laterite is fairly soft while it remains in the soil, but it hardens when it is exposed to air. It has been mined as a source of iron and nickel. Bauxite, the most important aluminum ore, is very similar to laterite. In some lateritic soils aluminum combines with silica to form the mineral kaolinite, also known as China clay, which is used in the manufacture of fine porcelain and as a whitening agent or filler in paper, paints, medicines, and many other products.

Laterite forms in well-drained soils under humid tropical conditions. The high temperature and abundant moisture accelerate the chemical reactions that break down rock—the process called *chemical weathering*—and many of the dissolved products of those reactions drain out of the soil and are lost. The remaining compounds are concentrated because of the removal of others. In a strongly lateritic soil, iron oxides and hydroxides may account for nearly half of the weight of soil and aluminum oxides and hydroxide for about 30 percent. There may be less than 10 percent silica—the most common mineral in many soils.

Lateritic soils are found in India, Malaysia, Indonesia, China, Australia, Cuba, and Hawaii and in equatorial Africa and South America. There are similar soils in the United States, but these are not true laterites.

## Water and grasslands

Grasslands thrive in climates that are too dry to support forests, and tropical grasslands grow in climates with wet and dry seasons (see "Dry seasons and rainy seasons" on pages 51–55). Rainfall on grassland is often heavy. The Great Plains of the United States, which were originally prairie grasslands, are renowned for their fearsome storms, and grasslands in other parts of the world also experience violent storms (see "Convection and storms" on pages 64–67). Although the rain is intense, once the storm ends and the sky clears, the ground dries fairly quickly. All of the water disappears. That is what it means to say that the soil drains well. Most grassland soils are well drained.

Soil drains best if its surface is covered by vegetation. After heavy rain water often lies on the surface of bare soil much longer because of the effect of heavy rain on unprotected soil. Big raindrops fall at about 20 MPH (32 km/h) in still air, and they strike the ground with considerable force. Typically, dry soil particles stick to one another to form crumbs, but the impact of the falling rain smashes the soil crumbs at the surface, separating the individual soil particles. These spread to form a layer over the surface. Continued pounding by the rain packs soil particles tighter until the layer becomes a waterproof "skin," called a *cap,* that prevents water from penetrating. Water then lies on the surface in pools that collect in hollows and depressions. While it lies there, the water evaporates, returning to the air without benefiting plants.

If plants cover the ground, however, they break the fall of the raindrops. Rain batters the plants, but they bend and bounce back, shedding the water so that it falls quite gently onto the soil. Raindrops intercepted by plants lack the force to smash soil crumbs, and consequently the water is able to penetrate the surface and drain away.

Water may drain by flowing downhill across the surface of the ground, following channels that it widens and deepens until they are worn into gullies. If the water is able to penetrate the soil, it drains downward under the force of gravity. Water moves between and around soil particles until it reaches a layer of material that it cannot penetrate. This impermeable layer may be solid rock or densely packed clay. Unable to

*Movement of water through soil. Water drains downward from the surface, saturating the soil above a layer of impermeable material. The water table is the upper boundary of the saturated layer. Above the water table, water is drawn upward by capillary attraction, moving through the spaces between soil particles in the unsaturated layer.*

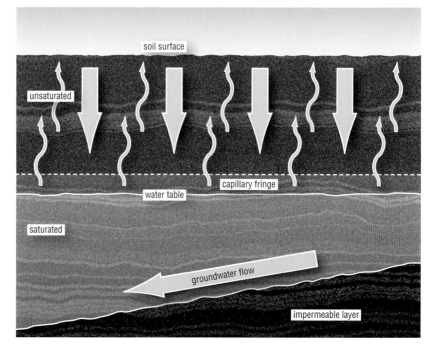

descend any deeper, the water accumulates above the impermeable layer, its level rising as it fills all the tiny air spaces between soil particles. When all of these spaces are filled, the soil is said to be saturated. The upper boundary of the saturated layer is called the *water table.* The diagram shows the arrangement, with the broad arrows indicating the downward movement of water through the unsaturated soil above the water table.

As the diagram shows, the surface of the impermeable layer is not horizontal; rock layers and layers of clay are seldom level. Because water always flows downhill, the water in the saturated soil also flows downhill, across the impermeable surface. Water moving through the soil in this way is called *groundwater.* Where groundwater flows for most of the time, the material through which it moves is called an *aquifer.*

Groundwater continues flowing downhill until it reaches a depression that it fills. The water table then rises. If it rises all the way to the surface, the water will form a pool or lake. If the impermeable layer beneath the groundwater occurs near the surface, water may flow onto the surface as a spring or seep and then continue downhill as a stream.

Besides draining downward, water is capable of rising up through the soil profile because of a property called *capillarity* or *capillary attraction.* Above the water table is a narrow layer called the *capillary fringe,* and water rises through this layer and into the unsaturated soil, as shown in the diagram. It is this upward movement that carries water from the saturated soil to within reach of plant roots.

To understand capillary attraction one must consider the water molecule. Water molecules are *polar;* that is, each molecule carries a small positive electromagnetic charge at one end and a small negative charge at the other. The attraction of opposite charges makes water molecules adhere to each other and to molecules of other substances. This attraction also draws water molecules into the configuration that requires the least energy to maintain it: the sphere. Water droplets are spherical and drops of water lying on a surface have curved surfaces because a sphere is the most energy-efficient shape.

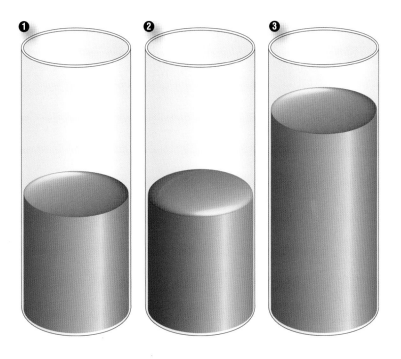

*Capillarity. 1. Attraction between molecules makes the water climb the sides of the tube. 2. The center rises to restore the most economical shape. 3. Water now rises farther up the sides.*

The diagram illustrates the capillarity of water in a tube. When water enters the tube, the attraction between the water molecules and the molecules of the tube itself draws the water upward. Water rises at the sides, where it is in contact with the tube, but not at the center; consequently there is a dip in the water surface. This is not the most efficient shape for the surface, however, and so the center rises to restore the spherical shape. Water at the sides of the tube is then able to rise a little farther. The process repeats itself and water continues to rise up the tube until the weight of the water in the tube is equal to the force of capillary attraction drawing it upward. Water will rise higher in a very narrow tube than in a wider tube, because the wider tube holds more water and therefore the weight of the water soon equals the force of capillary attraction.

Soil consists of particles with countless small air spaces between them. These spaces are linked, allowing water to move along them by capillarity. This movement takes water into the reach of plant roots.

## CHAPTER 3

# GRASSLAND CLIMATES

## Why there are seasons

Winters are cold and summers are warm. In some parts of the world the temperature changes little through the year, but winters are dry and summers are wet. These changes mark the seasons, but why do we have seasons at all?

Summer differs from winter because the Earth turns on an axis that is tilted by about 23.45° from the vertical. Imagine that the path the Earth follows in its orbit about the Sun marks the edge of a flat disk. That disk is called the *plane of the ecliptic,* because eclipses of the Sun and Moon occur only when the Moon crosses it. If the Earth's axis of rotation were at right angles to the plane of the ecliptic, the Sun would be directly above the equator every day of the year. Because the axis is tilted, however, there are only two days in the year—March 20–21 and September 22–23—when the Sun is directly above the equator. On every other day of the year sunlight illuminates more of one hemisphere than of the other.

The diagram shows the Earth's orbital path with arrows indicating the direction of the Earth's movement and the Earth at four positions in its orbit, in December, March, June, and September. The rotational axis, passing through the globe and connecting the North and South Poles, is tilted with respect to the Earth's orbital path. Sunlight travels across the plane of the ecliptic. In December more of the Southern Hemisphere than of the Northern Hemisphere is illuminated. The North Pole is in shadow, but the South Pole is fully lit. In June the situation is reversed, and it is the Northern Hemisphere that receives more sunlight. In March and September both hemispheres are illuminated equally. These differences are most pronounced near the North and South Poles. Although the Sun is directly overhead on only two days, places close to the equator are fully lit at all times of year.

Seen from a position on the surface at the equator, the height of the Sun in the sky at noon changes. Observed just after it has reached its lowest midday height, the Sun each day is a little higher until the day when at noon it is directly overhead. The following day it is not quite so high—and it has moved into the other hemisphere. Each day after that it is a little lower at noon until it reaches its lowest point, after which the Sun rises a little higher each day—it is returning. When it is not directly overhead at the equator, the noonday Sun is directly overhead a point some distance from the equator. On June 21–22 each year the noonday Sun is directly overhead at 23.45°N, the line of latitude that marks the tropic of Cancer. On December 22–23 each year it is overhead at 23.45°S, which is the tropic of Capricorn. These dates are known as the *solstices,* and the Tropics exist because of the axial tilt.

Our word *day* has two meanings. In the first a day is the length of time that the Earth takes to complete one rotation about its own axis—from midnight to midnight, or from noon to noon. In this sense one *solar day,* measured as the

*The seasons. Because the Earth's rotational axis is tilted with respect to the plane of the ecliptic, more of the Northern Hemisphere directly faces the Sun in June and more of the Southern Hemisphere faces the Sun in December. This variation produces the seasons.*

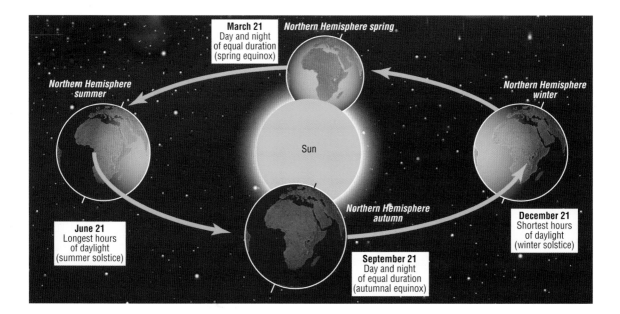

March 21
Day and night
of equal duration
(spring equinox)

Northern Hemisphere spring

Northern Hemisphere summer

Northern Hemisphere winter

Sun

Northern Hemisphere autumn

June 21
Longest hours
of daylight
(summer solstice)

December 21
Shortest hours
of daylight
(winter solstice)

September 21
Day and night
of equal duration
(autumnal equinox)

time taken for the Sun to return to a particular position in the sky, is 86,400 seconds. If it is measured against the position of a fixed star it is called a *sidereal day* and it is 86,164 seconds. This may sound confusing, but at least the general idea is clear enough: One day is the time the Earth takes to make one complete turn on its axis.

Day is also the opposite of night; in other words, it is the period between dawn and sunset, the hours of daylight. This sense of the word *day* is quite different from the first. The conditions that influence the length of this kind of day make the difference between summer and winter.

Because of the tilt in the Earth's axis the length of this kind of "day" varies according to latitude and the time of year. At the equator the Sun is above the horizon for 12.07 hours and below it for 11.93 hours on every day in the year. At New York City, latitude 40.72°N, the Sun is above the horizon for 15.1 hours at the summer solstice—Midsummer Day—but for only 9.9 hours on Midwinter Day—the winter solstice. The higher the latitude the more extreme the difference becomes. At Qaanaaq, Greenland, latitude 76.55°N, people enjoy a full 24 hours of sunlight at the summer solstice, for this is the "land of the midnight Sun." It is also the "land of midday darkness," however, and at the winter solstice the Sun does not rise above the horizon at all. The Arctic and Antarctic Circles mark the latitudes where there is one day in the year when the Sun does not sink below the horizon and another day when the Sun does not rise above the horizon. They are at 66.55°N and 66.55°S and, as the diagram shows, they and their location are determined by the angle of the Earth's axial tilt. The poles are at 90°, and the Arctic and Antarctic Circles are at 90°–23.45° = 66.55°.

On March 20–21 and September 22–23, when the Sun is directly above the equator, there are precisely 12 hours of daylight and 12 hours of darkness everywhere in the world. These dates are called the *equinoxes*.

Regardless of day length, while sunlight is shining on the ground, the Earth's surface absorbs its warmth. As its temperature rises, the ground warms the air next to it, and the warmth spreads upward. At night the ground loses warmth, radiating it into the sky, and its temperature falls. Much depends, therefore, on the duration of daylight and darkness. If, for instance, there are more hours of daylight than there are hours of darkness, the ground has more time to absorb heat than it has to lose it. Each night it cools down, but it does not cool quite as much as it did on the preceding night. The ground and therefore the air above it as well grow steadily warmer, and spring turns into summer. When, on the other hand, there are more hours of darkness than of daylight the ground and air grow cooler, and winter approaches. These changes—the seasons—become more pronounced with increasing distance from the equator. In the Tropics there is less difference between summer and winter temperatures than there is between the afternoon and predawn temperatures.

## Continental and maritime climates

Grasslands are found deep in the interior of continents, where the climate is fairly dry. The tropical grassland climate is hot and dry in winter, and the average temperature never falls below 64.4°F (18°C); this set of conditions is referred to as *Aw* in the Köppen classification (see the sidebar). Temperate grasslands grow where there is sufficient precipitation through the year for healthy plant growth. In some areas the average summer temperature is about 71.6°F (22°C), and in others summers are cooler, but during at least four months in each year the average temperature is higher than 50°F (10°C). In the Köppen scheme these climates are labeled *Caf, Daf,* and *Dbf.* All of them are continental climates.

Climate classification can become highly detailed and extremely complicated, but there is one major and quite simple distinction that defines two radically different types of climate: those that are *maritime* and those that are *continental.*

*Climate* and *weather* are words that have different meanings. Because weather varies from day to day and season to season, the climate of a place may not be apparent on any particular day. A visitor to the Sahara, for instance, might arrive on the day when it rains for the first time in months but would be quite wrong to conclude that the Sahara has a wet climate. The climate of a place reveals itself over time.

# How climates are classified

Throughout history people have devised ways of grouping climates into types. The Greeks divided the Earth into three climatic zones in each hemisphere, defined by the height of the Sun above the horizon. The torrid zone lay between the tropics of Cancer and Capricorn, the frigid zones lay in latitudes higher than the Arctic and Antarctic Circles, and the temperate zones lay between these. Today we still speak of the *temperate zone,* but the terms "torrid zone" and "frigid zone" are no longer used.

During the 19th century scientists began to develop more detailed classifications. Most of these were based on the types of vegetation associated with a climate. They introduced such terms as *savanna climate, tropical rain forest climate, tundra climate,* and *penguin climate.* Some of these terms are still used.

Modern classifications are more detailed. They are mainly of two types: generic or empirical and genetic. *Generic* or *empirical* classifications rely on aridity and temperature to identify climates that have similar effects on vegetation. *Genetic* classifications are based on features of the atmospheric circulation that cause particular climates to occur in particular places.

The most widely used classification scheme is the generic one devised by the German meteorologist Wladimir Peter Köppen (1846–1940). The Köppen classification begins by dividing climates into six categories: tropical rainy (A), dry (B), warm temperate rainy (C), cold boreal (northern) forest (D), tundra (E), and perpetual frost (F). These are further subdivided mainly according to the amount of precipitation they receive and identified by additional lowercase letters. For example, a warm-temperate rainy climate that has mild winters and warm summers and is moist throughout the year is designated *Cfb.* A C climate that is mild and dry in winter and hot in summer is *Cwa.* These categories are further refined by additional letters denoting other factors, such as a dry season in summer (*s*), frequent fog (*n*), or sufficient precipitation for healthy plant growth throughout the year (*f*).

The American climatologist Charles Warren Thornthwaite (1899–1963) devised another widely used generic system. It divides climates into nine moisture provinces and nine temperature provinces, based on calculations of the proportion of precipitation that is available to plants and on the effect of temperature on plant growth. These lead to a *precipitation-efficiency index* and a *temperature-efficiency index,* which are combined to indicate the *potential evapotranspiration*—a concept Thornthwaite introduced. When all the variations are included, this classification system identifies 32 types of climates, designating them by code letters and numbers.

*Climate* is the weather continued over many years and aver-aged. *Weather* consists of the conditions we experience day by day—warm or cool, wet or dry, calm or windy.

Cloud, rain, snow, wind, and all the other ingredients that make up our weather result from events that take place in the air. Imagine the air lying over the North Atlantic Ocean. Air at the bottom is in contact with the ocean surface, and heat passes between the air and water. If the air is warm, contact with the cold sea lowers its temperature, and if it is cold, con-tact with the warmer water raises its temperature. At the same time ocean water evaporates into the air. Air move-ments mix the air, so that after a time the air at any particu-lar altitude, anywhere over the ocean, is at approximately the same temperature and pressure and contains the same amount of water vapor. Air over the ocean is moist and nei-ther very hot nor very cold.

A large body of air, covering an ocean or continent, is called an *air mass*. If it covers an ocean, it is a *maritime* air mass. Air masses do not remain stationary. They are carried by the prevailing winds, and when a maritime air mass crosses a coast it introduces mild, moist weather conditions. The annual temperature range—the difference between the highest and lowest temperatures in a given year—is fairly small and rain or snow falls in every month. Seattle, Wash-ington, has a climate of this kind, produced by air that has crossed the Pacific Ocean with the prevailing westerly winds. The difference between the average temperature in the warmest and coldest months is 23.5°F (13°C), and the average annual rainfall is 33 inches (838 mm). Seattle has a maritime climate.

As the air mass continues its journey across the continent, its characteristics gradually change. Less water evaporates into it because the air is crossing land rather than sea, and lit-tle by little the air loses much of the moisture it gathered over the ocean. The air becomes drier, and, consequently, it introduces dry weather. The temperature of the air also changes as the air mass moves over land. Land warms up much faster than ocean in spring and summer and cools much faster in autumn and winter. Contact with the land surface makes the air much warmer in summer than it was while it remained over the ocean, and much colder in winter. The maritime air mass has become a *continental* air mass.

Continental air masses carry weather conditions that produce a continental climate. Continental climates have a wide annual temperature range and low rainfall. Omaha, Nebraska, has a continental climate. The annual temperature range at Omaha is 55°F (30.5°C) and the average rainfall is 29 inches (737 mm).

Although Omaha has a continental climate and Seattle a maritime climate, there are gradations of both. Climate scientists calculate the extent to which a climate is continental or maritime. On a scale on which a value of 0 or lower indicates a climate that is extremely maritime and 100 or greater indicates an extremely continental climate, Seattle scores 32 and Omaha scores 113.

Grasses tolerate low rainfall and a large temperature range, but they demand full sunshine and cannot grow beneath the shade of trees. Trees require higher rainfall and are less tolerant of extreme temperatures. Consequently forests prefer a more maritime climate and grasslands occupy the interior of continents, where the climate is of a continental type.

## Dry seasons and rainy seasons

In temperate regions winter is the season of cold weather. Tropical winters are not cold; instead, in many places they are dry. So far as plants are concerned, the effect is similar. Plants are unable to obtain the water they need when the ground is frozen, just as they cannot find water in dry soil. A dry winter is therefore equivalent to a cold winter and, as the cold winter does, it occurs because of the tilt in the Earth's rotational axis (see "Why there are seasons" on pages 45–48).

At the equinoxes the noonday Sun is directly overhead at the equator, and that is where the surface is heated more intensely than it is heated anywhere else. Air in contact with the surface is warmed. The warm air expands and rises, and cooler air from higher latitudes flows toward the equator at low level to take its place. Rising air produces low atmospheric pressure near the surface because warm air is less dense

*When it rains the storm is often intense. This is a rainstorm over the savanna grassland of the Serengeti Plain. (Courtesy of Mitsuaki Iwago/Minden Pictures)*

than cool air, so there is a smaller weight of air pressing down on the surface. The equatorial air rises to a height of 39,000–49,000 feet (10–15 km), carrying with it water that has evaporated from the ocean and from wet ground. The rising air cools (see the sidebar "Adiabatic cooling and warming" on page 59), and its water vapor condenses to form clouds, producing heavy rain. That is why equatorial regions have a wet climate. The rising air moves away from the equator and subsides at about latitude 30° in both hemispheres. When it reaches the surface, the air is hot and very dry because it released its moisture during its rise, and it warmed adiabatically as it sank. A body of air warms or cools adiabatically when the change in temperature involves no exchange of heat with the surrounding air. Subsiding air produces high atmospheric pressure at the surface because as the air subsides, air is drawn at high level to take its place, increasing the weight of air pressing down on the surface. At the surface air flows outward from the region of high pressure. That is why there is a belt of deserts in the subtropics of both hemispheres. Rising air produces a belt of low atmospheric pressure at the surface. Air is drawn into the low-pressure region, producing the trade winds that blow from the northeast in the Northern Hemisphere and from the southeast in the Southern Hemisphere.

This vertical circulation is called a *Hadley cell,* after George Hadley (1685–1768), the English meteorologist who first described it in 1735. The diagram shows the circulation of air in the Hadley cells. The belt around the Earth where the trade winds from the Northern and Southern Hemispheres converge is called the *Intertropical Convergence Zone* (ITCZ).

As the Earth continues along its orbital path, the Earth's axial tilt makes the Sun appear to move away from the equator. After the March equinox it appears to move into the Northern Hemisphere, and after the September equinox it seems to move into the Southern Hemisphere. Consequently, the region that is most strongly heated by the Sun—the *thermal equator*—also moves and the ITCZ moves with it.

*Intertropical Convergence Zone. Air rises where the trade winds from the Northern and Southern Hemispheres meet (converge). The warm air is moist, and as it rises and cools its water vapor condenses to produce clouds and rain.*

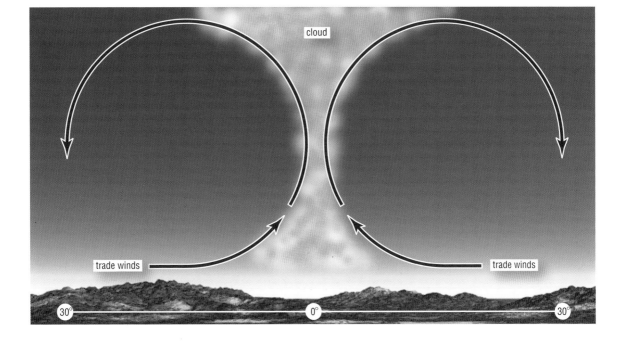

The location of the thermal equator varies with the seasons between 23°N and 10°–15°S. However, it does not form a straight line. In January the thermal equator and the ITCZ are both at about 15°S over Africa and South America and close to the geographic equator over the oceans. In July they lie at about 15°N over Africa, about 25°N over Asia, and at about 5°–10°N over the oceans.

In winter the ITCZ is on the opposite side of the geographic equator. Therefore, over those parts of the Earth located between about latitude 30° and 45° in the winter hemisphere, the weather is produced by the dry, subsiding air of the Hadley cell. The tropical grasslands receive very little rain at this time of year; it is the dry season. In summer, as the ITCZ approaches, the belt of heavy, tropical rainfall moves closer to the grasslands, and they experience a rainy season.

The trade winds always blow toward the ITCZ, but when the ITCZ moves away from the equator the trade winds in one hemisphere cross the equator, and as they do so, they change direction. Seen from above, a bend appears in the wind direction and the trade winds are then called the *hooked trades,* illustrated in the diagram. If it were not for the rotation of the Earth, winds flowing toward the ITCZ from each side of the equator would blow from due north and south. It is the Earth's rotation that deflects the winds to the right in the Northern Hemisphere and to the left in the Southern Hemisphere. The French physicist Gaspard-Gustave de Coriolis (1792–1843) discovered the reason for this in 1835 and it is known as the *Coriolis effect* (abbreviated *CorF*). When the ITCZ is some distance from the equator, the winds continue to blow toward it, but deflection due to the CorF changes direction as the moving air crosses the equator. If the ITCZ lies to the north, the southern trade winds, deflected to the left by the CorF, blow from the southeast on the southern side of the equator, but as they enter the Northern Hemisphere, they are deflected to the right instead of the left. Consequently, the southeasterly winds become southwesterly in direction. When the ITCZ moves south of the equator the northeasterly trades become northwesterly in the Southern Hemisphere. The "hook" is quite gentle, because

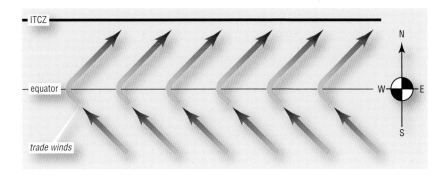

*Hooked trades. The trade winds blow from the northeast in the Northern Hemisphere and from the southeast in the Southern Hemisphere, but when the Intertropical Convergence Zone (ITCZ) moves north of the equator the southern trade winds swing until they blow from the southwest.*

the magnitude of the CorF is greatest at the North and South Poles, and zero at the equator.

## The Dust Bowl

Temperate grasslands also grow in a fairly dry climate, and droughts are not uncommon. There are some parts of the world, including the North American prairie, where droughts recur every few decades. On the Great Plains there is a drought every 20–23 years. The recurring droughts vary in their severity. Extreme droughts occurred in the 13th and 16th centuries—when the drought continued for 20 years—and more recently in the 1750s, 1820s, and 1890s. There were less severe droughts in the 1950s, 1970s, and 1990s. It is quite likely that there will be a drought in the 2010s.

The most severe North American drought of modern times began in 1931 and affected an area of about 150,000 square miles (388,500 km$^2$) in southwestern Kansas, southeastern Colorado, northeastern and southeastern New Mexico, and the panhandles of Oklahoma and Texas. This is the region, shown on the map, that came to be known as the Dust Bowl. It was the most seriously affected area, but three-quarters of the country suffered from the drought, and its effects were severe in 27 states.

Dried to powder, soil blew away from the farms, carrying with it the seeds that had been sown in it. Over large parts of the country the clouds of dust made the sky so dark that chickens roosted in the middle of the day. Geese and ducks choked to death as they flew through the dust, and dust set-

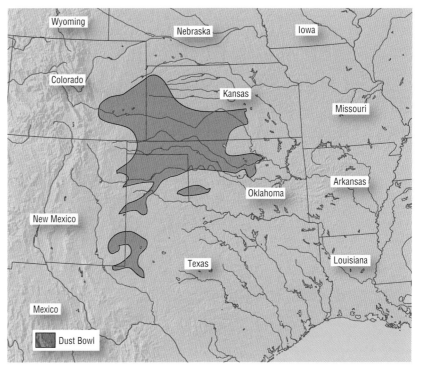

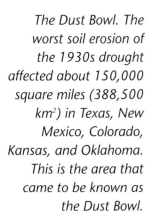

*The Dust Bowl. The worst soil erosion of the 1930s drought affected about 150,000 square miles (388,500 km²) in Texas, New Mexico, Colorado, Kansas, and Oklahoma. This is the area that came to be known as the Dust Bowl.*

tled on ships hundreds of miles out at sea. People called the dust storms "black blizzards," and they produced dunes of topsoil, in places up to 30 feet (9 m) high. The biggest of these clouds extended from Canada to Texas and from Montana to Ohio, covering an area of 1.35 million square miles (3.5 million km²).

Prairie grasses have deep roots that bind and hold the soil. The grasses die and wither away during a drought, but their roots remain to prevent the soil from blowing away, holding the soil particles together so they form large clods that bake hard as concrete. When the rains return, the grasses recover.

But farmers had plowed the prairie. Originally from the East, where the climate is different, farmers had worked very hard to break up the clods and produce a fine soil into which they could sow wheat and other annual crops. The Great Depression, which began in 1929, caused cereal prices to fall, prompting the farmers to plow still bigger areas of prairie in order to maintain their income. Despite this, the continuing fall in prices meant that by 1931 the poorest farmers were close to bankruptcy. Most of the farmers managed to survive, however, because the weather was favorable and yields were high. Over Nebraska, Iowa, and Kansas the average annual rainfall between 1927 and 1933 was five inches (127 mm) higher than the long-term average.

Then the rains began to fail, and within a few years the annual rainfall was well below the average. Yields dropped and then crops began to fail. The ground was left bare, and the clods that had once given the farmers so much trouble were no longer there to hold the soil. Instead of baking hard, the soil dried to powder. In 1931 the first of the black blizzards struck. There were 14 more in 1932 and 38 in 1933. By 1934 the storms were almost continuous. Scientists estimated that 850 million tons (772 million) of soil blew away from the southern plains in 1935 alone. The rains did not return until the winter of 1940–41. By then 2.5 million people had moved from their devastated farms, 200,000 of them to California.

There were further severe dust storms in the 1970s. At times the dust clouds rose to 12,000 feet (3,660 m), and a February 1977 storm in eastern Colorado removed about five tons of soil from every acre of farmland (11.2 ha). The lessons had been learned, however, and these storms were nowhere so severe as those of the Dust Bowl years. Nowadays farmers plant trees to reduce the force of the wind, and native grasses have been reestablished on parts of the prairie.

## Monsoons

Ordinary seasons can produce extreme conditions. The greatest contrast between dry and rainy seasons occurs in southern Asia, where the seasons are known as monsoons.

Our word *monsoon* is from an old Dutch word, *monssoen.* The Dutch derived it from the Portuguese *monção,* and the Portuguese took it from the Arabic word *mausim,* which means a season that returns regularly. There are two monsoon seasons. The winter monsoon is dry, and the summer monsoon is wet. Monsoon seasons occur in many parts of the Tropics, but they are especially associated with southern Asia. Chiengmai, for example, a city located amid the savanna grasslands of Thailand, receives an average 7.5 inches (190.5 mm) of rain between the beginning of October and the end of April. In most years it receives no rain at all during January. In contrast, during the rainy season, lasting from May to September, Chiengmai receives 35 inches (889 mm) of rain.

Monsoon seasons, even those that produce the extreme contrasts found in Asia, are simply dry and rainy seasons. As are those elsewhere in the subtropics and Tropics they are produced mainly by the annual migration of the Intertropical Convergence Zone (ITCZ) (see "Dry seasons and rainy seasons" on pages 51–55). However, the contrast is intensified by the geography.

Asia is a vast continent, and in winter the interior becomes very cold as the land rapidly radiates away the warmth it absorbed during the summer. Cold, dense air settles across a large area, producing high surface pressure—an *anticyclone.* Air flows outward from the high pressure. The air is dry, not only because the interior of the continent is dry but also because the air is cold, and cold air is unable to hold much water vapor. As the air moves southward, the air behind pushes it across the Himalayas, where it loses what little moisture it still manages to hold. The air then subsides down the southern side of the mountains, and, as it does so, it warms adiabatically (see the sidebar). The Himalayas divide the west-to-east airflow. This division produces another winter anticyclone over northern India and intensifies the winds blowing across the land.

Over the ocean pressure is relatively low. The oceans retain their summer warmth longer than the continents do, so air in contact with the water warms and rises. Warm air rising over the oceans is replaced by hot air from the Asian continent, which causes large amounts of moisture to evaporate. Winter rainfall is heavy over offshore and oceanic islands.

In winter, as the map shows, the ITCZ lies close to the equator, far to the south. With the ITCZ in this position the whole of southern Asia lies beneath the northeasterly trade winds, strengthening the winds blowing in the same direction from the mountains. The winter monsoon is dry, but it is not cold. Average daytime temperatures in Chiengmai

# Adiabatic cooling and warming

Air is compressed by the weight of air above it. Imagine a balloon partly inflated with air and made from some weightless substance that totally insulates the air inside. No matter what the temperature outside the balloon, the temperature of the air inside remains the same.

Imagine the balloon is released into the atmosphere. The air inside is squeezed between the weight of air above it, all the way to the top of the atmosphere, and the denser air below it.

Suppose the air inside the balloon is less dense than the air above it. Denser air will push beneath it and the balloon will rise. As it rises, the distance to the top of the atmosphere becomes smaller, so there is less air above to weigh down on the air in the balloon. At the same time, as the balloon moves through air that is less dense, it experiences less pressure from below. This causes the air in the balloon to expand.

When air (or any other gas) expands, its molecules move farther apart. The amount of air remains the same, but it occupies a bigger volume. As they move apart, the molecules must "push" other molecules out of their way. This uses energy, so as the air expands its molecules lose energy. Because they have less energy they move more slowly.

When a moving molecule strikes something, some of its energy is transferred to whatever it strikes, and part of that energy is converted into heat. This raises the temperature of the struck object by an amount related to the number of molecules striking it and their speed.

In expanding air, the molecules are moving farther apart, so a smaller number of them strike an object each second. They are also traveling more slowly, so they strike with less force. This means the temperature of the air decreases. As it expands, air cools.

If the air in the balloon is denser than air below, it will sink. As it sinks, the pressure on the air will increase, its volume will decrease, and its molecules will acquire more energy. Its temperature will increase.

This warming and cooling has nothing to do with the temperature of the air surrounding the balloon. It is called *adiabatic* warming and cooling, from the Greek word *adiabatos*, meaning "impassable," suggesting that the air is enclosed by an imaginary boundary through which heat is unable to pass.

reach 84°–89°F (29°–32°C) between November and February, and it is an uncomfortably oppressive heat, because the *relative humidity* is about 96 percent. The *relative humidity* is the amount of water vapor present in the air as a percentage of the amount needed to saturate the air.

The rains start to arrive in April as occasional thunderstorms, and the main monsoon rains commence early in May. The ITCZ is then moving northward, and by the middle of summer it lies north of the Himalayas. As they enter the Tropics of the Northern Hemisphere, trade winds originating in the Southern Hemisphere change direction as a result of the Coriolis effect—which deflects moving objects to the left in the Southern Hemisphere and to the right in the Northern Hemisphere. The southeasterly winds become southwesterly and therefore approach Asia across the Indian Ocean, Arabian Sea, and Bay of Bengal. Land warms up faster than the ocean and warm air rises over the land, producing a region of low surface pressure. Pressure is then higher over the ocean, which is warming more slowly, so air now moves from the sea toward the land, intensifying the trade winds. This air is moist, and when it rises to cross the hills, its water vapor condenses to form clouds that produce rain. September is the wettest month at Chiengmai, with an average 9.8 inches (249 mm) of rain. By October, however, the rainfall begins

*Asian monsoon seasons. During the winter monsoon, air from central Asia moves in a southwesterly direction, causing dry weather in southern Asia. This is the dry, northeasterly, or winter monsoon. In summer, moist air flows in a northeasterly direction, creating the wet, southwesterly, or summer monsoon.*

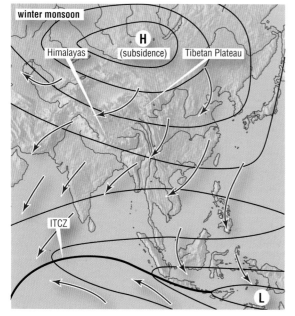

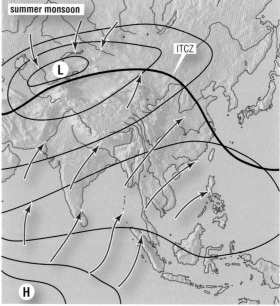

to decrease as the ITCZ moves southward and the land begins to cool. Chiengmai usually receives only 1.2 inches (30 mm) of rain in November.

## El Niño

Farmers depend on the monsoon rains, but the monsoons are not entirely reliable. In some years they arrive late. When that happens, the growing season is shorter and crop yields are reduced. Sometimes the rains do not arrive at all. A failure of the monsoon rains means a failed harvest and possibly famine.

Monsoon failures caused severe famine in India in 1877 and 1899. The 1899 failure prompted the British government—Britain then ruled India—to ask the head of the Indian Meteorological Service, Sir Gilbert Walker (1868–1923), to try to find a pattern in the monsoon seasons that would make it possible to predict crop failures. Reliable forecasts would enable the authorities to lay in stores of food and prevent famine. Walker failed to find any pattern in the monsoons, but when he examined detailed weather records from all over the world he discovered that events in one place often coincided with different events in places far away. Today these are known as *teleconnections*. In particular, Walker noted that the air pressure was usually low over Darwin, Australia, and high over Tahiti, but when the pressure rose over Darwin, it fell over Tahiti. After a time the changes would reverse, with pressure falling at Darwin and rising at Tahiti. Such changes occurred slowly at intervals of between two and seven years. Walker called the change a *Southern Oscillation*.

In 1969 the Norwegian-American meteorologist Jacob Bjerknes (1897–1975) became the first scientist to explain El Niño, which is another weather phenomenon that occurs over the tropical Pacific. Meteorologists now know that El Niño is linked to the Southern Oscillation. The technical name for a full El Niño cycle is an El Niño–Southern Oscillation (ENSO) event.

In the usual course of events high pressure over the eastern South Pacific and low pressure in the west generate a force that accelerates the southeasterly trade winds. The trade winds drive an ocean current—the South Equatorial Current—that flows from east to west just south of the equator, carrying warm surface water away from South America and toward northern Australia and Indonesia. A deep pool of warm water surrounds Indonesia, but in the eastern Pacific the layer of warm surface water is fairly shallow. Warm, moist air rises over Indonesia and cool, dry air subsides over the eastern Pacific. This circulation, illustrated in the diagram, produces heavy rain in the west but dry weather in the east, where the Atacama Desert, one of the world's driest deserts, lies along the Pacific coastal region of South America.

Winds over tropical South America blow from the southeast and have crossed the continent by the time they reach the west coast, losing their moisture in the process. That is why the western coastal belt has such a dry climate. But the winds have a second effect: They push water away from the coast. As the wind pushes the surface water away from the coast, the Coriolis effect and friction with deeper water set the upper water moving in a circle that very slowly draws up water to replace it all the way from the ocean floor. This is called *upwelling.* The deep water is rich in plant nutrients that have settled on the ocean floor and upwelling carries these close to the surface, where they nourish microscopic plants and animals known collectively as *plankton.* The plankton organisms feed huge populations of fish, which in turn provide food for marine mammals such as seals and for seabirds.

During a Southern Oscillation the pressure gradually changes. As pressure rises in the west and falls in the east, the force accelerating the trade winds weakens and the winds slacken. In extreme cases the trade winds cease or even change direction from southeasterly to southwesterly. The South Equatorial Current also weakens or, occasionally, reverses direction. Warm water starts to accumulate off the South American coast, and the pool of warm water around Indonesia becomes shallower. Weather conditions become much drier in the west, in Indonesia, Australia, and the Philippines, and there may be drought in these places. On the other side of the ocean heavy rain falls over the dry coastal regions of South America.

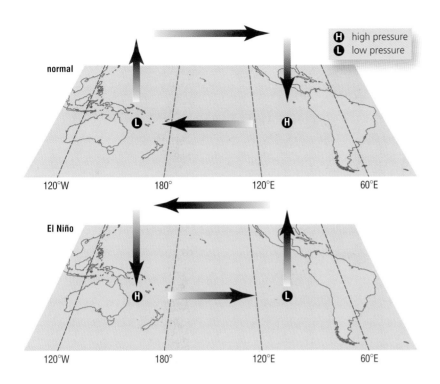

H high pressure
L low pressure

*El Niño. Every few years surface air pressure falls over the eastern South Pacific and rises in the west. This decrease in pressure changes the direction of the winds and surface current just south of the equator. Normally, warm surface water flows from east to west, but during an El Niño it flows from west to east.*

The change in pressure and winds develops over several months, but the resulting change in the weather arrives fairly abruptly, usually in December. The rains mean an abundant harvest for the farmers of Peru and Ecuador, and because they arrive around Christmastime the phenomenon came to be regarded as a Christmas gift and called "the [male or Christ] child"—El Niño. Strong El Niño events also generate bad weather, however. The rains can cause flooding and landslides in western South America, as well as wet, stormy weather in the western United States, the Gulf states, and Mexico, while the drought on the western side of the ocean can trigger bushfires and forest fires. The weakening of the southeasterly trade winds also prevents cold water from welling up to the surface along the Peruvian coast. When the upwellings cease, the fish and birds go elsewhere and the Peruvian fishing industry suffers.

After a few weeks of this weather pattern, the pressure distribution starts to return to normal. It may then swing too far, so that the pressure rises above its usual value in the east and falls below its usual value in the west. When this happens, the trade winds strengthen and the South Equatorial Current intensifies, producing conditions that cause very wet weather in Indonesia and extreme drought in South America. This condition is called La Niña, "the [female] child." A full ENSO event comprises an El Niño followed by La Niña.

## Convection and storms

When it rains on the grasslands, the rain often arrives as a fierce storm, with hail, gale-force winds, and usually thunder and lightning. Most of the prairie experiences thunderstorms on about 50 days each year.

Violent storms occur more frequently in summer than in winter, and they are most likely to begin in the late afternoon or early evening. Individual storms seldom last much longer than one hour, but as one storm dies down another storm is often beginning nearby. Sometimes storms develop side by side along a line that can extend for hundreds of miles. This is known as a *squall line*. Single storms and squall lines move across the ground.

Certain ingredients are needed to make a storm. Air close to the ground must be warm and moist. That is why storms often begin late in the day, after the ground has had time to warm up. Something must then make the warm, moist air start to rise and continue rising. Cold air pushing beneath warm air at a weather front makes the warm air rise, and some storms start this way. But most summer storms begin when air rises above an area of ground that is warmer than its surroundings. Air that ascends in this way is said to be *unstable* (see the sidebar). As the air rises, its temperature falls and the water vapor it contains condenses to form liquid droplets—cloud droplets. By the time it is fully developed, the storm cloud, called a *cumulonimbus* cloud, may extend from a base that is 5,000 feet (1.5 km) above the ground to a height of more than 30,000 feet (9.15 km).

Inside the cloud air is rising by *convection*, which is one of the three ways that heat can be transferred from one place to another. Warmth from the Sun travels to the Earth as *radiation*. The radiant heat warms the ground and passes by *con-*

*duction* to air that is in contact with the ground. The air expands as it grows warmer. Expansion makes it less dense, and denser air sinks beneath it, pushing it upward. The air continues to rise, growing cooler as it does so, until its density is the same as that of the air around it. Air that replaced it at ground level is also warmed and rises, and so warmth is transported upward. This is convection.

Convection generates vertical air currents, and vertical air currents strengthen storms. At first, when the cloud is still small enough to be classed as *cumulus,* the currents are fairly gentle, but by the time the cloud has grown to its full cumulonimbus size, air inside it may be rising at up to 100 MPH (160 km/h). The air currents carry water, which is constantly condensing and evaporating again. In the upper part of the cloud, where the temperature is below freezing, water vapor freezes directly, forming ice crystals, and some liquid droplets cool to below freezing temperature, but without turning to ice—they are *supercooled.* Water evaporates from these supercooled droplets and accumulates as ice on the ice crystals. The ice crystals grow and join together into snowflakes, which melt as they fall into the lower part of the cloud. As the droplets continue to fall, they collect others. Up currents carry some of them back to the top of the cloud, where they freeze and then fall again, gathering a thin surface layer of ice as they descend. When they are too heavy to be lifted by the up currents, they fall from the cloud as hailstones. The size of the hailstones that reach the ground is an indication of the strength of the up currents inside the cloud. The bigger and more violent the cloud, the larger the hailstones will be.

At this stage the cloud is delivering heavy rain. Not every storm cloud produces falls of hail, but those that do accumulate the hail and then drop all of it at once, producing a *hail streak* about one mile (1.6 km) wide and six miles (10 km) long.

Because its surface is exposed to the cold air, a water droplet freezes from the outside in. When the interior freezes a short time later, its expansion bursts the pellet, releasing tiny splinters of ice. The splinters carry a small positive electrical charge and the larger frozen droplets carry a negative charge. The splinters accumulate near the top of the cloud,

# Lapse rates and stability

Air temperature decreases (or lapses) with increasing height. The rate at which it does so is called the *lapse rate.* Although all air contains some water vapor, air that is not saturated with moisture—all of its moisture is present as vapor rather than liquid droplets or ice crystals—is said to be *dry.* When dry air cools adiabatically, it does so at 5.4°F for every 1,000 feet (9.8°C/km) that it rises. This is known as the *dry adiabatic lapse rate* (DALR).

When the temperature of the rising air has fallen sufficiently, its water vapor will start to condense into droplets. Condensation commences at the *dew-point temperature* and the height at which this temperature is reached is called the *lifting condensation level.* Condensation releases *latent heat,* which warms the air. Latent heat is the energy that allows water molecules to break free from each other when liquid water vaporizes or ice melts. It does not change the temperature of the water or ice, which is why it is called *latent,* meaning "hidden." The same amount of latent heat is released, warming the surroundings, when water vapor condenses and when liquid water freezes. Consequently, the rising air then cools at a slower rate, known as the *saturated adiabatic lapse rate* (SALR). The SALR varies, depending on the rate of condensation, but it averages 3°F per 1,000 feet (6°C/km).

The actual rate at which the temperature decreases with height in air that is not rising is called the *environmental lapse rate* (ELR). It is calculated by comparing the

and the droplets accumulate near the bottom, so cloud acquires a positive charge near the top and a negative charge near the bottom. The charge at the base of the cloud induces an opposite charge on the ground below. These charges increase until they are strong enough to overcome the electrical resistance of the air. Then they discharge as a spark—a lightning flash—between one part of the cloud and another, between two clouds, or between the cloud and the ground. A flash of lightning releases so much energy that in less than one second the air around the flash is heated by up to 54,000°F (30,000°C). This effect makes the air expand so rapidly it explodes, producing the shock waves that we hear as a crash of thunder.

Rain is melted snow and hail is ice. Both are cold, and as they fall from high in the cloud each raindrop and hailstone surface temperature, the temperature at the tropopause (it is about –85°F; –65°C at the equator), and the height of the tropopause (about 10 miles; 16 km over the equator).

If the ELR is less than both the DALR and SALR, rising air will cool faster than the surrounding air, so it will always be cooler and will tend to subside to a lower height. Such air is said to be *absolutely stable*.

If the ELR is greater than the SALR, air that is rising and cooling at the DALR and later at the SALR will always be warmer than the surrounding air. Consequently, it will continue to rise. The air is then *absolutely unstable*.

If the ELR is less than the DALR but greater than the SALR, rising air will cool faster than the surrounding air while it remains dry but more slowly once it rises above the lifting condensation level. At first it is stable, but above the lifting condensation level it becomes unstable. This air is said to be *conditionally unstable*. It is stable unless a condition (rising above its lifting condensation level) is met, whereupon it becomes unstable.

Stable air brings settled weather. Unstable air produces heaped clouds of the *cumulus* type. The base of these clouds is at the lifting condensation level, and the cloud tops are at the altitude where the rising air has lost enough water vapor to make it dry once more, so it is cooling at the DALR. If the air is sufficiently unstable, however, the clouds can grow into towering *cumulonimbus* storm clouds. Equatorial air is usually unstable.

drags a small amount of cold air with it. Rain and hail generate down currents of cold air. These emerge from the base of the cloud as a cold, gusty wind. The down currents also cool the up currents of warm air inside the cloud. Eventually the down currents completely suppress the up currents. When that happens, the storm ends and the cloud dissipates. As it dies, the cloud may release all of its remaining moisture at once, as a *cloudburst*. Cloudbursts are intense. A big cumulonimbus cloud holds up to 250,000 tons (275,000t) of water.

## Tornadoes

A set of up currents and down currents is called a *cell*, and most storm clouds contain several. Sometimes, however, the winds near the top of the cloud push the up currents to one side, making them bend over, and when this happens, a really huge cumulonimbus may contain only one cell, called a *supercell*. Because the up currents and down currents are separated, the cold down currents do not cool and suppress the warm up currents as they do in a multicell cloud. Consequently, supercell clouds survive much longer than do multicell clouds. The diagram shows a very simplified cross-sectional view of a supercell cloud. The cloud rises to about 50,000 feet (15 km) and its base covers an area of about 87 square miles (225 km²). Air in the cloud is rising so vigorously that it produces a bulge, called an *overshooting top*. The wind draws out the top of the cloud, at this height consisting entirely of ice crystals, into an overhanging sheet. Ice crystals that fall from the sheet evaporate instantly in the dry air, giving the sheet a shape like that of a blacksmith's anvil. Supercell clouds produce the most violent storms of all.

It is the wind in the surrounding air that draws out the top of the cloud into an anvil shape. This process sweeps away air that has risen through the cloud, drawing more air into the up current to replace it. Winds also blow horizontally inside

*Supercell. In most storm clouds there are several currents of warm, rising air, with currents of cold air sinking between them. If the rising air columns bend and become horizontal, however, they may merge and lie to the side of the cold, subsiding air. This is a supercell.*

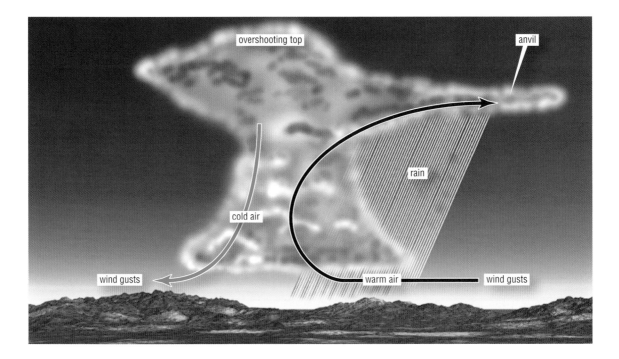

the cloud, and the speed or direction of the wind may change at different heights inside the cloud. This process produces *wind shear,* a force that exists when the wind at a particular height blows across the path of the wind below it and at a greater speed. Wind shear sets the column of rising air rotating, so the air is spiraling upward. The rotation begins in the upper part of the cloud, below the level of wind shear. The rotating center of the cloud is then known as a *mesocyclone.* The word *cyclone* describes air that rotates in the same direction as the Earth—counterclockwise in the Northern Hemisphere. Most mesocyclones rotate cyclonically (counterclockwise), but the reason for this is unclear and occasionally there are mesocyclones that turn in a clockwise direction (anticyclonically).

Gradually more and more of the inside of the cloud begins to turn, and the rotation extends downward. At this stage the mesocyclone is up to five miles (8 km) across. Eventually the rotation may extend to the air immediately below the cloud. Air that is drawn into the up currents now starts turning as it approaches the cloud, so the mesocyclone consists of air that is spiraling upward to where it is swept into the anvil and removed.

Because air is being removed, the atmospheric pressure inside the mesocyclone is low, and as air enters the spiral its pressure drops. The reduction in pressure allows the air to expand, causing it to cool, and its water vapor condenses. Condensation in the rotating air beneath the cloud base makes it look as though the cloud itself is descending. Its rotation is clearly visible from a distance, and fragments of cloud can be seen moving across it.

The rotation continues to extend downward, and as it does so it becomes narrower. Visible because of the condensation it produces, the rotating column of air extends below the storm cloud as a *funnel cloud,* widest at the top and tapering toward the lower end. Air accelerates as it enters the spiral and the wind speed is greatest around the core of the funnel. The acceleration is due to a property of spinning objects. When it spins, an object possesses *angular momentum* that is proportional to its mass, speed of rotation (called its *angular velocity*), and radius of rotation. Its angular momentum remains constant, so if one of its components changes, one or more of the others changes to compensate. This is called the *conservation of angular momentum*. Air cannot alter its mass, but as it approaches the center of the funnel, its radius of spin decreases and consequently its angular velocity increases in proportion. It means that the wider the funnel, the greater the wind speeds around the center.

If the funnel touches the ground it becomes a *tornado*—called a "cyclone" or a "twister" in some parts of the United States. Tornadoes sweep up dust and other debris to produce a dark cloud around the base of the funnel. As this material is carried upward and into the cloud, the tornado darkens. All tornadoes are dangerous. Even a mild one will lift debris and hurl it out of the spiral with great force, and all but the mildest tornadoes are capable of demolishing small buildings and throwing trailer homes and cars around as if they are toys.

Tornadoes can happen anywhere and at any time, but they are more likely in some places and at some times. More than half of all tornadoes occur in spring. The season begins in February in the Gulf states. In March and April there are often tornadoes in Georgia and Florida. The greatest number, however, occur in May and June across the Great Plains. A belt extending from northern Texas and the Texas Panhandle through Oklahoma and Nebraska suffers more tornadoes than any other part of the country—or of the world. It is known as "Tornado Alley."

## CHAPTER 4

# HISTORY OF GRASSLANDS

## Evolution of grasslands

Grasses first appeared on Earth about 60 million years ago. The earliest types, possibly related to modern bamboos, grew in the Tropics, in regions close to the forest edges where the climate was too dry for trees. As the map shows, at that time North America, Eurasia, and Africa were still joined and the early grasses were able to spread across the supercontinent. As the supercontinent broke apart, its animals and plants were carried away on the present-day continents.

Plants and animals on one continent cannot breed with those on another continent separated from them by an ocean, so once the supercontinent had broken apart, the species on each continent began to evolve independently. All of the main groups of grasses had appeared before the separation began, however, so each continent carried representatives of all the groups. No matter how living conditions changed, there was a good chance that among these groups there would be some types of grass that could prosper. The grasses thrived, and today there are about 9,000 species in the grass family (Poaceae). Some other plant families contain more species, but none dominates entire landscapes the way grasses do or thrives in such varied locations—everywhere from the edges of the Arctic and Antarctic Circles to the equator and from high in the mountains to sea level.

By about 45 million years ago there were grasses growing on all of the continents, but they were not yet abundant, especially in Australia, where grasses made up only a small proportion of the vegetation. Grasses were still confined to the Tropics, and they probably grew in forest clearings and around their edges. There were no grasslands like those of today.

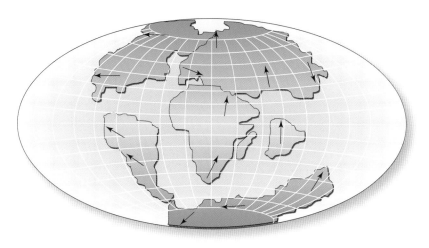

*The world 65 million years ago. At that time North America, Eurasia, and Africa were joined. This proximity allowed grasses to spread freely. When the continents separated, they carried the grasses with them. The arrows represent the movement of grasses.*

As the continents continued to separate, climates everywhere slowly changed. There were periods of warmer weather, but the general trend was toward cooler conditions. The slow but steady fall in temperatures continued for millions of years, leading to the series of ice ages that began about 2.5 million years ago.

Tropical climates remained warm, but the changes in wind patterns resulting from the redistribution of the continents and the widening of the oceans produced dry and rainy seasons over the interior of the tropical continents (see "Dry seasons and rainy seasons" on pages 51–55). Trees had difficulty adapting to dry winters and surviving occasional prolonged droughts. Grasses, however, were able to thrive in these conditions. The forests became smaller and grasses moved into the lands the trees had vacated.

About 15 million years ago there were tropical grasslands in South America, and by 14 million years ago grassland covered parts of what is now Kenya, in East Africa. These are the earliest grasslands for which scientists have fossil evidence. They were much less open than the modern savanna grassland. The landscape was more like parkland, with some isolated trees and shrubs, scattered stands of trees, and grasses, together with a variety of other herbs, growing on the open ground between them.

As the global cooling continued and forests outside the Tropics contracted, grasses expanded away from the equator and temperate grasslands started to appear. Around the time the Kenyan grasslands were expanding, some of the tropical grasslands in South America were changing into temperate grasslands.

Forests survived for much longer in North America. Grasses were widespread, but until about five million years ago they accounted for no more than about one-fifth of the total vegetation on the Great Plains. Then the grasses began to spread. It was not until about 2.5 million years ago, however, that they had developed into the prairie that greeted the first humans to make their homes on the continent. The Eurasian steppe formed and expanded at about the same time.

The continents continued to move, and about 3 million years ago North and South America met and joined. There were times when the climate grew warmer and tropical forests expanded through Central America, but at cooler times savanna grassland linked North and South America, allowing grassland animals to move from one continent to the other. Temperate grassland animals also migrated between North America and Eurasia, across a land bridge linking Alaska and Siberia across what is now the Bering Strait.

## Grasslands and past climate changes

Grasses tolerate a wide range of climatic conditions, but occasionally even they are overwhelmed. About 2.5 million years ago the continuing fall in average temperatures reached an extreme. An ice age began. We know very little about this ice age. Evidence for it has been found in Britain and northwestern Europe but not in North America. Nevertheless, it is likely that the ice age affected the entire Northern Hemisphere.

This was only the first of a series of ice ages that have been occurring ever since. There have probably been eight ice ages in all, and each one has lasted for tens of thousands or hundreds of thousands of years. Ice ages are separated by periods of warmer conditions, called *interglacials*. The most recent ice age—known as the Wisconsinian in North America, the Devensian in Britain, and the Weichselian in northwestern Europe—began about 75,000 years ago and ended about 10,000 years ago. Today we are living in the interglacial following the end of the Wisconsinian, called the Holocene. Scientists divide the history of the Earth into episodes, as a geologic time scale (see "Geologic time scale" on page 32). There were ice ages in the more distant past, but the present series began toward the end of the Pliocene epoch and continued through the Pleistocene epoch. We are living

## Holocene, Pleistocene, and late Pliocene glacials and interglacials

| Approximate date (1,000 years BP) | North America | Great Britain | Northwestern Europe |
|---|---|---|---|
| **Holocene** | | | |
| 10–present | *Holocene* | *Holocene (Flandrian)* | *Holocene (Flandrian)* |
| **Pleistocene** | | | |
| 75–10 | Wisconsinian | Devensian | Weichselian |
| 120–75 | *Sangamonian* | *Ipswichian* | *Eeemian* |
| 170–120 | Illinoian | Wolstonian | Saalian |
| 230–170 | *Yarmouthian* | *Hoxnian* | *Holsteinian* |
| 480–230 | Kansan | Anglian | Elsterian |
| 600–480 | *Aftonian* | *Cromerian* | *Cromerian complex* |
| 800–600 | Nebraskan | Beestonian | *Bavel complex* |
| 740–800 | | *Pastonian* | |
| 900–800 | | Pre-Pastonian | Menapian |
| 1,000–900 | | *Bramertonian* | *Waalian* |
| 1,800–1,000 | | Baventian | Eburonian |
| **Pliocene** | | | |
| 1,800 | | *Antian* | *Tiglian* |
| 1,900 | | Thurnian | |
| 2,000 | | *Ludhamian* | |
| 2,300 | | Pre-Ludhamian | Pretiglian |

*BP* means "before present" (present is taken to be 1950). Names in italic refer to interglacials. Other names refer to glacials (ice ages). Dates become increasingly uncertain for the older glacials and interglacials and the period before about 2 million years ago. Evidence for these episodes has not been found in North America; in the case of the Thurnian glacial and Ludhamian interglacial the only evidence is from a borehole at Ludham, in eastern England.

today in the Holocene epoch. The table lists the ice ages—the technical name for them is *glacials*—and interglacials from the present back through the Pleistocene and to the late Pliocene.

Ice ages begin when summer temperatures fall by a few degrees. When this happens, some of the snow that fell in the previous winter fails to melt. Because it is white, the snow reflects sunshine—which would otherwise warm the surface—and the ground beneath the snow remains cold. The following winter more snow falls on top of the snow that is still lying from the preceding winter, and the following summer a slightly bigger area of snow fails to melt. In this way the snow-covered area gradually expands. Year by year the layer of snow grows thicker and heavier until the snow at the base of the layer is compressed so tightly it turns to ice. The ice then starts to spread outward.

An advancing ice sheet scours away all of the soil and loose stones beneath it. Obviously no plants can survive beneath the ice—not even grass. Beyond the ice sheet there is a wide belt of tundra, where both the climate and the vegetation are similar to those found today in northern Canada and Siberia.

During an ice age the climate everywhere is relatively dry. Such a large amount of water is stored permanently in the ice sheets that sea levels fall, leaving a smaller area of sea surface from which water can evaporate. At the same time low temperatures reduce both the rate of evaporation and the amount of water vapor that air is able to transport. Consequently, rainfall decreases, even in the Tropics. Tropical forests shrink in area, and savanna grasslands expand. Deserts also expand; during the Wisconsinian ice age, for example, the Sahara was much more extensive than it is today.

When the ice age comes to an end, the ice sheets contract and the warmer conditions and rising sea levels mean that rainfall increases. The ground that was previously frozen throughout the year—the *permafrost*—thaws, and the tundra vegetation gives way to bushes and then to forest, except in the drier areas, where grassland predominates. Deserts also retreat. By about 9,000 years ago the Sahara had almost completely disappeared. The desert was replaced by savanna grassland, which continued to occupy the area until about 5,000 years ago, when the climate became drier again and the desert returned.

As the rainfall increased in the temperate regions and soils became deeper and richer, trees migrated northward. By about 7,000 years ago most of the lowlands throughout Western Europe and all of lowland Britain were covered by forest. During a period of warm, dry weather about 5,000 years ago, the prairie in North America expanded eastward as far as Ohio, with patches of grassland throughout the Midwest. But by about 3,000 years ago cooler, moister weather allowed forests of oak, chestnut, beech, and hemlock to become established.

## How forest can change into grassland

The catalyst that converts forest to grassland is usually a change in the climate, but other factors can also play a part. The increased rainfall that allowed the North American forests to begin expanding into the prairie from about 3,000 years ago might have allowed them to expand farther had it not been for the bison. Similarly the tropical savannas of Africa might occupy a smaller area than they do were it not for the herds of grazing animals that live there.

Large plant-eating animals, such as bison and antelope, feed on grass and herbs growing with the grass, but they will also eat the leaves and tender young shoots of trees and shrubs. They only eat those parts of the plants that they are able to reach, so the taller plants can survive, but not young seedlings. Those are destroyed when they are eaten or trampled.

Trees and shrubs grow from seeds, and destroying young plants reduces the number of future seed producers. As seeds stored in the soil sprout, grow a little, and are then killed, the store of seeds is steadily reduced. Thus when the mature plants that produced the seeds die of old age, there are no young plants to take their place.

Grasses actually benefit from grazing, so they thrive as the shrubs and trees disappear. Grazing animals feed on grass, so they also benefit. The increased food supply means that more of their young survive, and with more animals to graze, the woody plants are suppressed even more severely. Once the area of grassland is large enough to support large herds of grazers, the animals will prevent the grassland from changing to forest.

Fire also helps grassland remain grassland. During the dry season tropical grasses die down, covering the ground with dry grass that the smallest spark will ignite. Fires are common and beneficial. They remove the dead plant matter and leave behind a layer of ash, rich in nutrients, that is washed into the ground by the first rain. With no layer of dead grass to suppress the new growth, the rain yields a flush of lush, nutritious grass. Trees and shrubs are more likely to be killed by the fire. Although their seeds below ground remain unharmed, by the time they produce shoots above ground the grasses are flourishing and the grazers are feeding.

Humans may also play a part in maintaining grassland. They depend on the game animals and use fire as a tool to

*Fire on the Okavango delta, Botswana. Fires sweep unchecked across up to 70 percent of this grassland each year. (Courtesy of Frans Lanting/ Minden Pictures)*

hunt them. Large animals flee from fire, and hunters can exploit this behavior to make hunting easier. A group of hunters hides downwind of the herd, so the animals can neither see nor smell them; other members of the team then set a fire along a line at right angles to the wind; the wind directs the fire and the animals flee before it into the prepared ambush. After the fire has died down the grasses soon reappear. Over many years this technique will maintain the grassland and expand its area by pushing back the edges of the forest, thereby providing more food for game animals.

## The transformation of New Zealand

About 1,500 years ago Polynesian peoples were traveling across the Pacific Ocean and settling the habitable islands. In about the year 850 they reached New Zealand, the most southerly point in their explorations. They remained there, isolated from the rest of the world, for almost 1,000 years. Abel Janszoon Tasman (ca. 1603–ca. 1659), the Dutch navigator who also discovered Tasmania, Fiji, and Tonga, sighted South Island in December 1642, but when he attempted to land, the island's inhabitants drove off his party and killed several of his men. The next European to visit the islands was the English explorer Captain James Cook (1728–79). In 1769–70 Cook sailed around both islands, mapping their coastlines and charting their coastal waters. Cook landed and eventually established good relations with the Maori people.

Cook returned to New Zealand several times, exploring and mapping much of the country. He and other explorers found that approximately half of New Zealand was forested. Of the remainder, some was mountainous and lay above the tree line, but substantial areas were covered with grassland, scrub, and bracken. The map shows the area of forest in about 1850.

The amount of forest was surprising, not because it was so extensive, but because it was so restricted. New Zealand has a climate that is ideal for trees, ranging from moist subtropical in the northern part of North Island to cool temperate in

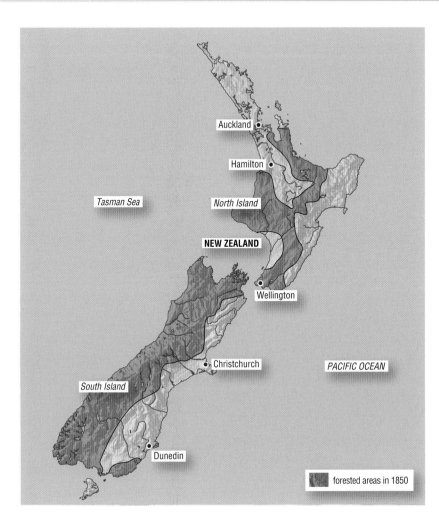

*Original forest in New Zealand. In 1850 much of New Zealand was forested, but much more had been forested in earlier times.*

Map labels:
Auckland
Hamilton
Tasman Sea
North Island
NEW ZEALAND
Wellington
Christchurch
PACIFIC OCEAN
South Island
Dunedin
forested areas in 1850

South Island. Winters are mild, summers warm, and rainfall is moderate and distributed evenly through the year. The mystery was why there was so much grassland, which is typical of a much drier climate. Scientists found the solution to the puzzle when they examined the grassland soils. Mixed in the soil they found charcoal—made by heating wood in airless conditions—and pieces of wood. More recent studies have found tree pollen in ancient soil samples. The evidence shows that originally almost the whole of New Zealand was covered by forest and that the forest started to disappear about the year 1000. It was cleared mainly by burning and replaced by tussock grasses.

When Captain Cook arrived, the people he met were farmers and the population was densest in North Island, where it was possible to grow sweet potatoes, their staple food. It was not the farmers who had cleared the forest, however. The deforestation was most severe in South Island, where the climate is too cold for growing sweet potatoes. In South Island the underground stems of a variety of bracken (*Pteridium aquilinum esculentum*) were one of the most important food items. Bracken cannot tolerate shade. Clearing the forest encourages its growth, and that is what the people did—but it may not have been their only reason for burning the trees.

New Zealand was once the home of up to 25 species of flightless birds called *moas*—the Polynesian word for "fowl"—ranging in size from turkey to ostrich and some standing 10 feet (3 m) tall. Moas fed on seeds, fruits, leaves, and grasses, and they lived mainly in the forests. The Maori hunted them, eventually to extinction, possibly burning the forest to drive the birds into the open.

The climate on the eastern side of South Island is somewhat drier than that in the west. This dryness might have made the forest burn more readily. The destruction reached a peak between about 1150 and 1350. By the time Captain Cook landed, half of the original forest had gone, and the people whom he met had no memory of it.

## CHAPTER 5

# LIFE ON
# THE GRASSLANDS

## What is grass?

A grass plant looks simple. It has roots, a stem, and leaves in the form of long, narrow blades. Its flowers have no petals, but they produce large amounts of pollen, which travels on the wind, and varying numbers of seeds. There are many variations on this straightforward theme. For example, grass flowers occur in all sizes. Some are tiny, but others are large and showy. For instance, pampas grasses have big flowers, and the flowers of uva grass (*Gynerium sagittatum*), found in the tropical grasslands of South America, form a plume up to 6.5 feet (2 m) long.

Grasses are useful to animals. Grazing mammals, such as cattle, sheep, and rabbits, eat grass leaves. Many birds and rodents feed on grass seeds—and so do people. Wheat, rice, corn (maize), barley, oats, millet, and sorghum are all grasses. So are sugarcane and bamboo.

The apparent simplicity of grass is misleading. In fact, grasses are very advanced plants that arose quite recently. Life on Earth began in water, and the first plants were probably green, single-celled organisms called *algae* (singular *alga*) that drifted near the surface. Plants first moved onto land about 450 million years ago. The earliest land plants were probably algae in which the cells are linked to make long filaments. You can still see algae like this, called blanket weed (usually *Cladophora* species), attached to stones in fairly narrow, slow-moving rivers, their dark green filaments gently waving in the current like long hair billowing in the wind. Algae like these grew on the edges of lakes and marshes. Approximately 390 million years would pass before the first grass plants appeared. Many changes took place in plants during that unimaginably long period.

As they spread onto land farther from the shore, plants developed a tough, waxy outer covering that helped them to retain water and specialized structures, called *gametangia* (singular *gametangium*), in which their sperm and eggs were produced, the eggs were fertilized, and the fertilized eggs grew into potential young plants, called *embryos.* These plants survive today. They are the mosses, liverworts, and hornworts.

As long as the plants remained very small, water and nutrients could enter their cells and spread to where they were needed. But after a time some mosses with tissues that conducted water and substances dissolved in it appeared. This innovation allowed plants to become bigger, and the conducting tissues continued to develop until they became vessels through which water and nutrients could be transported to every part of a much larger plant. About 410 million years ago a plant called *Cooksonia* stood erect, had branches, and produced spores in structures at the tips of the branches. It was a *vascular plant*—a plant with vessels.

At this stage plants reproduced by means of *spores,* which are very small particles, often consisting of just one cell, that carry the genetic material that will develop into a new plant if conditions are suitable. In addition to mosses, liverworts, and hornworts, ferns and horsetails reproduce in this way. During the Carboniferous period, around 350 million years ago, giant ferns and horsetails grew in vast swamp forests. Among them, however, were a few plants that reproduced more efficiently. Instead of spores, they produced seeds. A seed is a tiny plant, complete with rudimentary leaves and roots and provided with a food supply to give it a start in life, all wrapped securely inside a tough coat. The seed plants flourished after the end of the Carboniferous period, when the climate changed and the swamps dried out, because they were better than the spore producers at coping with dry conditions. The first seed plants developed into the *gymnosperms;* this group includes the cycads, the maidenhair tree or ginkgo, a group of plants called *gnetophytes,* and the *conifers*—plants such as firs, pines, hemlocks, and spruces that bear woody cones.

The innovations of the gymnosperms—the first plants to have a seed to protect a tiny but fully developed plant structure—were important advantages that promoted their survival. But another group of seed plants developed even more advanced equipment to improve their chances of producing offspring: flowers and fruit. Gymnosperms do not produce flowers and their seeds are enclosed only in a seed coat. The first flowering plants appeared about 130 million years ago, during the Cretaceous period—the age of the dinosaurs. Most flowering plants use their flowers to attract animal pollinators—usually insects—and they have ingenious ways to distribute their seeds. The seeds develop inside an *ovary* that becomes a fruit. Animals eat the fruit and either discard the seeds or distribute them in their droppings. The term *gymnosperm* is from the Greek words *gymnos,* meaning "naked," and *sperma,* meaning "seed." Botanists class all flowering plants as the division Anthophyta—*anthos* is the Greek word for "flower"—but they are often called *angiosperms* (the Greek word *angeion* means "vessel") to contrast them with gymnosperms. The angiosperms had a highly successful reproductive strategy. By about 65 million years ago flowering plants outnumbered the gymnosperms. Today there are approximately 235,000 species of flowering plants, but only 721 species of gymnosperms.

Very early in their evolution the angiosperms split into two distinctive types, called monocots (short for monocotyledons) and dicots (dicotyledons). The distinction is based on the leaves that are tucked inside the seed and emerge when the seed sprouts; these seed leaves are called *cotyledons.* Monocot seeds contain one of them and dicot seeds contain two. There are other important differences between monocots and dicots. Most monocots have leaf veins that are approximately parallel to one another, whereas the veins in dicot leaves form a network. Many dicots have a deep taproot with smaller roots branching from it; monocot roots are usually shallow and form a dense mat.

All grasses are monocots, along with such plants as orchids, lilies, bananas, and palm trees. The much larger group of dicots includes such plants as roses, cabbages, carrots, camellias, carnations, and cacti.

# How grasses work

Grasses appeared about 60 million years ago, quite late in the history of plants. Today they grow in almost every part of the world. We see them every day and tend to take them for granted. Yet despite being so common and apparently so simple, a grass plant is a complicated and highly developed living organism.

The upright stem—the botanical name is the *culm*—of a grass plant has distinct joints, called *nodes*. The culm is usually round, although in a few species it is flattened. The nodes are solid, but the *internodes*—the sections of the culms between nodes—are either hollow or filled with pith (as they are in maize and sugarcane). The diagram shows the culm and the way the leaves are attached to it.

At the base of each internode there are cells that divide rapidly, constantly lengthening the culm. These *meristem* cells are the first secret of every grass's success. They cause the culm to grow from each of its nodes. Consequently, if the plant loses the top of its culm—perhaps because an animal has eaten it—the grass continues growing from lower down. Grass is not in the least harmed by being grazed or mowed.

The meristem also helps the plant in another way. If the plant becomes flattened, such that the culm lies along the ground, the growth hormone that stimulates cell division accumulates on the lower side, causing the meristem cells there to divide faster than those on the upper side. This process makes the grass rise up again from one of its nodes until it is standing vertically once more.

As with all green plants, grasses have cells in their leaves and culms that contain *chloroplasts*. A chloroplast is a discrete unit—an *organelle*—inside a plant cell that specializes in converting sunlight to chemical energy. All cells in the green tissues of a plant contain chloroplasts; some have just a few and others have many. Structures inside the chloroplasts contain molecules of *chlorophyll,* a green substance that absorbs the photons of light energy that provide the energy for a series of reactions that use carbon dioxide and water to make sugars. The process is called *photosynthesis* (see the sidebar).

*Grass stem and leaf. The blade (leaf) grows from a node on the culm (stem). The lower part of the blade forms a sheath surrounding the culm. The ligule is a small structure at the top of the sheath.*

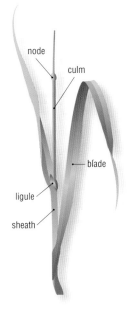

node

culm

blade

ligule

sheath

# Photosynthesis

Green plants and some bacteria are able to use energy from sunlight (photo-) to assemble (synthesize) sugars. The process is called *photosynthesis* and it depends on a pigment called *chlorophyll.* Chlorophyll is green and it is what gives plants their green color.

Photosynthesis proceeds in two stages. The first stage depends on light, and it is called the *light-dependent* or *light* stage. The second stage does not use light energy, so it is called the *light-independent* or *dark* stage (although it also takes place in the light).

***Light-dependent stage.*** When a photon (a unit of light) possessing precisely the right amount of energy strikes a chlorophyll molecule, the photon disappears and its energy is absorbed, allowing an electron (a particle carrying negative charge) in the molecule to break free. This leaves the chlorophyll molecule with a positive charge. The free electron immediately attaches to a neighboring molecule, thereby ejecting another electron that moves to a neighboring molecule. In this way electrons pass along an *electron-transport chain* of molecules. Each plant cell contains a number of chloroplasts and each chloroplast contains many molecules of chlorophyll, so while the plant is exposed to light there is a constant stream of photons being captured and electrons moving along the electron-transport chain.

Some of the transported energy is used to convert adenosine diphosphate (ADP) to adenosine triphosphate (ATP) by the addition of phosphate, after which the electron then returns to the chlorophyll. Converting ADP to ATP absorbs energy; converting ATP to ADP releases the energy. The ADP ↔ ATP reaction (the double arrow indicates the reaction can move in either direction) is used by all living organisms to transport energy and release it where it is needed.

Energy that is not used to convert ADP to ATP is used to split a water molecule ($H_2O$) into a hydrogen ion, which bears a positive charge ($H^+$), and a hydroxyl ion, which has a negative charge ($OH^-$). (An *ion* is an atom that has gained or lost one or more electrons, so it bears a positive or negative charge.) The $H^+$ attaches to a molecule of nicotinamide adenine dinucleotide phosphate (NADP), converting it to reduced NADP (NADPH). The $OH^-$ passes one electron to the chlorophyll molecule, restoring the neutrality of both chlorophyll and hydroxyl. Hydroxyls then combine to form water ($4OH \rightarrow 2H_2O + O_2\uparrow$). (The upward arrow in this chemical formula indicates that the oxygen is released into the air.) This completes the light-dependent stage.

*(continues)*

*(continued)*

**Light-independent stage.** Using ATP from the light-dependent stage as a source
of energy, the first in a series of chemical reactions attaches molecules of carbon
dioxide ($CO_2$) obtained from the air to molecules of ribulose biphosphate
(RuBP), a substance present in the chloroplast. The enzyme RuBP carboxylase
(the name is usually abbreviated to *rubisco*) catalyzes the reaction. In a cycle of
reactions the carbon atoms, originally from the carbon dioxide, are combined
with hydrogen obtained from NADPH; the NADP then returns to the light-
dependent stage. The cycle ends with the synthesis of molecules of glucose and
of RuBP. The RuBP is then available to commence the cycle again.

Glucose, a simple sugar, is the most common source of energy for living
things; its energy is released by the process of *respiration*. Glucose is also used to
synthesize complex sugars: starch and cellulose in plants and glycogen (also
called animal starch) in animals. Plants use cellulose to build cell walls; starch and
glycogen can be converted to glucose, releasing energy.

One leaf grows upward from each node and the lower part
of the leaf forms a *sheath* enclosing the internode. The sheath
protects the internode, and especially the sensitive meristem
cells at the base of the internode. In most grass species the
edges of the sheath are not joined, so the leaf can be prized
open. At the top of the sheath is a small structure called a
*ligule*. In some species the ligule consists only of hairs or is
absent altogether.

Above the ligule the upper part of the leaf, called the *blade,*
grows outward from the culm. Blades grow on alternate sides
of the culm, such that each projects from the culm on the
opposite side to the blades above and below it. The blades are
usually long, narrow, and smooth-edged and have a pointed
tip. Some grasses, such as bamboos, have wider leaves, and
some tropical American grasses have leaves that are two inches (5 cm) or more wide. Regardless of their width, all grass
leaves have veins that run parallel to each other along the
length of the leaf; this is a feature of all monocots. Because the
leaf grows from the node at its base, if grazing or mowing
removes the upper part of the blade, the leaf soon grows back.

Most grasses have a single culm, but some tropical grasses, especially bamboos, produce branches from the nodes along the upper part of the culm. Some tropical grasses are climbers that cling to trees. Tussock grasses produce many culms from the base of the plant. This type of growth, called *tillering,* is also typical of wheat, barley, oats, and rye. The branches grow inside the leaf sheath on the main culm, eventually pulling the sheath away from the culm.

Grass roots have many offshoots that spread widely to form a dense mat. As well as absorbing water and nutrients, the roots anchor the plant securely. At the same time grass roots bind the soil together. This binding prevents soil erosion, and grasses are often planted in order to stabilize coastal sand dunes and loose soil on sloping ground.

All grasses are capable of growing from seed, and for some this is the only method of regeneration from year to year. Grass species that die at the end of one season and arise again from seeds the following year are described as *annual.* Cereal grasses are annual. Other grasses do not die at the end of the growing season, although they become dormant and their brown and wilted blades make the plants look as though they are dead. Plants that live for more than two seasons are said to be *perennial.* Perennial grasses, such as bluegrass (*Poa pratensis*), live for many years, and many perennial species produce horizontal stems that are called *rhizomes* if they run below ground and *stolons* if they run along the surface. Rhizomes and stolons have nodes, from which grow culms and roots—called *adventitious* roots because they emerge from nodes rather than from the base of the plant. The drawing of Bermuda grass (*Cynodon dactylon*), a tropical species, shows the stolon, adventitious roots, and tillering of the culms. Buffalo grass (*Buchloe dactyloides*) is a prairie grass that produces stolons. Quack grass, also called couch, twitch, or witch grass (*Elymus repens*), is a weed of cultivated ground that is difficult to remove because its rhizomes are so tough.

The Bermuda grass shown here is in flower, the flowers being the structures branching from the tips of the culms. In most grass species, whether annual or perennial, many flowers are grouped together to form an *inflorescence,* in which the

*Bermuda grass, showing stolon and tillering. Bermuda grass (Cynodon dactylon) has a stem (stolon) that lies on the ground. Adventitious roots grow from the nodes and bunches (tillers) of culms (stems) grow at intervals along the stolon, producing new plants.*

basic unit is called a *spikelet*. The tassel of a corn plant and an ear of wheat are examples of grass inflorescences.

A spikelet, illustrated in the drawing, comprises several flowers, called *florets*. The spikelet consists of a series of modified leaves or *bracts* in two ranks borne on either side of a short axis called a *rachilla* (hidden in the drawing). The two lowest bracts are called *glumes*, and one is higher on the spikelet than the other. The bracts above the glumes are called *lemmas*, and they bear flowers in their *axils*—the places where the lemmas are attached to the rachilla. The culms and blades of all grasses are very similar, but there are many different arrangements of the spikelets, and these are important aids to identifying species.

The flowers are pollinated by the wind and each floret produces a single seed. The seed usually is small and incorporates part of the floret, but not always. Some bamboos, for instance, bear nutlike fruits, and others produce berries that are the size of small apples.

Grasses have various ways of dispersing their seeds. In tumble grass (*Schedonnardus paniculatus*) the inflorescence remains intact and is blown along by the wind, scattering seeds as it goes. Tumble grass has appeared in many western movies, in which it adds to the feeling of desolation in abandoned towns. Most grasses disperse their seeds individually, however. Seeds of some species have plumes of hairs that allow them to be carried long distances by the wind. Others have hooked or barbed bristles, called *awns,* at the ends of their glumes. These bend and straighten in response to wetting and drying; as they do so, they pull the seed away from the parent plant and then tuck it below the soil surface.

Equipped as grasses are with such an impressive set of survival characteristics, it is no wonder that they have spread to almost every corner of the world. Not only do they survive being nibbled or cut to ground level—treatment that would kill most plants—they thrive on it. Their roots anchor them so firmly they can withstand the fiercest winds. Rhizomes and stolons allow perennial grasses to spread, with a new plant emerging at each node. They grow rapidly: Some bamboo species can grow by up to three feet (90 cm) in 24 hours. Finally they are able to distribute their seeds widely, and some species have seeds that sow themselves.

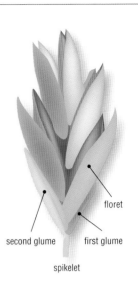

floret

second glume    first glume

spikelet

*Grass five-flowered spikelet. The grass flower forms a spike consisting of several spikelets. Each spikelet contains individual flowers, called florets. In this spikelet there are five florets. The glumes are leaflike bracts.*

## Prairie grasses

Prairie grasses vary in height according to the amount of moisture in the soil. Short grasses grow where only the uppermost 12 inches (30 cm) of soil is moist and the ground is completely dry for some of the time. Short grasses predominate in the midwestern prairies, in a belt extending approximately from southern Alberta and Saskatchewan to New Mexico and Texas, but restricted to the eastern side of the mountains. Generally too dry to cultivate, these are the rangelands of North America.

Buffalo grass (*Buchloe dactyloides*) and grama grasses (*Bouteloua* species) are typical of the short prairie grasses. They are usually no more than eight inches (20 cm) tall, although blue grama (*B. gracilis*) forms dense tufts that can grow to 18 inches (46 cm). Both are edible to grazing animals and both are cultivated. Galleta or curly grass (*Hilaria jamesii*) is three to 20 inches (8–50 cm) tall, has coarse rhizomes, and reproduces from the rhizomes and also from seed. Cattle, horses, and sheep feed on it, and it can withstand heavy grazing. Prairie June grass (*Koeleria macrantha*) has loose tufts of leaves that resist drought and seeds that will sprout in dry soil. Its growth begins early in spring, 10–15 days after the snow disappears, and it is in full flower by June—hence its name. It is one of the earliest grasses to flower in the southern United States; flowering is later farther to the north and west.

Prairie June grass is widely distributed and occurs in the palouse prairie or bunchgrass prairie as well as the short-grass prairie. Palouse prairie occurs mainly between the Rocky Mountains and the Cascade Range, and between the Coast Ranges and Sierra Nevada in California. Bluebunch wheatgrass (*Agropyron spicatum*), a typical grass of the palouse prairie, is used as an official state symbol by both Montana and Washington. It grows in erect tussocks, up to 2.5 feet (76 cm) tall, often with short rhizomes linking tussocks, but reproduces mainly from seeds and its tillers and seldom from the rhizomes. Cattle, sheep, horses, and deer graze it.

Tallgrass prairie forms the eastern section of the grassland, where the climate is moister than it is farther west. Tall grasses also occur on the coastal prairie that lies along the Gulf Coast of Texas, where the climate is moist.

Big bluestem (*Andropogon gerardii*) grows two to 10 feet (0.6–3 m) tall and is the most prominent of the tall grasses. It occurs across Canada from Quebec to Saskatchewan and in the United States as far south as Arizona and Florida and is most common in the eastern part of its range, especially in the lowlands. The name *bluestem* refers to its blue-green culms. The leaves, up to 12 inches (30 cm) long and 0.5 inch (1 cm) wide, develop a red tinge in late summer and turn to bronze in the fall. They sometimes have a hairy look. Big bluestem flowers from June through September. The flowers form three or four straight inflorescences, up to three inches

(7.6 cm) long, attached to a stem. The botanical name for this type of inflorescence is a *raceme,* and the raceme's appearance gives the plant one of its other common names: turkey feet. It is also known as beard grass, because its fertile lemmas have awns up to 0.8 inch (2 cm) long that bend downward. Big bluestem forms tussocks and grows in dense stands that suppress other grasses by shading the ground. Consequently, there are large areas where big bluestem is the only grass. This grass reproduces by seed or sometimes from rhizomes, although rhizomes are not always present. In sandy areas big bluestem is replaced by sand bluestem, a variety of bluestem (*Andropogon gerardii* var. *paucipilus*) that is adapted to sandy soils.

Bison feed on big bluestem, as do deer and antelope, but it does not respond well to grazing. Early settlers discovered that corn grows well on land that supports big bluestem, but when they cleared the natural grass they removed its deep roots, which held the soil together. This made the soil prone to wind erosion (see "The Dust Bowl" on pages 55–57).

Indian grass (*Sorghastrum nutans*), also known as wood grass, yellow Indian grass, bushy bluestem, and wild oat grass, grows on deep, moist soils, often alongside big bluestem grass. It grows four to eight feet (1.2–2.4 m) tall, appearing either as single culms or, more commonly, in large clumps. Its flat, pointed leaves are 0.2–0.5 inch (0.5–1.3 cm) wide and up to 24 inches (61 cm) long. They are rough to the touch and often blue-green in color. Indian grass flowers in summer and reproduces from rhizomes and from seed. Though it prefers moist soil, Indian grass can tolerate dry conditions and will establish itself on ground that has been disturbed. It is very nutritious for livestock.

Slough grass or cord grass (*Spartina pectinata*) grows throughout the prairies on wet ground, in marshes, and along the shores of lakes. It grows upright from long rhizomes and stands three to 6.5 feet (1–2 m) tall. Its leaves are one to six feet (0.3–1.8 m) long and 0.2–0.4 inch (0.5–1.0 cm) wide, tapering to a long, slender point, and have rough edges that can give a nasty cut if they are handled carelessly.

Switchgrass (*Panicum virgatum*) is found beside streams and along roadsides, especially in low-lying, moist areas and in upland prairie. It is especially common on the western side of the tallgrass prairie. Also known as wobsqua grass, blackbent, wild red top, and thatchgrass, it is three to seven feet (0.9–2.1 m) tall and forms clumps that arise from short rhizomes. It is an important food plant for many animals.

Needle-and-thread grass (*Stipa comata*) forms dense, erect tufts—"needles"—and its nodding heads of flowers bear awns that are four to six inches (10–15 cm) long—"thread." Its leaves are four to 12 inches (10–30 cm) long and taper to a sharp point. This structure gives the plant its alternative common name of speargrass, or common or western speargrass. It occurs throughout the short-grass and palouse prairies and beyond them, from Indiana to California and from Texas to the Yukon, and it is especially common in mixed prairie, the transitional zone between the tallgrass prairie to the east and the short-grass prairie to the west.

Little bluestem (*Andropogon scoparius*) is a close relation of big bluestem. They often grow side by side, but little bluestem is a typical grass of the mixed prairie. It grows up to five feet (1.5 m) tall under ideal conditions but is often smaller, and it flowers from late summer through fall. Grazing animals feed on it and birds eat its seeds.

Spike dropseed (*Sporobolus contractus*) is found in dry, sandy, and rocky areas of the mixed prairie, where it grows up to four feet (1.2 m) tall. Its name refers to the fact that each spikelet holds one flower, which breaks away from the glumes and falls to the ground when the seed is ripe.

Wild ryegrasses (*Elymus* species) also occur in mixed prairie. Canada wild rye (*E. canadensis*) and Virginia wild rye (*E. virginicus*) are typical. They stand erect, up to five feet (1.5 m) tall, and each culm bears a single seed head about eight inches (20 cm) long with awns about 1.25 inches (3 cm) long. The seed heads resemble those of wheat but are bigger. Ryegrasses form tussocks and reproduce by tillering as well as from seed.

## Pampas grasses

The South American pampas is a temperate grassland similar in many ways to the prairies of North America. As on the prairies there are regions with a relatively moist climate supporting tall grasses and drier regions with short grasses (see "Steppe grasses" on pages 94–95). The moist pampas lie on the eastern side of the continent, and the climate becomes progressively drier farther to the west. Despite the similarity, however, there is one important difference: The moist pampa has a wetter climate than the eastern, tallgrass prairie. Consequently, South American tallgrasses are rather taller than their prairie equivalents. When the first Spaniards arrived at the mouth of La Plata River in the 16th century, they looked across an apparently endless sea of waving grasses that grew so tall they had to stand on the back of a horse to see over them.

It is likely that at one time low trees and shrubs covered the moist pampa, with grasses between them. Toward the end of the dry season, when the grasses were highly flammable, hunters set them alight in order to drive game. This treatment gradually removed the woody plants and created the grassland (see "How forest can change into grassland" on pages 76–78). The European settlers introduced cattle and horses—animals that are not native to South America—and with them European grass seeds. These grew well and before long they replaced the original grasses over large areas.

The tall grass that the Spaniards saw covering the level, low-lying plain was *Cortaderia selloana*—silver pampas grass or Uruguayan pampas grass. It is now the most popular of the grasses that are cultivated simply as "pampas grass." It was first grown outside South America in France and Ireland in the 19th century, from seeds obtained in Ecuador.

Silver pampas grass grows in giant tussocks. Its leaves grow mainly from the base of the culms and are three to six feet (0.9–1.8 m) long. The leaves have sharp edges. The botanical name *Cortaderia* is derived from the Spanish word *cortadura,* meaning "cut" or "cutting." The culms grow up to 12 feet (3.7 m) tall and the inflorescences form violet or silvery white, feathery plumes one to two feet (30–70 cm) long. There are 24 species of *Cortaderia,* of which 19 are found naturally in South America and the Caribbean region, four in New Zealand (where they are known as toetoe or kakaho), and one in New Guinea.

*Cortaderia* tussocks shade the ground around them and crowd out other plants. Consequently, silver pampas grass once covered hundreds of acres of pampas, with no other plants except herbs that grew between the tussocks.

Andean pampas grass, also known as jubata grass and purple pampas grass (*C. jubata*), is very similar in appearance but has pink or purple plumes that turn white as the seeds mature. It grows in the mountains of northern Argentina, Bolivia, Peru, and Ecuador at elevations of 9,200–11,000 feet (2,800–3,350 m). Its leaves are wider than those of silver pampas grass but equally sharp.

Both species grow rapidly. Andean pampas grass produces copious quantities of seeds that travel long distances on the wind. All the plants are female and all bear flowers that produce seeds without needing to be fertilized. This method of reproduction, called *apomixis,* makes a single, isolated plant capable of reproduction. This species has become a very invasive weed in California, New Zealand, and South Africa. Silver pampas grass has separate male and female plants, and therefore an isolated plant is incapable of reproducing. Consequently this species is much less invasive.

Wild cane or uva grass (*Gynerium sagittatum*) is a similar plant that grows on wet ground and beside streams all the way from Mexico to subtropical South America, including the tropical forests. It is even taller than the *Cortaderia* grasses. Its leaves are 0.2–0.3 inch (4–8 mm) wide and up to 6.5 feet (2 m) long and have sharp teeth along their edges. The culms grow to a height of 6.5–33 feet (2–10 m).

## Steppe grasses

Some plant geographers divide all temperate grasslands into prairie and steppe. Prairie has a moist climate and tall grasses; steppe has a drier climate and short grasses. The dry pampa of South America can therefore be described as steppe. Dry pampa is found in central Argentina, where the average annual rainfall is about 27 inches (685 mm).

The most widespread grasses of the South American steppe, or dry pampa, are feather grasses, needle grasses, or tussock grasses (*Stipa* species), many of which are known simply as *flechilla* in South America. All of them grow in dense clumps 12–24 inches (30–60 cm) tall. Puna grass, or pasto puna (*S. brachychaeta*), has leaves that are 0.04–0.08 inch (1–2 mm) wide and 15–24 inches (40–60 cm) long. All feather grasses have very narrow leaves that give the tussocks a feathery appearance, and they have been introduced to other parts of the world as ornamental plants. As with many such introductions, some have become invasive and persistent weeds. Serrated tussock grass (*S. trichotoma*), for example, is an attractive plant, with tussocks about 20 inches (50 cm) high and 10 inches (25 cm) wide, but each plant produces about 100,000 seeds, so it spreads rapidly.

Ichu or bunchgrass (*S. ichu*) grows on the higher ground in the pampa. Where the rainfall is sufficient, ichu grows at elevations above 10,000 feet (3,050 m) and up to the snow line. Farmers graze their livestock on it, although it provides only sparse pasture.

Feather grasses are also widespread on the Eurasian steppe. In places they cover the land from horizon to horizon with their delicate, waving flower plumes. In the western steppe, in Kazakhstan and around the Black Sea, the predominant grasses are Lessing's feather grass (*S. lessingiana*) and Ukrainian feather grass (*S. ucrainica*). Viviparous bluegrass or bulbous bluegrass (*Poa bulbosa*) also grows in this area. All three species grow about 18 inches (45 cm) tall. Sheep's fescue (*Festuca ovina*) grows throughout the southern steppe, where the climate is warm and moist.

In the drier eastern steppe there is June grass or koeleria (*Koeleria macrantha*), four to 20 inches (10–50 cm) tall. This grass also grows on the North American prairie, where it is known as prairie June grass (see "Prairie grasses" on pages 89–92). The sea of grass that composes the Mongolian steppe also has crested wheatgrass (*Agropyron cristatum*), black lyme-grass (*Elymus chenensis*), and bridlegrass (*Cleistogenes squarrosa*), as well as steppe needle grass (*Stipa krylovii*).

## Savanna grasses

Savanna (or savannah) is the name originally applied to a type of grassland found on Caribbean islands. Today it is also applied to the tropical grassland that extends across Africa as two belts, one on each side of the equator. Grasslands of this type also occur in South America, southern Asia, and Australia.

Red (or red oat) grass (*Themeda triandra*) is perhaps the most distinctive grass of the tropical savanna, and in Africa it is the most common grass species. It grows on clay soils in the moister parts of the savanna, where the average rainfall is 24–40 inches (600–1,000 mm), and it is the dominant species in areas where fires occur regularly. Red grass recovers well from fire, growing rapidly as soon as rain moistens the ash-covered ground and shading and crowding out other grasses. It grows in dense tussocks, and where it is the dominant species, the tussocks are fairly widely spaced, making the area resemble a vast field of cultivated cereals.

As all other savanna vegetation does, red grass grows vigorously during the rainy season but wilts and shrivels as the dry season advances. As it dries, its color changes to dark red. This gives it the name *red grass*. While it is growing, however, its culms and leaves are blue-green, and they give it another of its names—*bluegrass*. It is also called red oat grass because its large, drooping seed heads resemble those of oats.

Red grass usually grows to a height of 12–35 inches (30–90 cm), but where conditions are especially favorable it can be as high as 12 feet (3.5 m) tall. The leaves are up to 20 inches (50 cm) long and about 0.1 inch (3 mm) wide. Individual tussocks average 20 inches (50 cm) across.

Animals find red grass palatable and will readily graze it while it is young, but it is not very nutritious and by the time it flowers they no longer find it palatable. Wildebeest—the most numerous grazers in the African savanna (see "Grazing animals" on pages 119–124)—will usually feed on it only after they have eaten the more nutritious grasses. Red grass does not grow back very quickly after it has been grazed, and consequently it is easily overgrazed. It does not grow well in areas that are protected from fire or areas that are heavily grazed.

Elephant grass (*Pennistum purpureum*), also known as Napier grass and Uganda grass, is found along the edges of rivers and beside lakes in the African savanna, where the soil is rich. It grows in dense tussocks. Its pointed leaves are about one inch (2.5 cm) wide, up to three feet (91 cm) long, and very sharp along the edges. The coarse, hairy culms are about one inch

(2.5 cm) wide at the base and grow to a height of up to 10 feet (3 m). The culms and seeds are yellow or purple. Elephant grass reproduces from rhizomes—horizontal underground stems that produce new culms and leaves from their nodes (see "How grasses work" on pages 84–89). It develops into almost impenetrable thickets that provide shelter to many birds.

Pan dropseed (*Sporobolus ioclados*) and crabgrass (*Digitaria macroblephora*) are short grasses that grow in those parts of the African savanna where grazing is very heavy during the rainy season. Trampling by the animals packs the soil into a dense, hard layer just below the surface, which prevents the grasses from producing the deep roots that would allow them to grow taller.

Bermuda grass (*Cynodon dactylon*) is another short grass, which grew originally on the East African savanna but now grows throughout the Tropics and beyond. Its name refers to the fact that it was introduced to the United States from Bermuda. It is also called Bahama grass, kweek grass, devil's grass, couch grass, wire grass, dhob, dhub, doob, and Indian doab. It produces stolons—horizontal stems that run along the ground surface—with new plants growing from each node, so that one plant spreads to form a thick mat. It also has deep roots, with most of the root system lying 24 inches (60 cm) below the surface. It prefers a warm climate with more than 16 inches (410 mm) of rain a year, but in times of drought some of its roots extend to a depth of four to five feet (1.2–1.5 m) in search of moisture. Bermuda grass has gray-green leaves that are one to four inches (2.5–10 cm) long with rough edges.

*Themeda triandra* is known in Australia as kangaroo grass. Probably the most widespread of all native Australian grasses, kangaroo grass is found in most parts of the dry and semiarid regions of Australia, growing on a wide variety of soils. It is especially common in places where moisture collects, fires occur from time to time, and there is little grazing. This adaptability accounts for part of its prominence—it grows well beside roads and railroad tracks, where it is highly visible.

Oat kangaroo grass (*T. avenacea*) is a closely related and very similar grass that is common in central Australia. Its tussocks are about four to eight inches (10–20 cm) across, and it grows 24–48 inches (60–122 cm) tall.

The most common grasses in the South American llanos are species of *Trachypogon* and *Axonopus*: they have no common names. In some places *T. plumosum* and *A. canescens* account for more than 80 percent of the vegetation. *Trachypogon* grasses have long, narrow leaves and culms that grow one to 6.5 feet (0.3–2.0 m) tall. *Axonopus* species grow about six to 40 inches (15–100 cm) tall. *Trachypogon plumosus* appears to recover from fire better than *Axonopus canescens* does, but where fire is prevented, *A. canescens* often replaces *T. plumosus*.

*Savanna baboons (Papio cynocephalus) live in troops of up to 150 individuals. They spend most of their time on the ground but climb acacia trees in search of food. They eat grass, seeds, fruit, insects, and small mammals.* (Courtesy of Fogstock)

## Grassland trees and shrubs

Pictures of the African savanna show a flat landscape stretching into the far distance, but with the monotony broken by scattered trees that have a very characteristic flat-topped shape. These are acacia or thorn trees (*Acacia* species). The most typical thorn tree is the umbrella thorn (*A. tortilis*). As the name suggests, it is an umbrella-shaped tree. It grows 13–50 feet (4–15 m) tall and is distributed throughout most of Africa and the Middle East.

There are about 1,200 species of acacias, and most are able to survive prolonged drought. This is a necessary characteristic for any savanna plant, but most woody plants—trees and shrubs—lack it. Consequently, acacias are often the only trees to be seen in the savanna. In the drier parts of the savanna they are widely scattered, because each tree needs a large volume of soil in which to find water. Many animals feed on the leaves, young shoots, and seedlings of trees, and their isolation leaves acacias very exposed. Thorn trees protect themselves by means of the big, fearsomely sharp thorns that give them their name.

Some acacias, including the whistling thorn or ant-galled acacia (*A. drepanolobium*) found on the African savanna, have recruited ants as allies. These trees have a pair of swollen thorns at the base of each leaf. Ants hollow out the thorns and then live inside them, feeding on nectar from *nectaries* at the base of each leaf stalk (*petiole*) and on oils and proteins produced in sausage-shaped organs called *Beltian bodies* at the tips of the leaves. Worker ants swarm all over the tree, defending their own territories and biting and stinging any animal within their reach. The ants also cut away any part of a neighboring plant that touches their own tree. This prevents any other plant from shading their acacia, thus allowing it to grow rapidly. It is a very successful alliance that benefits both parties.

About half of all acacia species are native to Australia. There they are often known as wattles, because early settlers used their wood to build huts they then plastered with mud, a building technique known as wattle-and-daub.

Thorn trees have an attractive shape, but the candelabra tree (*Euphorbia candelabrum*) has an extraordinary one. Its many branches all emerge at the same level, about eight feet (2.4 m) above the ground, and then curve until they, and all the smaller branches growing from them, point directly upward. As do the acacia, the candelabra tree protects itself with thorns. In addition, its sap is poisonous. Any animal that took a bite from it would feel so ill it would not make the same mistake a second time.

The sausage tree (*Kigelia africana*) produces succulent, sausage-shaped fruits up to three feet (90 cm) long and weighing up to 11 pounds (5 kg). Sausage trees are scattered sparsely across the African savanna, but they are now being cultivated in some areas because the fruits have medicinal properties (as purgatives). The flowers are pollinated by bats.

The sagebrush (*Artemisia tridentata*) is the most famous shrub of the North American prairies. A shrub is a woody plant that produces many branches at ground level and has no main stem, unlike a tree, which has one or more main stems. Sagebrushes have many branches. They grow three to six feet (0.9–1.8 m) tall, but occasionally taller, and have silver-gray leaves with a strong, spicy smell. Most of the leaves have three teeth at the tip, giving the plant its botanical species name: *tridentata*—"three teeth."

Close relatives of the prairie sagebrush are also widespread on the Eurasian steppes, where they are known as wormwood. There are several species of *Artemisia,* all known as wormwood, and areas in which these shrubs are especially common are known as wormwood steppe.

## Grassland herbs

The word *grassland* conjures a picture of grasses bowing in the wind and stretching to the horizon in every direction—a seemingly boundless sea of grass. Grasslands are like that for much of the time, but grasses are not the only plants that grow there. In spring, before the grasses have grown to their full height and started to flower, the grassland is briefly transformed into a dazzling riot of color. The other nonwoody plants, called *forbs,* are in flower and the grasses provide a background to their display. Although spring is the most colorful season, forbs continue to flower, creating a changing sequence of colors throughout summer and fall.

Although many of the species are different, all the world's grasslands are rich in flowering herbs and produce similar carpets of color throughout the year. The forbs of the Eurasian steppe include the Chinese lantern or winter cherry (*Physalis alkekengi*), whose berries are enclosed by a red or orange papery structure resembling a Chinese lantern. The steppe lupine (*Thermopsis lanceolata*) stands eight to 10 inches (20–30 cm) tall and in summer bears yellow flowers. There are two species of peashrub, both of which also produce yellow flowers in summer across the plains of central Asia. The littleleaf peashrub (*Caragana microphylla*) grows up to eight feet (2.4 m) tall and about 10 feet (3 m) across. The pygmy peashrub (*C. pygmaea*) is up to three feet (90 cm) tall and five feet (1.5 m) wide.

The flowers of the North American prairie are typical of all temperate grasslands. Prairie buttercup (*Ranunculus rhomboideus*) appears in spring in well-grazed parts of the tallgrass and mixed prairie. Its bright yellow flowers are no more than 0.5 inch (1 cm) across, and the plant is only three to five inches (7.5–13 cm) tall. The very similar early buttercup (*R. fascicularis*), known as prairie buttercup in some places, also appears in spring.

Shooting star (*Dodecatheon meadia*) is also known as American cowslip, Indian-chief, rooster-heads, Johnny-jump, and pride-of-Ohio. It grows to about 10 inches (25 cm) tall and bears pink or mauve flowers at the top of a long stem. Shooting star is a member of the primrose family (Primulaceae), and as do most primroses—the name is from the Latin *prima rosa*, "first rose"—it flowers early in the year. Bluejacket, or Ohio spiderwort (*Tradescantia ohiensis*), grows throughout the eastern and midwestern prairies. It is a much bigger plant, growing up to 30 inches (76 cm) tall and with leaves up to 16 inches (40 cm) long. Its blue, lavender, or occasionally white flowers have three petals and are about 1.6 inches (4 cm) wide. They also appear in spring.

Wild bergamot (*Monarda fistulosa*) produces whorls of slender, tubular, purple scented flowers from July through September. It is a tall plant that grows in clumps up to two to four feet (0.6–1.2 m) tall. A close relative called bee balm or Oswego tea (*M. didyma*) was once used to make a drink, by infusing the leaves. New Jersey tea (*Ceanothus americanus*) was used in the same way. A small shrub up to three feet (90 cm) tall, it bears masses of small white flowers in middle to late summer.

Prairie coneflower, also called yellow coneflower and grayhead coneflower (*Ratibida pinnata*), grows naturally over most of the midwestern and eastern United States. It is three to four feet (0.9–1.2 m) tall and produces yellow flowers in June and July. The petals droop, giving the flower a conical shape, hence the name *coneflower*. The color of the flowers give it the name *yellow coneflower,* and its gray seed heads give it the name *grayhead coneflower.*

Fine hairs cover the leaves, stems, and unopened flower buds of *Amorpha canescens,* producing the gray color that gives the plant its common name *leadplant.* Unlike the metal, which is very poisonous, leadplants make good, nutritious food for grazing animals. The plant grows up to three feet (90 cm) tall but is often shorter. Its inflorescences consist of dark purple spikes of flowers and appear in early summer.

Butterfly milkweed (*Asclepias ruberosa*) grows to a height of two feet (60 cm) and has bright orange or red flowers; the plant is also known as orange milkweed. Its flowers appear in early summer and attract butterflies, as the plant's name suggests, but butterfly milkweed also has medicinal uses and used to be called pleurisyroot. The milkweeds, of which there are about 120 species, earn their name from the white, milky latex present in all parts of the plant. The drug asclepias was formerly obtained from the latex of *A. tuberosa*. Asclepias was used to make patients perspire, urinate, and cough to clear mucus from the respiratory passages.

*Eryngium yuccifolium* also had a medicinal use in times past. People used to believe its roots contained an antidote to snake venom, so some called it rattlesnake master and others called it button snakeroot. It had no obvious effect on snakebites, but it is a very attractive plant. It stands two to five feet (60–150 cm) tall and has stiff, spiny leaves with prickly edges that are one to four inches (0.5–10 cm) wide and up to three feet (90 cm) long. Botanists find the leaves interesting because the veins running through them are parallel; this is an unusual feature in a dicot plant (see "What is grass?" on pages 81–83). The flowers of rattlesnake master are greenish white and resemble those of thistles. The plant flowers from late summer to early fall. Culver's root (*Veronicastrum virginicum*) flowers at about the same time. It grows to about 40 inches (1 m) tall and bears tall spikes of pale lavender flowers. It, too, once had a medical use, as an extremely violent purgative and emetic.

Rough blazing star (*Liatris aspera*), a plant about two feet (60 cm) tall, flowers in the fall, when its spikes of lavender flowers color large areas of the drier prairies. Narrow-leaved blazing star (*L. punctata*) is smaller, reaching 10–18 inches (25–45 cm) in height, but otherwise similar. It grows on short-grass prairie, from western Minnesota and Alberta to Arkansas and New Mexico.

## Grassland insects

Animals feed on plants, but plants take steps to protect themselves. One way to avoid being eaten is to poison any animal that takes a bite. This strategy is often successful, and there are many poisonous plants. But occasionally the tables are turned: Not only does the animal become immune to the poison, it uses it in its own defense.

The monarch butterfly (*Danaus plexippus*) is the most famous practitioner of this strategy. Its caterpillars feed on milkweed plants; the insect is sometimes called the milkweed butterfly. Caterpillars have soft bodies, are unable to move quickly, and are highly visible while they munch their way across leaves. They offer a tasty snack to some insects and to many bigger animals, especially birds. But the monarch's milkweed diet protects it. Any bird that ate a monarch caterpillar would be so ill it would never touch another. Just to make sure the birds make no mistakes, the caterpillar is brightly marked with black, white, and yellow bands. The milkweed poison that accumulates in the caterpillar's body remains there during the metamorphosis that transforms the larva into the adult butterfly. Consequently the monarch butterfly is also poisonous and remains so throughout its life, although adult monarchs feed only on nectar from flowers.

Adult monarchs are as brightly and distinctively marked as their caterpillars are to warn the world that they are not good to eat. Viceroy butterflies (*Limenitis archippus*) mimic this coloration. Monarchs are large butterflies, with a wingspan of about four inches (10 cm), and viceroys are only 2.5–3 inches (7–8 cm) across, but apart from that the two species closely resemble one another—and well enough to deter a hungry bird. Viceroys are not poisonous, but they are well protected for as long as the monarchs outnumber them. If there were more viceroys than monarchs, their enemies would soon learn that more often than not, butterflies with those markings were good to eat.

Monarchs are also famous for their migrations. They spend the summer scattered through the countryside, but toward

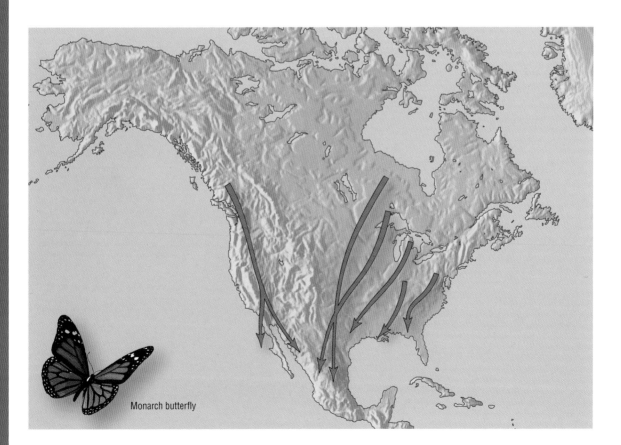

Monarch butterfly

the end of summer they gather in vast numbers and fly south, from southern Canada and the northern United States all the way to Mexico. There they spend the winter packed together, several thousand crowding into a single tree. In spring they make the return journey, but this time as individuals, not as a crowd. Monarchs breed in the north and spend the winter resting. The map shows the routes they follow.

Other butterflies remain in the same place through the year, mating in late summer and laying eggs on the plants that will feed their caterpillars. The eggs hatch and the caterpillars feed for a time before hibernating for the winter. Caterpillars feed on a wide variety of plants. For example, those of Leonard's skipper (*Hesperia leonardus*) eat the leaves of switchgrass (*Panicum virgatum*), little bluestem (*Andropogon scoparius*), love grass (*Eragrostis alba*), and bent grass (*Agrostis* species). Adult butterflies feed only on nectar—the sugary syrup produced by flowers. Adult Leonard's skippers take nectar from thistles, teasels, asters, and blazing star (*Liatris* species).

The blazing star borer moth (*Papaipema beeriana*) is totally dependent on blazing star plants. A small moth, one to one and one-half inches (25–38 mm) across, with brown front wings and gray hind wings, the blazing star borer moth lays its eggs in the soil close to a blazing star plant. When the eggs hatch, the caterpillars find their way to the base of the plant and bore into the stem and root, where they feed until it is time for them to return to the soil to pupate. The closely related ironweed stem borer (*P. cerussata*) and rattlesnake master stem borer (*P. eryngii*) live similar lives, based on ironweed (*Vernonia baldwinii*) and rattlesnake master (*Eryngium yuccafolium*), respectively.

Dragonflies are another group of silent flying insects of the prairie; they breed in ponds. Other prairie insects are not so quiet. Day-flying insects, such as butterflies and dragonflies, have good vision and can recognize potential mates by sight. During the day, however, insects that are highly visible—and edible—make easy targets for insect-eating birds. Nocturnal insects are much safer, but unable to find mates visually. Some, such as moths, emit perfumes called *pheromones* that drift with the wind; males can detect just a few molecules of a pheromone, and by flying in the direction of the highest concentration they use the attractant to locate the female emitting it. Other insects, especially those that live mainly on the ground, use sound. They "shout" to announce their presence to any members of the other gender in the vicinity. These are the noisy ones, and long-horned grasshoppers or katydids are the noisiest of all.

The sword-bearing conehead (*Neoconocephalus ensiger*) is a typical and widespread long-horned grasshopper. It is a large green insect with a conical head and long antennae—the "horns." The handsome grasshopper (*Syrbula admirabilis*) is a short-horned species. Both these grasshoppers feed on plants. Most grasshoppers escape from their enemies by hiding— they are well camouflaged—and, if that fails, by using their long and powerful hind legs to jump out of reach. In addition, the adults of many species are able to fly. Mole crickets are different. They hide in tunnels below ground. They are called mole crickets because their front legs are adapted for digging as are the front legs of a mole. Mole crickets are fairly large insects and noisy, despite spending most of their time below ground, because their tunnels amplify the sounds all grasshoppers and crickets make by rubbing their legs against their body. The northern mole cricket (*Neocurtilla hexadactyla*) is a typical prairie species, about 2.5 inches (6 cm) long, that emerges from its tunnel at night. It can fly as an adult and at all stages in its life it feeds on leaves.

Many species of flying and nonflying insects inhabit the African savanna; tsetse flies (*Glossina* species) are the most notorious. Adult tsetse flies feed only on blood, and in doing so some species transmit the organism that causes sleeping sickness, or trypanosomiasis, in humans and a similar disease called nagana in grazing animals. This is a severe and sometimes fatal disease. Tsetse flies are not widespread, however. There are about 20 species, but most inhabit tropical forests. Of those that live in savanna woodlands—around the edges of the grassland—there are two, *G. morsitans* and *G. swynnertoni,* that are sometimes called game tsetses because they feed on grazing animals. Still, the ease with which the flies can carry nagana from wild animals to domestic cattle makes raising livestock on the savanna difficult.

Nothing is wasted on the savanna, and this includes animal waste: Hordes of insects quickly descend on the dung dropped by game animals. Dung beetles, also known as scarab beetles, specialize in dung. A beetle seizes a piece of dung that is bigger than its own body and, walking on its back legs and pushing with its front legs, rolls its dung ball along the ground until it is clear of all rival insects. Then the beetle digs a burrow and drags the dung inside. It feeds on the dung and lays its eggs in it. Their habits may strike people as unwholesome, but dung beetles are very important. By burying dung they accelerate its decomposition and the recycling of plant nutrients, and their burrows allow air and moisture to penetrate the soil.

Termites are also nonflying insects of the savanna. They are soft-bodied and most of the time they remain out of sight. Despite this they are by far the most visible of all the

*The bat-eared fox* (Otocyon megalotis) *of southern and eastern Africa follows herds of grazing mammals but feeds mainly on insects, especially termites. Its big ears help it to keep cool.* (Courtesy of Frans Lanting/ Minden Pictures)

savanna insects because the mounds they build form a prominent feature of the landscape. There are more than 2,000 species of termites. Not all of them build mounds, but those that do, build on a grand scale. The compass or magnetic termite (*Amitermes meridionalis*) of Australia builds wedge-shaped mounds, about 11.5 feet (3.5 m) high, that are aligned north to south. In the early morning and evening the Sun shines on the flat sides, warming the interior, but at midday the Sun shines on the pointed edge, preventing the mound from overheating. Another Australian termite, *Nasutitermes triodae,* builds mounds that are 20 feet (6 m) tall.

Many of the mounds on the African savanna are built by *Macrotermes* and *Odontotermes* species. Individual termites are specialists. Some are workers of various kinds, and others are soldiers that protect the nest from invaders. At night columns of workers, guarded by soldiers, emerge to forage for food—plant material of all kinds, including paper and even rubber—which they carry back to a store inside the nest. Unlike many termites, however, *Macrotermes* and *Odontotermes* species cannot digest the cellulose in wood. To compensate for this, these termites have developed a close relationship with particular species of fungi that are able to break down cellulose. The insects use their own feces to make "combs" on which they cultivate the fungi, and when the termites eat them, the fungi supply the insects with vitamins.

The illustration shows a *Macrotermes* mound. The important part of the structure is below ground. That is where the insects tend the fungi and where they store food. The king and queen live there in a chamber called the royal cell, where they are fed and groomed by workers. The king is much bigger than the workers and soldiers, and the queen is much bigger than the king. The royal cell is also where the queen lays eggs—an *Odontotermes obesus* queen is capable of laying more than 80,000 eggs in a single day. Workers remove the eggs, and when they hatch, the larvae are raised in galleries below the royal cell.

A medium-size *Macrotermes* mound houses about 2 million individuals. Their bodies generate a considerable amount of heat, and a termite population of that size needs about 4,000 cubic feet (1,200 l) of fresh air a day. What makes this

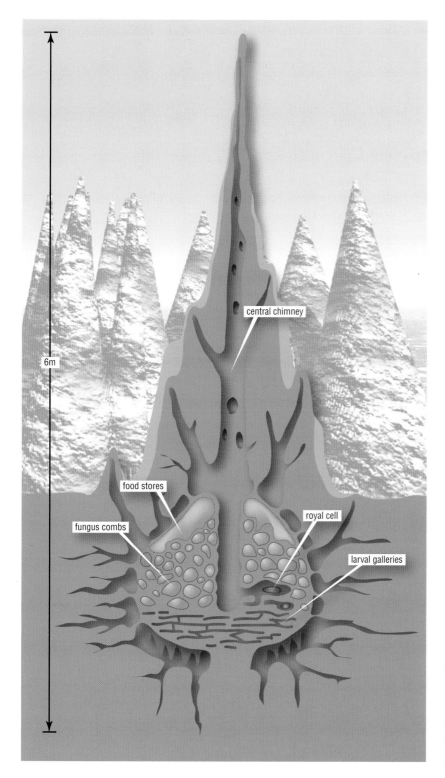

6m

central chimney

food stores

fungus combs

royal cell

larval galleries

Cross section through a termite mound. This mound was built by Macrotermes termites, which are common on the African savanna. The part above ground is a chimney that allows fresh air to enter and provides air-conditioning. The termites—about 2 million in a mound of this size—live below ground.

much fresh air circulate through a termite mound? Good architecture does.

The structure above ground is a chimney that provides air-conditioning. The workers build it from soil particles stuck together with saliva to make a kind of cement, and it is very strong. Ridges on the outside of the mound are hollow. Inside each ridge there is a network of six or more passages leading from the central chimney, which rises from the underground nest. The ridge passages lie beneath a very thin skin of cement. Warm air rises from the nest. When it reaches the tops of the ridges, the air seeps through the cement and is replaced by air seeping in from outside at the bottom of the ridges. This air is then drawn downward through other passages and into the nest. In this way the air in the nest is kept fresh and cool.

Although a termite mound looks permanent, in fact it is always a "work in progress." The workers are constantly repairing it and adding to it, and their maintenance includes the vital task of keeping the ridge passages clear and operating properly.

## Mongooses, prairie dogs, marmots, ground squirrels, and pocket gophers

Termites build strong defenses that protect them from marauding ants, which are their worst enemies, but no termite mound can withstand a determined assault from a pack of banded mongooses (*Mungos mungo*) that have decided to set up house at the mound. There are 31 species of mongooses. Most live a solitary life, but some live in groups, including the banded mongoose and the suricate or gray meerkat (*Suricata suricatta*), an animal found close to the desert's edge. A pack of banded mongooses comprises approximately a dozen adults and their young. At dawn the adults set out in single file, led by the dominant female and male, then separate to forage for food. They feed on small animals, insects—especially dung beetles—and occasionally fruit. As they move around, the mongooses maintain contact by means of a variety of calls, each with a particular meaning. They can cover a considerable distance, depending on the abundance of food.

In drier parts of the short-grass savanna a pack will range over about six square miles (15.5 km²); where there is more food they cover about 0.4 square mile (1 km²).

One male stays at home to look after the young. A few hours later the pack return. The mothers suckle their infants and some of the mongooses take them beetles. Then they head off on another foraging expedition.

The savanna is a dangerous place for small animals—an adult banded mongoose is about 22 inches (56 cm) long, including its 8.5-inch (22-cm) tail—but mongooses are alert, quick, and brave. They frequently stand upright on their hind legs to look for danger, and if one animal spots trouble, it will alert the others. When youngsters are old enough to leave the nest, there is always a baby-sitter to keep an eye on them until they are experienced enough to fend for themselves. A group of mongooses will drive off most threats. A jackal (*Canis* species) can catch a solitary mongoose, but if it approaches a pack, the mongooses crowd tightly together and move toward the aggressor, one mongoose standing upright from time to time to get a better view. This apparition is enough to make the jackal turn tail and run, pursued by the mongooses, now working as individuals, snapping at its tail and legs. Banded mongooses were once seen to climb a tree and attack an eagle that was holding a member of their pack. They forced the eagle to release its victim and the mongoose fell to the ground, landing unharmed.

There are no mongooses on the prairie or steppe. Instead there are prairie dogs (*Cynomys* species) and sousliks (five species of *Citellus*), which are squirrels that live on the ground. Both prairie dogs and sousliks live in large underground colonies that comprise chambers linked by extensive systems of tunnels. In the case of the sousliks, communal housing is about as far as cooperation goes. Each souslik has its own chamber, where it lives an independent life. Prairie dogs are much more social. The black-tailed prairie dog (*Cynomys ludovicianus*), which is found throughout the mixed prairie, is an animal about 12 inches (30 cm) long with a short tail. It is called a "dog" because of the bark it utters to warn of danger.

*Black-tailed prairie dogs* (Cynomys ludovicianus) *are highly social animals that live in colonies linked by tunnels to form "townships." They were once found throughout the prairies but are now much less common.* (Courtesy of Fogstock)

Prairie dogs live in groups called *coteries*. Each coterie has its own system of chambers and tunnels, but there are also tunnels linking neighboring coteries. Several coteries form a township, and a township can occupy 150 acres (60 ha) or more. Within a coterie, all the individuals are free to use any tunnel, but in winter the dominant male, sometimes with help from an assistant, defends the coterie's boundaries by chasing and screeching at outsiders who try to enter. The boundaries are relaxed in summer, and when members from different coteries meet, they greet each other cordially. When a coterie becomes too crowded the older members leave and start a new coterie nearby, leaving the old coterie to the younger and less experienced individuals.

Coteries have to be defended, and there are usually sentries on the lookout for hunters—especially for snakes, which can move easily through the narrow burrows. To guard against invaders, prairie dogs clear all the shrubs and other tall plants from a wide area around the coterie so that any approaching animal must cross open ground where there is no cover.

Marmots are also social animals. American marmots, which are also known as woodchucks or groundhogs, are animals of forest edges and mountains, but two of the seven species of Eurasian marmots inhabit the steppes. The bobak (*Marmota bobac*) lives on the western steppe, and the Siberian marmot (*M. sibirica*) lives in the east, around Lake Baikal. Marmots are stocky animals, weighing about nine pounds (4 kg), but they have very flexible bodies that allow them to squeeze into narrow spaces and to dig complicated networks of long tunnels with many sharp bends. Burrows average 85 feet (26 m) in length, and some are 197 feet (60 m) long. There are winter burrows and summer burrows as well as chambers, usually about 6.5 feet (2 m) below ground, where the young are born. Marmots hibernate—and their hibernation chambers, where they spend six to nine months of the year, are up to 23 feet (7 m) below ground. Marmots are the biggest animals to hibernate (see "Hibernation" on page 141). Bears (which are not grassland animals) become dormant in winter, but they do not enter true hibernation in which the body temperature falls to about 2°F (1°C) above the air temperature. A bear dies if its body temperature falls below 59°F (15°C).

The steppe marmots live in colonies similar to those of prairie dogs, with connecting tunnels that link individual colonies—equivalent to prairie-dog coteries—into "townships." Marmots communicate with each other constantly, both vocally and in body language, and they use a very piercing cry to warn of approaching danger. They feed on a wide variety of plant material, but because they do not digest it very efficiently, they augment their diet with insects and other invertebrate animals.

Thirteen-lined ground squirrels (*Spermophilus tridecenlineatus*) also live in large colonies, but colonies in which individuals largely ignore each other. They are much less social than prairie dogs or marmots. The thirteen-lined ground squirrel is a little smaller than a prairie dog. Its name refers to the lines and rows of spots that run the length of its body. These animals are active by day, often in large numbers. They frequently sit up on their haunches to look out for hunters in search of a meal, and if they see danger they vanish into their burrows. They feed on seeds, roots, fruit, insects, and some-times birds' eggs and mice. In winter they hibernate (see the sidebar "Hibernation" on page 141).

Pocket gophers also live below ground and are well equipped for digging. There are 34 species of pocket gophers, but all gophers are built on the same lines. A gopher has a big head and strong jaw muscles; a stout, tubular body; short, powerful limbs; very loose skin; and incisors—the teeth at the front of both jaws—that protrude through the lips, so the teeth are exposed when the animal has its mouth closed. This characteristic allows the gopher to use its teeth for digging and cutting through roots without filling its mouth with dirt, although gophers dig mainly with their forelimbs; they use their teeth only when their claws are inadequate. The *pocket* in their name refers to their cheek pouches, in which they carry food.

Unlike prairie dogs, pocket gophers are solitary animals. Each individual has its own burrow system. Males and females move in together during the mating season, and females live with their offspring until they are old enough to leave—usually when they are about nine weeks old—but for the rest of the time they live alone. An individual obtains its food from a territory of about 3,000 square feet (280 m²) and feeds on the leaves of forbs and grasses, and on roots and tubers from below ground. They live wherever the soil is loose enough for digging, from southwestern Canada through the western and southeastern United States, and as far south as the Colombian border.

## Snakes and lizards

Snakes evolved from lizard ancestors, and lizards and snakes are very similar. They are reptiles and as such they need to bask in sunlight until their muscles are warm enough to work properly and in very hot weather they cool themselves by sheltering in the shade. In contrast, mammals and birds are able to generate heat inside the body, for example, by shivering, and to rid themselves of excess heat, for example, by sweating and panting. This ability to regulate their body tem-perature allows them to be active almost regardless of the outside temperature. Regulating their body temperature gives them a major advantage over reptiles, but they pay a high price for it: A mammal or bird needs to eat approximately 10 times more food than a reptile of similar size.

Reptiles are highly adaptable and many thrive on the world's grasslands. Those living on the temperate prairie, pampa, and steppe spend the cold winters lying inactive in sheltered places such as caves. They move little, but they are not hibernating (see the sidebar "Hibernation" on page 141). Many species congregate in large numbers to spend the winter together, emerging in spring to disperse in search of food.

Vipers (*Vipera* species) are venomous snakes that occur throughout Europe, Asia, and Africa. They vary in size, and the typical viper of the steppe is one of the smallest. Ursini's viper, also known as the meadow viper, steppe viper, and Renard's viper, averages 18 inches (45 cm) in length and is never more than three feet (91 cm) long. Most scientists now believe that this snake, found over much of southern Europe and central Asia, in fact comprises several species. The steppe viper (*V. renardi*) has dark, zigzag markings along its back, making it easy to recognize. It is an irritable snake that is likely to strike if it is approached. The Central Asian viper, also known as the Asiatic pit viper or manushi (*Agkistrodon halys*), found throughout the steppes, is less than three feet (91 cm) long and not very dangerous to humans. It hunts mainly at night and hibernates through the winter.

The Montpellier snake (*Malpolon monspessulanus* ) is much bigger. It grows to 6.5 feet (2 m) and hunts small mammals, birds, and other reptiles. It is a fast-moving, venomous snake that is active by day.

All snakes are carnivorous—they eat only animals. Some feed on prey small enough to be caught and overpowered easily. Other species feed on bigger prey, including other snakes, which they need to kill before they can swallow it. Venomous snakes use their venom mainly to subdue prey that might otherwise be too quick or powerful for them to overcome—although they will also use it to defend themselves. Other grassland snakes are nonvenomous and use an alternative to venom: constriction. A constrictor snake seizes the prey with its teeth, then throws a section of its body around it in a coil. It tightens the coil and keeps such a tight grip that the victim is unable to draw breath. Some constrictor snakes can kill several rats or mice at the same time, by throwing a coil around each.

Sand boas are constricting nonvenomous snakes that feed on small mammals and lizards. They are rarely more than three feet (91 cm) long, and they spend most of the day in their burrows below ground. All sand boas have thick bodies and blunt snouts and tails. This shape helps them in burrowing, and the javelin sand boa (*Eryx jaculus*) of the steppe uses its shape in self-defense. When threatened, it hides its head and raises its tail, waving it in a threatening fashion and making striking movements with it. Many of these sand boas bear scars on their tails as evidence of the success of this technique.

Prairie dogs and pocket gophers keep careful watch for snakes, especially the gopher snake (*Pituophis melanoleucas*). It is a thick-bodied snake that grows to about eight feet (2.4 m) long and kills by constriction. As well as ground squirrels, these snakes feed on rabbits, birds, and lizards. Gopher snakes are themselves liable to attack by kingsnakes. The common kingsnake (*Lampropeltis getulus*) is up to 6.5 feet (2 m) long and also kills by constriction. It feeds on small animals of all kinds, including snakes—even young rattlesnakes; kingsnakes are immune to rattlesnake venom.

There are about 30 species of rattlesnakes. All are pit vipers. Small depressions (pits) on a pit viper's face contain organs that are highly sensitive to small differences in temperature. No matter how good a bird's or mammal's camouflage, a rattlesnake can accurately pinpoint the animal's position by the difference between its body temperature and that of the background. Prairie rattlesnakes include the western diamondback (*Crotalus atrox*) and prairie rattlesnake (*C. viridis*). These are "true" rattlesnakes and both grow to more than 6.5 feet (2 m) long. Though not a "true" rattlesnake, the massasauga (*Sistrurus catenatus*) is closely related and has rattles in its tail. It is up to 40 inches (1 m) long. Rattlesnakes feed mainly on small mammals.

There are many species of snakes living on the African savanna, but they are rarely seen and many are active only at night. Pythons tend to be large snakes, but the royal python, or ball python (*Python regius*), is only three to six feet (91–180 cm) long. Found throughout much of Africa, it feeds mainly at night and sees well in dim light. It eats rodents and thus helps control the rodent population. It is becoming rare, however, because local people hunt royal pythons for food, and the small size of these snakes, combined with their attractive markings and the ease with which they can be tamed, make them popular in the pet trade.

The coral snake (*Aspidelaps lubricus*) also emerges at night, having spent the day in its burrow below ground. It feeds on rodents, lizards, and other snakes. The coral snake is 15–30 inches (40–80 cm) long and venomous, but it is not very dangerous to people. It is most active after rains, and at these times many coral snakes are killed on the roads.

Puff adders (*Bitis arietans*) are active by both day and night, but they become especially active soon after sunset. A thick-bodied snake, averaging three feet (91 cm) in length but sometimes longer, a puff adder moves slowly and relies on its camouflage to remain hidden as it lies on the ground, waiting for prey to approach within its reach. It feeds on any small animal it can catch, often striking and then following its victim by scent, waiting for it to die. Puff adders are very venomous and bad tempered. If threatened, a puff adder expands its body to make itself look bigger—hence its name—before striking. The horned adder (*B. caudalis*) lives in the drier parts of the savanna and is also active by day and night. It is about 10–20 inches (25–50 cm) long and often hides by burying itself in sand with only the top of its head, with its two "horns," and its eyes exposed. Although venomous, it is not very dangerous. The berg adder (*B. atropos*), a bad-tempered snake that is slightly bigger than its relative the horned adder, lives only in South Africa.

The two savanna snakes with the most dangerous venom spend most of their time in trees and are not aggressive toward people. Both the boomslang (*Dispholidus typus*) and the eastern green mamba (*Dendroaspis angusticeps*) can be up to 6.5 feet (2 m) long and feed on lizards and birds.

Grassland lizards feed on small animals that they catch either by chasing them or by waiting in hiding to spring on any prey within reach. Agamid or chisel-teeth lizards have long tails, plump bodies, and triangular heads, and they feed mainly on insects. Some have heads rather like those of toads, including two steppe species, the toad-headed agama (*Phrynocephalus mystaceus*) and the spotted toad agama (*P. guttatus*). There are several species of racerunners, found from southern Europe to Mongolia and in Africa. These are small, fast-moving lizards that have long tails and strong legs and shelter in crevices among rocks. They feed on insects, spiders, and other small animals. They are often gray, and many have fringes along their toes that improve their grip when they run across loose sand. The rapid fringed-toed lizard (*Eremias velox*) is one of the most widespread species. The steppe racerunner, also called the Mongolian racerunner and desert lacertid (*E. argus*), has a pointed snout. It lives in a region extending from Romania to Mongolia.

Several species of skinks (family Scincidae) live on the prairie. Skinks are lizards that have a long, round body and short legs—many skinks have no legs at all. The Great Plains skink (*Eumeces obsoletus*), however, has strong legs. It is six to 14 inches (15–35 cm) long and feeds on insects, spiders, and small lizards. It hunts by day and will bite if it is disturbed. Unlike most lizards, female Great Plains skinks actively care for their young. They guard the eggs, turning them from time to time to make sure they warm evenly, and when the eggs are ready to hatch, the mother rubs against them to stimulate the young to start wriggling free. She continues to care for them for several days after they hatch, cleaning them regularly. The Great Plains skink lives in drier, rockier parts of the prairies. Brown skinks, also called ground skinks (*Scincella lateralis*), inhabit the moister regions. They do not tend their young.

The most curious lizards of the savanna are its chameleons. All chameleons have a body that is flattened from side to side, bulging eyes that can move independently of each other, a muscular tail that can grip tree branches, toes that provide a viselike grip, and a long tongue with a sticky pad at the tip. The chameleon's most famous talent, though, is its ability to change color to match its background rapidly. Its camouflage helps the lizard as it moves slowly toward an insect until it is close enough to shoot out its long tongue. Jackson's chameleon (*Chamaeleo jacksonii*) is about four inches (10 cm) long and has three large horns on its head. Meller's chameleon (*C. melleri*), at about 22 inches (56 cm) long, is the largest chameleon outside Madagascar. It feeds on small birds as well as insects. It has a tiny horn on its snout and is marked with yellow stripes and black spots.

## Grazing animals

When Europeans first ventured onto the prairie, they saw immense herds of animals they called "buffalo." At that time there were probably at least 60 million buffalo. The Native Americans living on the plains depended on these herds for meat and for their hides, which they used for clothing and covering of their tepees. When European settlers moved onto the prairies, they also killed buffalo for meat and hides—and later for sport. Sometimes buffalo were killed merely for their tongue, which was considered a delicacy and commanded a

*"Buffalo," more correctly called bison (Bison bison), once roamed the prairies in vast herds. They were hunted almost to extinction but were rescued in time, and their population is now recovering.* (Courtesy of Fogstock)

good price in the cities, and the remainder of the carcass was left to rot. William F. Cody (1846–1917) earned his nickname "Buffalo Bill" for supplying buffalo meat to the crews building railroads. He once killed 4,280 of the animals in 17 months. This large-scale destruction of buffalo herds by non Native Americans wrecked the economy of the Plains peoples and led to much of the conflict between them and the settlers. By 1900 the buffalo was almost extinct. Thanks to the efforts of conservationists and the American Bison Society, the species was saved, and there are now some tens of thousands of buffalo—but not the tens of millions that once existed.

Although it resembles the true buffalo of Africa and the Asian water buffalo, the North American animal is not closely related to them, and nowadays it is known as the bison (*Bison bison*). Bison are big animals. An adult bull stands more than six feet (1.8 m) tall at the shoulder and weighs about one ton (908 kg). Cows are smaller. Bison live as family groups, each family consisting of a cow, several generations of her descendants, and one or more bulls. Varying numbers of family groups feed and travel together in herds that can number thousands of individuals. All the adults protect the calves.

Grass is their preferred food, although they will eat leaves and twigs from trees and shrubs. Bison are cattle and all cattle are very regular in their habits. They feed early in the morning, rest while they digest their meal, feed again in the early evening, and rest through the night. A herd may remain in the same area for several days and then move to fresh pasture, or it may wander apparently aimlessly.

Although bison were the most famous of the prairie animals, they were not the only large grazing mammals. At one time there were also approximately 40 million pronghorns (*Antilocapra americana*), also known as the prongbuck and the pronghorned antelope. Their name refers to the small forward-pointing spur—the prong—on each of their horns. In fact, the prong is part of the sheath of specialized hair that covers the bony horns; the sheath is shed every year. Most of the year pronghorns move around in small groups, but in winter they congregate in herds of up to 100 individuals.

They feed, mainly in the early morning and evening, on forbs and shrubs as well as grass. They are fleet of foot, escaping from danger by running at up to 40 MPH (64 km/h), and they swim well. Hunting reduced their numbers severely, and they have also suffered from loss of the open grassland on which they depend. Consequently, pronghorns are now rare.

Most deer live in forests, but the natural habitat of the pampas deer (*Ozotoceros bezoarticus*) is the South American grasslands. Now that much of the tall pampas grass has been replaced by pasture for cattle, however, the pampas deer has been driven into more wooded areas. For most of the year pampas deer live alone or in pairs, but they form larger groups in spring. They eat grass and feed mainly in the evening.

Countless television wildlife programs have made the grazing animals of the African savanna famous. They now provide the basis of a major tourist industry. The most spectacular, and certainly the tallest of them, is the giraffe (*Giraffa camelopardus*). It stands up to 11 feet (3.3 m) tall at the shoulder, and the top of its head may be more than 18 feet (5.5 m) above the ground. The Romans thought the giraffe resembled a cross between a camel and a leopard and called it *camelopardalis,* and the English name used to be *camelopard.* That is how the giraffe acquired its scientific name, *camelopardus.* Giraffes feed on the leaves, buds, and fruit of trees, but they also eat grass.

Antelope belong to the cattle family (Bovidae), and the common or Cape eland (*Tragelaphus oryx*) is the largest of them. A bull eland stands about five feet (1.5 m) tall at the shoulder. Both males and females have long spiral horns. Eland will eat seeds, fruits, flowers, leaves, tree bark, and any other nutritious plant material. Constantly on the move, they travel in groups of up to about 24 individuals for most of the year, but sometimes they form herds of several hundred animals.

The brindled gnu, also known as the blue wildebeest (*Connochaetes taurinus*), is an antelope that feeds on grass. A strange-looking animal, with its black face and wispy beard, it is highly successful. During the dry season gnus gather in herds numbering tens of thousands and migrate up to 1,000

*A male impala (Aepyceros melampus) in East Africa. Male impala spend much of their time alone, whereas females live in herds of up to 100 adults with their young. Impala are the most numerous antelope of the dry, woodland savanna. (Courtesy of Frans Lanting/ Minden Pictures)*

miles (1,600 km) in search of water and better pasture. It is a perilous journey, and many perish crossing rivers. Gnus prefer short grass, but the haartebeest (*Alcelaphus buselaphus*) is an antelope that eats coarse grass, although it is particularly partial to the lush young grass that springs up after a fire. Haartebeests live in herds of up to 30 individuals and often mingle with gnus and zebras to form mixed herds.

Gazelles are related to the antelope but are smaller. Thomson's gazelles (*Gazella thomsoni*) are probably the most abundant. They form herds of up to 200 animals, and when migrating in search of better pasture the herds number thousands. Gazelles feed mainly on short grass, grazing in the morning and evening, and when the grass is fairly lush they do not need to drink.

The springbok or springbuck (*Antidorcas marsupialis*), another animal that does not need to drink, is a rich tan color, with a darker stripe along each side of its body and long, slightly wavy horns. It earns its common name from its ability to leap up to 11.5 feet (3.5 m) into the air several times in succession. This behavior, called "pronking," is a considerable feat for an animal only 30–33 inches (75–83 cm) tall at the shoulder and with a body only four to four and a half feet (1.2–1.4 m) long. The springbok's species name *marsupialis* refers to a pouch extending from about halfway along its back to the root of its tail. When the animal is alarmed the pouch opens, revealing a row of stiff, white hairs. Springboks are very social and at one time formed herds numbering tens of thousands. In times of drought these vast herds used to migrate, consuming all the pasture and all the farm crops along the way. Consequently, large numbers were killed, and today they are much less numerous than they once were.

Zebras are striped horses, very closely related to the domestic horse, which are found only in Africa. They feed mainly on grass. There are three species. The plains or common zebra (*Equus burchelli*) occurs throughout eastern and southern Africa. Grevy's zebra (*E. grevyi*) is found in northeastern Africa, and the mountain zebra (*E. zebra*) lives in the upland grasslands.

The saiga (*Saiga tatarica*) lives on the steppe, where it feeds on grass and low shrubs. It was once classed as a kind of goat, then as an antelope; nowadays it is regarded as a gazelle. It

*Zebras (Equus species) are close cousins of the horse but have never been domesticated. Herds of them graze the savanna, mixing with herds of wildebeest when it is time for the seasonal migration. This is a female mountain zebra with her foal. (Courtesy of Fogstock)*

stands about 28–30 inches (70–80 cm) tall and has a sandy-colored coat that grows very thick in winter. The saiga's most remarkable feature is its long, drooping nose with nostrils that point downward. Its curious nose may moisten the air the saiga inhales and filter out dust from it, and in winter it may warm the air before it reaches the respiratory passages. Male saigas have horns, which are amber colored and translucent. Saiga horns are used in Chinese medicine, and the value of their horns led to the saiga's being hunted almost to extinction. It has been protected since 1917 and its numbers increased to more than 1 million by the 1980s. But today there are fewer than 600,000 animals as a result of poaching for meat and horns, and the saiga is again considered endangered.

## Hunters of the grasslands

Dogs and cats are the principal hunters of the grasslands, and the coyote (*Canis latrans*), also known as the prairie wolf or brush wolf, is the most successful hunter on the prairies. A coyote stands about 20 inches (50 cm) high at the shoulder and weighs on average 30 pounds (13.6 kg). These dogs are highly adaptable. They feed mainly on rabbits and rodents but will eat almost anything they can find, including snakes, insects, fish, frogs, carrion, fruit, and grass. Unfortunately they also attack farm livestock, especially sheep and lambs. This behavior has led to their persecution, but coyotes are now protected and are expanding their range. Coyotes are social as are all dogs. Breeding pairs live and hunt together, and their offspring sometimes remain with them, producing a family group of about six closely related animals. Members of the pack share food and cooperate in defending it from intruders. They use urine to mark the boundaries of their territory and howl to communicate with each other.

The coyote occurs only in North and Central America. Its South American equivalent is the maned wolf (*Chrysocyon brachyurus*), a beautiful animal that stands about three feet (91 cm) tall at the shoulder and has very long legs that allow it to see over the top of the tall grasses. Its "mane" is a patch of stiff, dark hair across its shoulders. The maned wolf feeds on any small animal it can catch.

*The coyote* (Canis latrans) *hunts on the prairie grasslands of North America.* (Courtesy of Fogstock)

The dingo (*Canis dingo*) is the wild dog of the Australian grasslands. Scientists now believe that all present-day dingoes are descended from a pair of domesticated dogs, or perhaps even a single pregnant bitch, that entered Australia from Indonesia about 5,000 years ago. Dingoes feed on insects, lizards, and rabbits, and dingo packs hunt larger prey, including kangaroos and sheep. Their social life resembles that of coyotes. The dingo breeds with domesticated dogs. In fact, it has done so to such an extent that there is a serious risk the dingo may become extinct, producing offspring that are indistinguishable from domestic dogs.

The African hunting dog (*Lycaon pictus*) is possibly the most social of all the grassland dogs. Although it is now threatened with extinction, the hunting dog once lived throughout the savanna. Unlike other dogs, it eats only meat—most dogs occasionally eat fruit and other plant material—and its short muzzle harbors very powerful jaws and strong, sharp teeth. Hunting dogs live in groups of two to 20 adults. They maintain a fixed base while they are raising pups, but at other times they are nomads, ranging up to 30 miles (50 km) a day in search of prey. They hunt mainly around dawn and dusk but also at night when the Moon is bright. The hunt begins with ritualistic behavior in which all the dogs rush around excitedly, greeting one another, probably in order to reaffirm their group identity. Then they set forth, locating a herd of prey by sight and then stalking it until they have identified a young or weak individual they are confident they can catch; wildebeest and gazelles are their usual prey. Once they have selected a target, they give chase, working as a team. They can keep running at about 35 MPH (56 km/h) for three miles (5 km). Life on the open grassland is a constant evolutionary contest between hunters and the hunted, between predators and their prey (see the sidebar). After a successful hunt the dogs share the food; pups are allowed to eat first.

Hyenas have powerful jaws. In fact, the spotted hyena (*Crocuta crocuta*) has the most powerful jaws of any mammal. Its jaws can crush bone, and its body can digest it. Hyenas eat the whole of their prey, leaving nothing for other animals, and later they regurgitate and spit out pellets made from the indigestible parts, such as hooves, horns, and hair. The spotted hyena lives in packs, usually of 10–30 animals but some-

*The gray wolf* (Canis lupus), *the largest member of the dog family, has been driven from most of its original range and now survives only in remote areas.* (Courtesy of Kevin Tate)

times more, and hunts mainly at night. Antelope and zebras are among its prey, but hyenas also feed on carrion. There are three species of hyenas. The striped (*Hyaena hyaena*) and brown (*H. brunnea*) hyenas are smaller than the spotted hyena and less social.

Hunting dogs and hyenas are impressive hunters, but the lion (*Panthera leo*) is by far the most famous meat eater of the savanna. Nowadays lions are found only in Africa and in a very small part of northwestern India, but at one time they lived throughout most of Europe and the Middle East.

Lions live in family groups, called *prides,* which comprise up to three adult males and up to 15 adult females together with their young. Known since ancient times as the "king of beasts," a male lion is about four feet (1.2 m) tall at the shoulder and 10 feet (3 m) long, not counting the tail, and it weighs 330–530 pounds (150–240 kg). It is a truly formidable animal, but in fact the male seldom takes part in the hunt. His job is to defend the family's territory and keep rival males away from the females. Hunting is left mainly to the lionesses. Lions will eat small birds, lizards, and animals as small as mice, but their diet consists mainly of gazelle, antelope, and

*The spotted hyena (Crocuta crocuta) inhabits grasslands over most of Africa south of the Sahara. A highly social animal, it lives mainly by scavenging, but it is also a formidable hunter.* (Courtesy of Fogstock)

*Lions* (Panthera leo) *resting on the African savanna. On the open grasslands where there is little cover, lions must hunt by stealth.* (Courtesy of Fogstock)

zebra. A single lion can kill any of these, but when several lions work together, they can kill bigger prey, such as buffalo and giraffes. Lions stalk their prey, slowly advancing until they are within about 100 feet (30 m) of the target before charging. If a lion is lucky—and three of every four lion attacks fail—it will be able to grab its victim or knock it to the ground with a blow from its paw before the prey animal has time to escape. When several lionesses hunt together, they try to surround the prey, cutting off its escape routes.

Cheetahs (*Acinonyx jubatus*) also stalk their prey, and this part of the hunt can last several hours. Once it charges, however, a cheetah can outrun its prey. It can accelerate rapidly to about 60 MPH (96 km/h), but it cannot maintain this speed long. Most chases last no more than about 20 seconds and cover about 560 feet (170 m). Cheetahs hunt hares, small antelope, gazelles, wildebeest calves, and birds, including ostriches. Centuries ago wealthy people in the Middle East and India kept cheetahs for hunting antelope. They are elegant animals and a cheetah is easily distinguished from other

(opposite page) *The cheetah* (Acinonyx jubatus) *is a cat built for speed. It stalks its prey until it is close enough to give chase, when it can reach 60 MPH (96 km/h) over a short distance.* (Courtesy of Fogstock)

cats by its long legs, light and agile build, and small head. The cheetah's spine is much more flexible than the spine of other cats. Combined with its long legs, this gives it a very long stride, and unlike other cats it has claws that do not retract, which give it a better grip when accelerating.

Cheetahs hunt mainly by day, when other cats are resting in the shade. The caracal (*Felis caracal*), or African lynx, hunts in twilight and at night. It measures two to three feet (60–90 cm) from its nose to the root of its tail and is recognizable by its long, tufted ears. Caracals feed on rodents and small deer and will also kill domestic sheep, goats, and poultry. They are found throughout the African savanna and much of the Middle East as far as northwestern India.

The jaguarundi (*F. yagouaroundi*) of North and South America is slightly smaller than a caracal, with a red or gray coat lacking any patterned markings. It is found on savanna grasslands and in scrub from Arizona to northern Argentina.

## Hunter and prey: The evolutionary arms race

In order to catch their prey, hunting animals—called *predators*—must either chase them, ambush them, or set traps for them. Hunting dogs, coyotes, and cheetahs chase their prey. Ambush calls for concealment, and it is the strategy many snakes use. Some have markings that make them almost invisible against the background. Where the ground is soft, certain snakes bury themselves with only their eyes and nose projecting above the surface. When a victim is within range they launch a very fast attack. Spiders set traps—their webs. Engineers have calculated that if strands of spider silk were the thickness of a pencil, a spider's web could catch and hold an airliner.

If they are to evade capture, prey must be wary to avoid ambushes, alert to possible traps, and able to outrun any hunter that gives chase. They can also confuse the enemy. One way to do so is to gather in herds; there is safety in numbers. This is partly because a hunter can attack only one individual, and it is almost impossible to select a target from a herd of animals that are not only crowded together and moving together, but swerving erratically from side to side. What is more, it is very difficult to approach a herd without being noticed. It may appear that all the animals are feeding, but at any moment there are always a few with their head raised, alert to any movement. If a prey animal detects danger, it starts to run, and so do all the others. As they run, many gazelles leap into the air. This leaping alters the outline of the herd and adds to the confusion of the pursuer.

It feeds on rodents, poultry, frogs, and fish. Farther south, the pampas cat (*F. colocolo*) lives among the pampas grass. A small, stocky cat with a thick, bushy tail, it hunts at night, feeding on small mammals.

### Grassland birds

Most birds fly, but not all do. Flying consumes large amounts of energy, and several groups of birds have abandoned flight and spend their entire life on the ground. This presents them with a problem but also gives them an advantage. Flying birds can avoid capture by dogs, hyenas, and cats by escaping into the air, but flightless birds must find an alternative means of defense. Consequently, some of those living on the

A herd of animals can also turn and fight. When hyenas chase eland, for example, the eland cows that have calves move ahead of the herd. Then the herd turns, and the animals that have no calves advance on the hunters. An eland is a big animal with big, sharp horns and hard hooves. In an encounter with a hyena, the eland usually wins.

One of the smartest strategies is to exploit the hunter's habits. Small birds often nest close to the nest of a bird of prey. They get away with this because a bird of prey travels away from its nest before commencing its hunt, so the small birds close to the nest are quite safe. They are also safe from other predators, because those hunters prefer not to approach the nest of a bird of prey.

Prey animals have other ways to prevent themselves from being eaten. They may make themselves objectionable. For example, monarch butterflies are poisonous, ladybugs are not good to eat, and wasps and bees have stings. Poisonous or inedible species usually have distinctive markings so predators can recognize them. Edible species can take advantage of this form of advertisement by acquiring similar markings.

Over many generations predators acquire more effective weapons and techniques, and prey animals acquire better defenses. As hunters and the hunted try to keep ahead of each other, this competition turns into an evolutionary arms race that ends only when it reaches a stable situation in which the predators are able to catch enough food to survive, but not so much as to wipe out the prey.

open grasslands are fast runners. Their advantage is that since they do not leave the ground there is no restriction on their weight, and flightless birds can be large and heavy enough to defend themselves against most attackers.

The ostrich (*Struthio camelus*) of the African savanna is the fastest, and it is also the world's largest living bird. Newly hatched, an ostrich chick is about 12 inches (30 cm) tall and already can run. An adult bird is six to nine feet (1.8–2.7 m) tall, and it can run at 44 MPH (70 km/h). Ostriches have keen eyesight and never sleep more than 15 minutes at a time. They have to bend their heads to the ground while feeding, but they look up frequently. They are so alert to danger that grazing mammals tend to keep close to them and use them as an early warning system. There is no truth in the old joke

*The ostrich* (Struthio camelus) *is the largest living bird, inhabiting the savanna grasslands of eastern and southern Africa and the area along the Atlantic coast of North Africa.* (Courtesy of Louis Azevedo)

about ostriches' burying their heads in the sand. The idea probably arose because when an ostrich is crouched on its nest it holds its head close to the ground, where the head is often partly hidden. Ostriches wander the savanna in small groups, feeding mainly on plant material, although they sometimes eat small reptiles.

The emu (*Dromaius novaehollandiae*) is the Australian equivalent of the ostrich. It is about 6.5 feet (2 m) tall and can run at about 30 MPH (48 km/h). Emus also swim well. These birds travel in small groups and feed on plant material and insects. They cause considerable damage to farm crops, and many were killed between 1932 and 1965 during a campaign to exterminate them. They are now protected in most areas and are found throughout Australia.

The rhea (*Rhea americana*) lives on the pampa. It is smaller than the ostrich or emu, standing about five feet (1.5 m) tall, and can run at up to 37 MPH (60 km/h). Old males usually live alone, but most rheas live in groups of up to 30 birds. They feed on plant material and insects. Male rheas raise the chicks and will defend them ferociously. A rhea has a powerful kick and is armed with hornlike spurs on its ankles. A rhea will charge a horse, and gauchos take dogs with them for protection. Rheas have even been known to attack taxiing airplanes!

Ostriches, emus, and rheas are too heavy to fly, but they are not the only large birds of the grasslands. Cranes, which do fly, live on the grasslands of every continent except South America. They breed in wetlands, however. The draining of these areas, combined with hunting, have contributed to a drastic decline in their numbers so that most cranes are now endangered, although they may be recovering as a result of sustained conservation efforts. The whooping crane (*Grus americana*) of North America is one of the largest, standing about 4.5 feet (1.4 m) tall. The demoiselle crane (*Anthropoides virgo*), one of the most beautiful of all birds, spends the winter in Africa and southern Asia and returns to the Eurasian steppe to breed. The crowned crane (*Balearica pavonina*), a bird about 3.2 feet (1 m) tall, is found over most of the African savanna.

No prairie bird has lost the ability to fly, but sage grouse and prairie chickens are very reluctant to do so and postpone escape until the very last moment. The sage grouse (*Centrocercus urophasianus*) lives on the drier short-grass prairies in the west, and the greater (*Tympanuchus cupido*) and lesser (*T. pallidicinctus*) prairie chickens live on the tallgrass prairie in the east.

During the breeding season sage grouse and prairie chickens gather in large numbers in traditional *lekking areas*. Each male occupies and defends a patch of ground called a *lek*, where he spreads his feathers, struts around, and utters loud calls. Females move among the leks, choosing the best performer, and the winning male mates with most of the females.

Other birds defend themselves by confusing attackers, using a version of the herd strategy of grazing mammals.

Although they can fly, small birds need to drink, and while they are on the ground beside a water hole they are vulnerable. Consequently, some birds, such as budgerigars (*Melopsittacus undulatus*) and cockatoos (family Cacatuidae) of Australia, arrive at water holes in large flocks that whirl around with individuals flying in all directions, making it very difficult for a predator to select a target, while below them individual birds take turns to drink.

Weavers are small birds that knot and weave grass blades to make intricate nests that hang from the trees of the African savanna. There are 94 species of true weavers, of which the red-billed quelea (*Quelea quelea*) is the most abundant. Queleas defend themselves with a version of the herd strategy, moving around in flocks numbering thousands. At breeding time queleas gather in even larger flocks, sometimes numbering millions, and a single tree can carry several hundred nests. There are so many birds and they are so vigilant that predators have little hope of approaching without raising the alarm and sending the flock scattering. When the queleas are airborne a predator becomes confused and abandons the hunt. Consequently, queleas breed more successfully than most small birds. They feed only on seeds—including those of wheat, millet, and other farm crops—and damage crops on a scale that is comparable to the devastation caused by locusts.

Many of the grassland birds are predators that feed on small animals. The secretary bird (*Sagittarius serpentarius*)—the name refers to its crest of feathers, which resembles a bunch of quill pens—spends most of its time on the ground. It eats a variety of animals, including snakes, which it kills by stamping on them. It is a large bird, up to 3.3 feet (1 m) tall and with a wingspan of 6.5 feet (2 m), that flies well and nests in the top of acacia trees. Secretary birds are found only in Africa and no other bird is quite like them.

Most hornbills eat fruit or insects, but some eat small mammals and also snakes. These include the Abyssinian and southern ground hornbills (*Bucorvus abyssinicus* and *B. cafer*, respectively) and the yellow-billed hornbill (*Tockus flavirostris*). These very social birds, named for their large bill, are found throughout the African savanna.

Several eagles also eat snakes. The short-toed eagle (*Circaetus gallicus*) is a snake-eating eagle of the steppe, and the bateleur (*Terathopius ecaudatus*) is a snake eater of the African savanna, although this species feeds mainly on carrion. The tawny eagle (*Aquila rapax*) will also eat carrion and spends much of its time on the ground. It is very widely distributed, occurring throughout the African savanna and the Eurasian steppes.

Vultures are the most famous eaters of carrion. They circle high in the air, constantly looking for food, and when hunters take down a prey animal the first vulture to see the event begins to circle lower. Other vultures notice this and converge on the meal—most vultures locate food by watching other vultures. The vultures land and wait until the killer has eaten its fill then take the remains. Different species eat different parts of the animal, allowing several species to feed together without competing, although there is much squabbling among individuals. Vultures can strip a small animal such as an antelope to the bone in 20 minutes. The two most common African vultures are Rüppell's griffon (*Gyps ruppelli*), which lives on the African savanna mainly north of the equator, and the lappet-faced vulture (*Torgos tracheliotus*), found south of the equator. Although they are highly efficient at locating food, vultures cannot fly at night, and they are easily driven away by large mammals such as hyenas and jackals.

American vultures are not closely related to Old World vultures, but they live in much the same way. The turkey vulture, also called the turkey buzzard (*Cathartes aura*), is found throughout the prairies and the South American pampa, and it is unusual among birds in having a keen sense of smell. This allows it to find carcasses lying on the forest floor, and American vultures are consequently able to enter forests, unlike Old World vultures, which have no sense of smell and live only in open country. In South America, where their ranges overlap, turkey vultures are often seen in the company of black vultures (*Coragyps atratus*). Whenever the two quarrel, the black vulture wins. King vultures (*Sarcoramphus papa*), of Central and South America, have a poor sense of smell and rely on their eyesight, but they find food in the forest by following other vultures.

## Coping with drought

Grasslands have a dry climate, often with a season when almost no rain falls, and droughts are common (see "Dry seasons and rainy seasons" on pages 51–55). Plants must survive these periods—and, of course, they do.

Water enters a plant through its roots and travels from the roots to every other part along channels called *vessels*. Photosynthesis (see the sidebar "Photosynthesis" on page 85) is the process by which green plants make sugars from water and carbon dioxide. Carbon dioxide must enter the photosynthesizing cells, and oxygen, a by-product of photosynthesis, must leave those cells. Gases are exchanged through tiny pores, called *stomata,* in the surface of leaves. Stomata can be open or closed, but while they are open for gas exchange, water can evaporate through them and be lost from the plant. This process is called *transpiration.* Ordinarily the water is immediately replaced by water drawn up from the soil, but if the soil is dry, the plant may lose water by transpiration faster than it can be replenished, with serious consequences. Water fills the spaces inside and between plant cells, making plant tissues rigid. Woody plants have solid stems that keep them upright even after the plant has died, but grasses and forbs are not woody and without water they wilt—become limp. When it rains the plants recover quickly, but if they remain without water for more than a certain length of time the wilting becomes permanent and the plants die.

Plants cannot control the weather or the amount of moisture in the soil, but they can reduce the rate of transpiration. Water evaporates fastest when it is exposed to direct sunlight. Consequently, grassland plants tend to have many more stomata on the shaded underside of their leaves than on the exposed upper side. This arrangement does not work so well for grasses, however, because their long, narrow leaf blades point upward and are lit from both sides. Instead, on warm, bright days many grasses, especially the feather grasses (*Stipa* species) that are so common on grasslands, roll their leaves into long tubes, with the stomata on the inside.

Plants keep their stomata closed on hot, sunny days. This prevents water loss by transpiration, but it creates another problem: Food production is disrupted. The light-independent stage of photosynthesis can continue with the stomata closed, using carbon dioxide that was absorbed earlier when the stomata were open, but the store of carbon dioxide in the cells is soon depleted and then another chemical reaction becomes dominant.

Rubisco (ribulose biphosphate carboxylase), the enzyme that attaches to carbon dioxide at the start of the light-independent stage of photosynthesis, will accept either carbon dioxide or oxygen, and when the concentration of carbon dioxide falls below a certain level, rubisco takes up oxygen rather than carbon dioxide. It then attaches oxygen instead of carbon dioxide to RuBP (ribulose biphosphate). The resulting process is called *photorespiration: photo-* because it takes place in light and *respiration* because it uses oxygen. Unlike ordinary respiration, however, it releases no energy for the plant, and it reduces photosynthesis by removing carbon compounds from the cycle. Plants in temperate regions of the world can tolerate photorespiration because although it slows the rate of photosynthesis, the hot, sunny conditions that cause it seldom continue long enough to do serious harm.

That is not the case in the Tropics, and several thousand species of plants, including corn (maize), sugarcane, and many grasses of the tropical savannas, have evolved a modified version of photosynthesis that precludes the problem of photorespiration. When an atom of carbon is added to a molecule of RuBP, the resulting compound (3-phosphoglycerate) has three carbon atoms in each molecule; plants using this version of photosynthesis are known as $C_3$ plants. Plants that use the modified version of photosynthesis absorb carbon dioxide into *mesophyll* cells lying just below the leaf cells that contain chlorophyll. In the mesophyll cells the enzyme PEP carboxylase catalyzes a reaction that attaches carbon dioxide to phosphoenolpyruvate (PEP), producing oxaloacetate, a compound with four carbon atoms in its molecule. Oxaloacetate is then converted to malate, another four-carbon compound. Plants using this reaction are known as $C_4$ plants. Malate leaves the mesophyll cells and passes through passageways between them, called *plasmodesmata,* to enter *bundle-sheath* cells packed tightly around leaf veins. Inside the bundle-sheath cells, the malate gives up its carbon dioxide, which combines with rubisco and enters the ordinary light-independent stage. PEP carboxylase has no affinity for oxygen, so it can capture carbon dioxide even when the concentration is very low, and because carbon dioxide accumulates in the bundle-sheath cells, its concentration there is always high enough to ensure that it wins the competition with oxygen for rubisco, thus preventing photorespiration. A $C_4$ plant is able to perform photosynthesis efficiently in hot, sunny weather when its stomata are closed—conditions in which $C_3$ plants suffer stress.

At the start of the rainy season the grassland is ablaze with color, which reveals an alternative strategy by which plants survive drought. Annual plants produce seeds that lie dormant in the soil throughout the dry season but sprout very quickly once the soil around them is moist. The plants grow, flower, and produce a new crop of seeds during the rainy season, then die. In fact, these plants do not survive drought—they avoid it.

Many grassland animals also avoid drought. They do so by migrating in search of water and the better pasture that grows where the ground is moister (see "Mammal migrations" on pages 155–157).

Many of the African grazers can survive long periods without drinking, obtaining all the liquid their body needs from the vegetation they eat. The sassaby or tsessebi (*Damaliscus lunatus*), for example, can live without drinking for 30 days. Thomson's gazelle (*Gazella thomsonii*) drinks only when the pasture is very dry. The haartebeest (*Alcelaphus buselaphus*) can also survive for a long time without water, although it drinks readily when water is available.

Some animals do not need to drink at all. These include the Beira antelope (*Dorcatragus megalotis*), springbok (*Antidorcas marsupialis*), gerenuk (*Litocranius walleri*), and Grant's gazelle (*Gazella granti*). Their ability to retain water, thereby making do with very little, allows animals such as these to venture into the driest parts of the savanna, where most animals would perish from thirst, and they have no need to migrate in search of water during the dry season. This confers an added advantage: The predators that hunt them during the rainy season do need to drink, and they follow the migrating herds in search of water, leaving the nondrinkers in peace.

## Coping with heat and cold

Animal bodies function only within a specific range of temperatures. The normal body temperature of a person is between 96.4°F (35.8°C) and 99.5°F (37.5°C). If the temperature rises or falls outside this range the body will respond in ways aimed at moving the temperature back within the tolerable range, and if the temperature wanders far outside this range the person will become severely ill. Death is likely if the body temperature falls below 78.8°F (26.0°C) or rises above 109.4°F (43.0°C). Most mammals have a similar tolerable range. Birds have a higher average temperature, of about 104°F (40°C).

Birds and mammals are able to maintain a constant body temperature by internal means. If we are cold, we shiver, for example, thus warming the body, and if we are hot, we sweat, cooling the skin by allowing the sweat to evaporate. Reptiles are unable to shiver, sweat, or control their body temperature in any other internal way. Instead, they must absorb warmth from outside the body when they are cold and find cool surroundings when they are hot.

Birds and mammals are sometimes described as "warm-blooded" and reptiles as "cold-blooded," but this description is misleading, because while a reptile's body is active it is quite warm—sometimes warmer than the body of a mammal. Reptiles are active when their body temperature is between about 88°F (31°C) and 100°F (38°C). They are unable to move if their temperature falls below about 45°F (7°C) or rises above 109°F (43°C). Birds and mammals are more accurately described as *endotherms* and reptiles as *ectotherms; endo-* means "internal" and *ecto-* means "external." Amphibians and fish are *poikilotherms*.

On the tropical savanna most animals seek shade during the hottest part of the day. They remain fairly still, resting. Reptiles and small mammals retreat into burrows. Toward evening, as the temperature falls, they emerge to feed, and soon after dusk, as the temperature falls still further, many become inactive once more. Early in the morning most animals enjoy feeling the warmth of the rising Sun. Reptiles need that warmth and must bask in the sunshine until their muscles reach working temperature.

Basking and sheltering make it possible to control body temperature within fine limits. If a lizard is too warm, it will move alternately from sunshine to shade or turn to face into the Sun to minimize the area of its body that is directly exposed. This prevents its body from overheating. Where there is no shade, many large mammals that rest during the middle of the day turn from time to time so they are constantly facing the sun, rather than letting it beat down on their flanks, thus minimizing the area of body surface directly exposed to the sun. They may also choose to lie close together, so they shade one another.

Some animals adopt a more radical strategy for avoiding extreme heat. They enter a condition called *torpor,* in which they lose consciousness, their breathing and heartbeat slow, and their temperature rises. This technique, known as *estivation,* allows the animals to survive prolonged periods of high temperature and drought; it is more common among desert animals than grassland species, however.

Animals living on the temperate grasslands have no need to escape the extreme summer heat of the savanna. Instead, they must survive long, cold winters. As the temperature starts to fall reptiles retreat for the winter into secure hiding places, sheltered from the wind, where the temperature is unlikely to fall so low that they die. Once the temperature falls below 45°F (7°C), reptiles become immobilized and utterly helpless. Winter temperatures define the boundaries of the regions reptiles can inhabit, although the adder (*Vipera berus*) and common garter snake (*Thamnophis sirtalis*) live in latitudes up to about 68°N.

Birds often have difficulty maintaining their high body temperature when the air temperature is very low. Those that are active by day must find enough food to provide the energy to keep them warm through the night, and a bird that fails to do so may not survive. Consequently, many birds solve the problem of winter cold by migrating.

# Hibernation

An animal that hibernates in winter begins its preparations early in the fall by eating voraciously in order to lay down a thick layer of body fat as an energy store. At the same time the animal prepares a nest in a hidden, sheltered place and stocks the nest with food. When the air temperature begins to drop, the animal retreats to its nest, curls up in its normal sleeping position, and falls asleep.

Then its body starts to change. Blood vessels in its skin and legs constrict, confining most of the animal's blood to the center of its body, where the blood pressure remains high. The composition of the blood plasma changes to allow the circulation to slow without causing the blood to clot. Then the heartbeat slows to a few beats every minute; breathing also slows, in ground squirrels from about 100 to four breaths per minute. Then the body temperature falls within about 2°F (1°C) of the temperature of its surroundings, usually stabilizing at around 40°F (5°C).

The hibernating animal is now much more deeply unconscious than it would be during normal sleep, and its body is functioning at about one percent of the normal rate. It continues to produce waste products, but in very small amounts that a small animal stores in its body until hibernation ends. Marmots wake every three to four weeks to urinate and defecate. The nervous system continues to function and the animal adjusts its posture from time to time, moving very sluggishly.

If the air temperature falls so low as to endanger the animal's life, its nervous system responds at once. The animal starts shivering, its body temperature rises, and it wakes. This saves the hibernator's life, but it consumes a large amount of energy, derived from its body fat, and the animal may need to eat some of its food stores before returning to its comatose state.

As the outside temperature starts to rise, the animal emerges from hibernation. Its heartbeat accelerates, its constricted blood vessels dilate, and the animal starts shivering in the front part of its body, thereby warming its head and respiratory system ahead of the hind part of its body. How fast its temperature increases depends on its body size. A very small animal, such as a bat weighing 0.4–1.4 ounce (10–40 g), can be fully active within about 30 minutes. An animal the size of a ground squirrel, weighing about four ounces (100 g), requires more than two hours, and a marmot, weighing about 11 pounds (5 kg), requires several hours. Arousal uses up much of the remaining fat store, and the amount of energy used is much greater for a large animal than for a small one because of the greater body mass that must be warmed.

Large mammals grow thicker coats for the winter. Without its warmer coat, the animal would need to eat more food to supply the energy to maintain its body temperature. The insulation provided by its winter coat helps keep it warm without more food. Food is harder to find in winter, and many animals would perish without their warm coat.

Small mammals, such as mice, spend the winter below the snow. They sleep much of the time in nests made from grass and other bedding material and stocked with food they gathered in the fall, but when necessary they can move about along tunnels they make along the ground, beneath the snow. Down there they are sheltered from the wind, hidden from predators such as owls, and able to keep warm.

Some animals go to even greater lengths to conserve energy, spending the winter in hibernation. Hibernation involves radical changes in the way the body functions (see the sidebar). Few birds hibernate, but one that does is the poorwill (*Phalaenoptilus nuttalli*). Its Hopi name is *holchko,* meaning "sleeping one." Turkey vultures (*Cathartes aura*) fall into a deep sleep in very cold weather, but they do not hibernate in the true sense.

Many bats and rodents hibernate. Marmots (*Marmota* species), weighing about 11 pounds (5 kg), are the largest animals to hibernate in the true sense. For a larger animal the entry into hibernation would take so long and the amount of energy needed for arousal would be so great that hibernation would not be practicable. Although some big animals, such as bears, sleep much of the winter, they do not hibernate.

Large animals do not need to hibernate, because they tolerate cold much better than small animals. The rate at which a body loses heat from its surface depends on the ratio of body surface area to volume of the body. The bigger the animal, the smaller is its surface area in relation to its volume and the more slowly its body loses heat. In very cold weather a small animal would lose body heat so rapidly that it might not be able to eat enough food fast enough to remain active, and consequently it would die.

## CHAPTER 6

# GRASSLAND ECOLOGY

## How the plant eaters help the grass

Every animal alters the environment around it. Prairie dogs clear away shrubs that might interrupt the view, removing cover that might hide a stalking hunter. Grazing mammals destroy tree seedlings. As a result, together the prairie dogs and the grazing herds prevent grassland from becoming scrub or even forest. They maintain the grasslands, and in doing so they create the conditions that support all the other grassland plants and animals.

*Ecology* is the scientific study of the relationships among living organisms such as mammals and the plants around them, and between living organisms and the nonliving environment—the climate, water, and soils. Those relationships form very intricate networks called *ecosystems* that regulate themselves. For example, if good weather makes the plants grow more abundantly, the grazing animals will be able to feed more of their own young. This will increase the number of grazing animals. The larger herds will eat the surplus plant food, and there will be less for the animals to feed to their own young, so their numbers will decrease once more.

In the case of grasslands the relationships are a little different, because grasses are very special kinds of plants: Being eaten makes them grow more. Grasses produce leaves from the base of the plant (see "How grasses work" on pages 84–89). When an animal eats the upper part of a leaf, a new leaf grows from the base to take its place. But that is not all.

Perennial grasses are those that live for many years, rather than dying at the end of one season and growing anew from seed the following season. Most perennial grasses have horizontal stems, called *stolons* or *rhizomes,* depending on whether they run above or below ground. When animals trample the grass, they stimulate it to produce new roots and stems from the nodes along the horizontal stem. Trampling one part of the plant makes new plants grow nearby.

These are ways in which the grasses benefit the grazers. After all, these responses are the way grasses have of repairing the damage caused by grazing. It just so happens that in doing so they produce more food. The grasses could manage perfectly well without being eaten—or could they?

At the end of the growing season—summer in the temperate grasslands and the rainy season in tropical grasslands—plants die down. The aerial parts of forbs—the parts above ground—are fairly small. They die and fall, and the dead leaves and stems are out of the way in time for the plant to start growing again the following season. It is not quite so simple for grasses. They are tall and their leaves are tough. When the plants die down at the end of the season they form a thick mat of dead brown leaves and culms that decomposes very slowly. It just lies there on top of the growing part of the plant. The dead grass shades the plant, preventing photosynthesis, and so it suppresses the new growth. Unless it is removed, the grassland deteriorates.

Grazing helps prevent the grasses from growing so tall that dead grass suppresses the following year's growth. That is how grazing animals help the grass.

Grazing animals do not eat all of the grass, however, and there are mats of dead grass on the tall grass prairie and savanna at the end of the season. That is where people can help the grass. They cannot eat grass, of course, but setting fire to dead grass clears it away, encouraging new growth to provide food for the grazing animals on which the people depend.

## Food chains and food webs

Relationships among the plants and animals within an ecosystem depend largely on diet. For example, some birds and rodents eat seeds; larger mammals such as rabbits eat grass and other leaves; and eagles eat rabbits. The seed eaters can live peacefully side by side with the animals that eat leaves, because the two groups are not competing for food.

Although the eagles kill some of the rabbits, provided they do not take too many, the rabbit population does not decrease. The relationships, defined by what the organisms eat, are stable.

These relationships are sometimes shown as a sequence linked by arrows. A typical prairie sequence might be: Grass → prairie dog → gopher snake → kingsnake. The sequence tells us that prairie dogs eat grass, gopher snakes eat prairie dogs, and kingsnakes eat gopher snakes. A sequence of this type is called a *food chain*. It is useful, because it illustrates relationships very simply, allowing scientists to identify places where something might go wrong and disrupt the ecosystem. If, say, there were a disease epidemic that killed many of the prairie dogs, there would be less food for the gopher snakes, so some of them would starve and fewer of their young would survive to become adults. If there were fewer gopher snakes, there would be less for the kingsnakes to eat, and their numbers would also decrease. Smaller numbers of prairie dogs would also mean less grass was being eaten. If prairie dogs were the only animals eating grass, the grass would grow taller and at the end of the season the dry dead grass would fall on top of the grass plants. This would suppress grass growth the following spring, so there would be less food for the surviving prairie dogs the following year (see "How the plant eaters help the grass" on pages 143–144). If prairie dogs were not the only grass eaters in the area, a decline in their numbers would mean more food for their competitors, and another population—perhaps of rabbits— would increase.

Food chains are useful in another way. Since the 1960s, ecologists have known that certain poisons can accumulate along food chains. This happens because animals do not eat just one individual—one grasshopper, say—but many. Certain chemical substances, including a class of insecticides that are no longer used for this very reason, are chemically stable and soluble in fat. Chemical stability means that their molecules do not break down readily into smaller molecules of a harmless substance. Their solubility in fat makes them liable to be absorbed into body fat. Suppose grasshoppers have absorbed such an insecticide, but in amounts that are

*Prairie food web. A food web is a diagram that illustrates how different species are linked, and as this one shows, it can be very complicated. For example, the diagram shows that prairie falcons eat meadowlarks and sparrows; meadowlarks eat grasshoppers, and sparrows eat grass and forbs (seeds); grasshoppers eat grass.*

too small to harm them. They continue eating grass and are picked off by insect-eating birds. These birds eat many grasshoppers, and each bird's body absorbs and retains the insecticide from each grasshopper. Even so, the amount of insecticide accumulated in their body fat is not enough to harm them, so the birds go on eating grasshoppers. Falcons prey on these small birds, and a falcon catches several of them every day. Again the insecticide from each small bird dissolves in the falcon's body fat. The falcon is now storing all of the insecticide from all the grasshoppers eaten by many small birds. This is enough to cause harm. Scientists found that birds of prey suffering from accumulated insecticide poisoning were laying eggs with shells so thin they broke before the young could hatch from them. Consequently, the birds were not producing young, and their numbers declined. Once researchers had identified the route by which the poison was reaching the birds of prey, the problem could be solved. The route was the food chain, and it taught ecologists that animals high in a food chain—the hunters—are especially at risk.

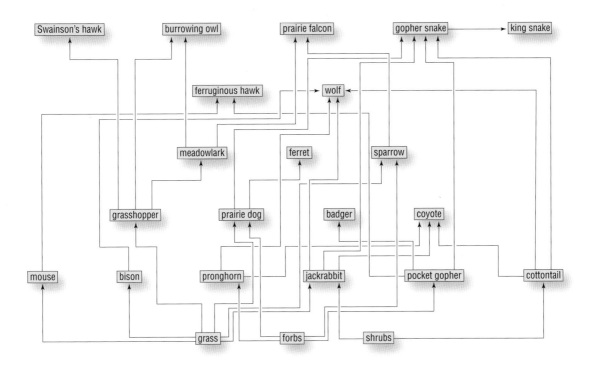

Food chains are useful, but they are very limited, because no animal eats just one kind of food. Animals eat different foods in different seasons, and most predators eat a wide variety of prey species. A food chain cannot describe the complexity of food relationships that exist in a real ecosystem. Relationships in the real world are more like webs than chains—they are *food webs*. Diagrams can be used to illustrate food webs, but, as the figure shows, even very simplified food webs yield extremely complicated diagrams. Nevertheless, food webs are much more useful than food chains, because a diagram of one provides an impression of the way a particular ecosystem works.

## Ecological pyramids

Lions hunt zebras. They are not very efficient hunters, probably because they fail to appreciate that if they approach in the same direction as the wind, the zebras can smell them coming. Suppose, though, that lions were so good at hunting they could catch zebras whenever they chose to do so. Might they be tempted to kill and eat all of the zebras? Obviously there is a limit to how much meat an individual lion can eat, but a limitless food supply would allow the lion population to expand greatly. If they did catch all of them, the zebras would disappear, because there would be no adults to breed and produce young. Then the lions would starve unless they could find an alternative animal to hunt—and if they found an alternative, might they not reduce its numbers to zero as well?

It does not happen. Lions never catch all of the zebras. In fact, averaged over a long period, lions never catch so many zebras that the zebra population declines.

It is possible for a predator to catch all of the prey, and people have been exploiting this possibility for centuries by keeping cats to hunt mice. We expect the cats to catch all the mice in and around our home, and the cats usually oblige. This is an artificial situation, however; we know that to make it possible we must feed the cat regularly. Unless we feed the cat, the cat will leave to find a better home, and it will not be long before the mice are back.

There are also contrived circumstances in which *herbivores*—plant-eating animals—totally destroy the vegetation on which they depend. It is called *overgrazing* and it occurs when herds of livestock are confined in too small a space too long and hunger forces them to eat all of the leaves, buds, and young shoots, killing all of the plants.

This does not happen in the natural world, where plant and animal relationships develop by themselves, without interference from outside. No predator ever eats all of the prey, and no herbivore ever eats all of the plant food. The herbivores eat approximately 10 percent of the plant material and the predators eat approximately 10 percent of the herbivores.

Many years ago the British ecologist Sir Charles Elton (1900–91) devised diagrams to show these relationships. He drew a rectangle to represent the plants. On top of this rectangle he set a second, the same height but about one-tenth the width, to represent the herbivores. A third rectangle, one-tenth the width of the one below, represented the meat eaters, or *carnivores*. The resulting diagram looked like a pyramid. It is known as an *ecological pyramid* or *Eltonian pyramid.* The Greek word *trophe* means "nourishment," so relationships based on diet are described as *trophic*. Each level in an ecological pyramid is known as a *trophic level.*

The pyramid demonstrates one fact very clearly. At each level, there can be no more than about one-tenth as many organisms as there are in the level below. Consequently, there are comparatively few carnivores, and carnivores that prey on other carnivores—sometimes called *top predators*—are very rare indeed.

The pyramid categorizes organisms according to their feeding methods; it does not name species. The plants use photosynthesis (see the sidebar "Photosynthesis" on pages 85–86) to make carbohydrates out of carbon dioxide and water. This is the food eaten by animals, and since plants produce it they are identified as *producers*. Herbivores then become *consumers,* but because they eat plant food directly and are the first level of consumers, they are known as *primary consumers*. Carnivores feed on the primary consumers, so they are *secondary consumers*. If there are top predators, they are *tertiary*

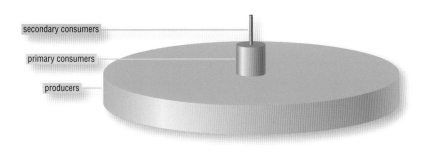

secondary consumers

primary consumers

producers

*Ecological pyramid. The three blocks represent feeding, or trophic, levels. Producers are green plants that produce food from inorganic ingredients. Primary consumers are plant eaters (herbivores); secondary consumers are meat eaters (carnivores that feed on the herbivores). The width of each block is proportional to the number, mass, or energy equivalent of the organisms at that level.*

*consumers.* The illustration shows a pyramid of this type, drawn approximately to scale. It indicates that if there were any tertiary consumers, their rectangle would be so narrow as to be almost invisible.

There is a difficulty, however. A *pyramid of numbers* represents the number of plants and animals at each trophic level, but this may be misleading. Elephants are herbivores—primary consumers—but an area of vegetation cannot support as many elephants as it can rabbits. The numbers mean very little unless we name the species, but if we did that, we would have to show the amount of food each species consumes. A simple diagram would then become extremely complicated—if it were possible to draw it at all.

The *pyramid of biomass* offers one solution. Take all the organisms of every kind at a particular trophic level and measure their combined mass. This is called the *biomass* at that level. If the pyramid shows the biomass at each level, whether the herbivores are elephants, rabbits, zebras, or any other kind of animal makes no difference. It is only their combined mass that interests us, and this should be more or less the same regardless of its composition: A ton of herbivores is a ton of herbivores. Biomass is usually given as the dry weight of organisms. It is measured in the first instance by heating samples to drive off all the moisture. The resulting values are then made available in tables, so that scientists can look up the dry weight of, say, an elephant weighing so much, without having to incinerate any animals.

Again, though, there is a problem. In order to maintain a constant body temperature, small mammals must eat much more than big animals in relation to their size. A ton of mice eat much more than a ton of elephants. This fact can distort the pyramid, in some cases to such an extent that the biomass of primary consumers appears to be greater than the biomass of producers, and that is clearly absurd.

There is a much better way to depict trophic relationships: the *pyramid of energy*. Green plants, the producers, use the energy of sunlight to drive photosynthesis. Biologists have measured the amount of energy photosynthesis uses, so it is possible to represent the consumers, or first trophic level, as an amount of energy. Consumers receive a proportion of that energy at each level, so the pyramid illustrates the flow of energy, originally from the Sun, through the ecosystem. It makes no difference whatever how big the animals are or what they weigh alive or dead.

Plants absorb energy from the Sun. Primary consumers utilize about 10 percent of that energy. They use most of it to provide themselves with the energy they need to move, grow, for bodily repair and maintenance, to digest their food, and reproduce. Only about 10 percent of the energy they receive is available to the next trophic level. The pyramid remains the same shape, with each level one-tenth the width of the level below, but the pyramid of energy is the most useful of the three illustrations because it is the most accurate.

In addition to these *producer* pyramids there is a second set of ecological pyramids, which describe the organisms and transfer of energy involved in decomposition. When plants and animals die, each individual body decomposes, and the *decomposers* form trophic levels similar to those of producers and consumers.

Dead organic matter, which is known as *detritus,* includes animal feces, fallen leaves, twigs, fruit, and dead plants and animals. Organisms that feed on such material are called *detritivores.* Instead of green plants, dead organic matter forms the base of the decomposer pyramids. The primary consumers are detritivores, such as snails, slugs, earthworms, millipedes, fungi, and bacteria. Predators, such as spiders, centipedes, and many species of beetles and other insects, feed on the detritivores, and *microbivores,* such as protozoa, nematodes, and rotifers, feed on bacteria and fungi. This group forms the second consumer level in the pyramid.

Birds, small mammals such as shrews and hedgehogs, frogs and toads, and certain reptiles feed on the secondary consumers and form the tertiary consumer level, and larger predators, such as dogs and snakes, feed on the tertiary consumers, making a fourth trophic level.

Dead organic matter enters the decomposer pyramid from every level of the producer pyramid because at every level organisms produce wastes and individuals die. Dead organic matter also enters the decomposer pyramids at every level, but here the effect is different because dead organic matter is immediately available for consumption by the detritivores. The decomposers recycle dead organic matter repeatedly until the material has been reduced to simple chemical compounds that dissolve in water in the soil, from which plant roots absorb them and they stimulate plant growth. The decomposers are extremely efficient. Researchers have calculated that of the total amount of energy stored in grassland plants, about 15 percent passes through the herbivores and carnivores feeding on that grassland but about 85 percent passes through the decomposers. The decomposers live mainly below ground, out of sight, and many of them are microscopically small, but they are immensely important.

## Do predators control their prey?

Lions eat zebras, so the lions regulate the number of zebras. If the zebra population increases for any reason, there will be more food for the lions and the lions will eat it, restoring the zebra population to its former size. It sounds obvious that ecological pyramids are controlled from the top, by the predators.

Suppose, though, that in a particular year the rains fail. If that happens, the vegetation will die back and there will be less for the zebras to eat. Some of them may starve, and fewer of their young will survive to become adults and have young of their own. In that case, the pyramid is being controlled from the bottom, by the abundance of producers, and the effects are felt all the way to the top. If there is less vegetation, there will be fewer primary consumers and in turn there will be fewer secondary and tertiary consumers— the carnivores.

Which is correct? Do predators control the size of the prey populations, or is it the other way around, with the prey population controlling the number of predators? Ecologists have been arguing about this for years, unfortunately, and there is no simple answer. It all depends.

The simplest food webs are found in the Arctic, where foxes, snowy owls, skuas, and stoats prey on lemmings. Investigations have shown that the predators regulate lemming numbers, but the way this happens varies from place to place. Stoats specialize in hunting lemmings, and the other three species largely leave the lemmings alone unless lemmings become very numerous. When this happens, the foxes, owls, and skuas turn their attention to the lemmings and lemming numbers fall dramatically. As a result, lemming numbers rise and fall in a cycle. This is what happens in northern Greenland, but not in Canada. Canadian lemmings are hunted by a variety of predators, and cumulatively these hunters prevent lemming numbers from increasing, so there is no cycle. Clearly, then, it is the predators that control the pyramid in both cases, and not the other way around.

Life is much more complicated on the tropical savanna. There are 28 species of hoofed grazing mammals on the African savanna, and 10 species of large carnivores to hunt them. The carnivores vary in size and therefore in the size of prey they are capable of attacking. Jackals and small cats hunt only small animals. A cheetah will hunt animals weighing up to about 220 pounds (100 kg); hunting dogs and hyenas will take prey up to 550 pounds (250 kg); and lions hunt prey up to 1,100 pounds (500 kg).

Big predators will also take small prey animals, however; therefore, the smaller grazing animals have more enemies than the large ones. Lions prefer to hunt wildebeest and zebras, but nearly half of their diet consists of smaller animals. Lions, cheetahs, wildcats, servals, caracals, jackals, hunting dogs, hyenas, and several smaller carnivores all hunt small antelope. Big animals are much safer. Lions are the only animals big enough to hunt buffalo and giraffe, although these account for only a small part of the lions' diet. Predators kill young elephants and hippopotamuses, but once these animals are fully grown they have little to fear. An adult African bull elephant weighs up to 6.6 tons (6 tonnes) and an adult male hippopotamus up to 3.5 tons (3.2 tonnes). Females of both species weigh about half as much as the males. It is very unusual for a predator to kill an animal of this size.

Scientists have discovered that on the savanna there is a critical body size for grazing animals, of about 330 pounds (150 kg). Animals smaller than this are much more likely to be caught by a predator than are bigger animals. Consequently, it is the hunters that regulate their populations. In this case the pyramid is controlled from the top.

Grazers weighing more than about 330 pounds (150 kg) have few predators and are much less likely to be killed by them. They have big appetites, however, and it is the availability of food that limits the size of their populations. The pyramid containing them as primary consumers is therefore controlled from the bottom.

## How herding provides safety in numbers

Over large areas of the open grasslands there is no place a large animal can hide. A watchful grazing animal will see the slight movement that betrays the presence of a camouflaged predator long before the hunter is close enough to launch an attack.

It sounds as though the hunters stand no chance at all. Unfortunately for the grazers, life is not quite so simple, however, because grazing animals must graze, and to do that an individual must lower its head and look at the ground. Its attention may be occupied for only a few seconds before it raises its head and resumes its watch while chewing the food it took, but the hunters are patient and skillful and are concentrating intensely. Those few seconds provide time enough to advance a few steps and then freeze, body flattened against the ground. It may take hours, but eventually these repeated small advances will put the hunter within range—close enough to outrun its prey—and the long time the hunt has taken will have been worthwhile, because the resulting feast will be highly nutritious.

Clearly the grazers are at a disadvantage, because while they eat they are vulnerable to attack. The hunters also have a weakness, however, and it is one that allows the grazers to survive: Hunters can attack only one prey animal at a time. This applies even to the predators that hunt as a team, such as lionesses, wolves, and hunting dogs. Their hunt involves running down or ambushing an individual. Teamwork allows them to hunt animals much bigger and stronger than they and to hunt more successfully, but it does not allow them to attack more than one individual at a time.

The grazers exploit this weakness by making it as difficult as they can for the predators to choose an individual as a target. They do not graze alone, scattered widely across the landscape, but together, as a herd. The approaching hunter sees not a solitary animal, but a crowd of animals, all of them moving, quite slowly, so they are constantly crossing and recrossing each other's paths. No sooner does the hunter choose an individual than another animal has crossed in front of it and the target has disappeared into the herd. From the hunter's point of view this is highly confusing behavior—as, indeed, it is meant to be.

There is another advantage to the grazers: A herd is much more alert than a solitary animal. An animal has to relax its guard while it is taking food, but in a herd there are at any time some animals each with its head down, biting, and others, each with its head up, watching. What is more, those with their heads up are looking in different directions so that together they are alert to any movement anywhere on the landscape around them. There is no way for a hunter to approach a herd unobserved.

When a member of the herd spots trouble, it starts to move away. Other members of the herd move with it and the entire herd starts to move. If the trouble is serious and close, the herd will run. The individual raising the alarm is simply protecting itself, but in doing so it is warning all of the others.

Herding is highly successful, provided members of the herd stay together in a tight bunch. The hunter moves with the herd, watching for an individual to wander away from the others. When that happens, it tries to move between that individual and the rest of the herd, preventing it from rejoining. Once it has done that the hunter has a good chance of making a kill. If the herd starts to run, a solitary hunter may abandon the chase, but a pack of wolves or hunting dogs regard the stampede as an opportunity and set off in pursuit. As the herd runs, one or two old or sick animals, or young animals that become separated from their mothers, may fall behind. One of those is the individual that will not survive.

As soon as the hunter or hunters seize their quarry they lose interest in all the other grazers. Then they, too, must concentrate on eating. The herd stops running, the stragglers rejoin the group, and they all resume grazing.

## Mammal migrations

Many grassland animals are nomads. Ostriches travel long distances in the course of their foraging for food, although they spend the dry season within easy reach of particular water holes. Similarly bison on the prairies wander over large areas. In the days when they were free to wander anywhere, the bison herds used to spend the winter approximately 400 miles (644 km) to the south of their summer grazing grounds, following an approximately circular route between the two. These animals and many others are migrants; the most famous migrants are found on the African savanna, however, where every year at the start of the dry season they move to the remaining areas of lush pasture.

Today many of their traditional routes are closed to them, but at one time African elephants used to make regular seasonal migrations. Large herds, often of 100 animals or more, traveled in search of shade, food, water, and salt. During the rainy season the elephants wandered as nomads, but in the dry season their journeys took them very much farther. Herds of breeding elephants, comprising individuals from a number of herds, used to make a round-trip of about 400 miles (645 km) that took three years. Their calves would be born two-thirds of the way along the route so the herds returned to their starting point with calves that were one year old. Even today African elephants prefer to spend the dry season in the forests and the rainy season on the open plains.

The Serengeti Plain in Tanzania lies between the Rift Valley in the east and Lake Victoria in the west. Wildlife on the plain has been protected since 1940, and the plain was made a national park in 1951. The Serengeti National Park covers 5,698 square miles (14,763 km²) and within it the animals are allowed to move around as they please. This is where the

*The African elephant (Loxodonta africana) lives on the savanna in herds, each herd led by the oldest female, called the "matriarch." This calf will continue suckling from its mother for three or four years (sucking with its mouth, not its trunk) before advancing to an adult diet of grass and leaves during the rainy season and twigs, branches, and tree bark during the dry season.* (Courtesy of Fogstock)

world's most spectacular annual migration takes place. The principal players are the wildebeest.

Throughout the rainy season the wildebeest live in herds that are scattered across the plain. There are few rivers in the Serengeti, and as the rainy season draws to a close the eastern part of the plain begins to dry out and the pasture deteriorates. Wildebeest herds in the northeast start moving southward, joining with herds from the southeast, moving westward out of the Ngorongoro area. Herds of Burchell's zebras inhabit the same areas as the wildebeest, both species feeding on red grass (*Themeda triandra*; see "Savanna grasses" on pages 95–98). The zebras also join the wildebeest herds and move with them. By the start of the dry season, usually in early June, the combined herds comprise about 1.5 million wildebeest, 300,000 Thomson's gazelles, and 200,000 zebras, as well as other species of antelope and some buffalo. The herd is accompanied, of course, by lions, leopards, cheetahs, hyenas, hunting dogs, and jackals—the predators and scavengers that hope to live well off this vast source of meat.

The herds spend the dry season in the moister west of the plain, and as the dry season nears its end in about November, they continue along their circular route, back to the northern and eastern plains. The complete circuit is about 500 miles (800 km) long, and many animals die along the way.

Soon after the migration begins, the wildebeest mating season commences. Each bull attempts to establish a territory it defends against rivals and in which it can contain a herd of females. This is possible only while the vast herd pauses in its journey. Once the animals start moving again, the females disperse. Consequently, mating takes place for only a few days at a time. Nevertheless, many of the cows become pregnant and give birth to their calves just as the rainy season is about to begin.

The wildebeest sometimes deviate from this pattern. If the rains are light or uncertain, they may leave earlier or later. They may even begin the westward movement, only to return after a few weeks. When it follows its usual course, however, the wildebeest migration is one of the most impressive sights in the world.

*Wildebeest* (Connochaetes taurinus), *also called the brindled gnu, are antelope that graze the savanna in immense herds. When they migrate in search of better pasture, up to 1.5 million of them may travel together. These wildebeest are crossing the Serengeti.* (Courtesy of Mitsuaki Iwago/Minden Pictures)

## CHAPTER 7

# PEOPLES OF THE GRASSLANDS

## Peoples of the prairie

Told of a country full of riches more marvelous than any he had seen, in the summer of 1541 the Spanish explorer Francisco Vázquez de Coronado (1510–54) set out from his camp to the north of present-day Albuquerque to explore the Great Plains. He reached the great bend in the Arkansas River in Kansas but did not find the gold or silver he had expected. The people he encountered lived as nomads. They traveled on foot, their dwellings were tents that they transported on frames dragged along by dogs, and they depended on the bison for food, clothing, and skins to cover their tents. The Spaniards introduced horses to North America, and by the end of the 18th century the use of horses had transformed the way of life of the Plains Indians. The culture portrayed in Western literature and movies is that which developed after the Native Americans had acquired European horses.

Horses allowed people to travel farther and transport their belongings more efficiently. Horses and their riders need equipment, such as saddles, bridles, blankets, and saddlebags to carry personal possessions. The making and decorating of these led to the development of craft skills, and trading in horses led to much more complex economic structures and relationships among groups than had existed previously. Horses also revolutionized hunting and warfare. The Plains Indians became expert riders and equally skilled breeders, and the possession of horses became a mark of status. Before the arrival of the Spaniards some tribes had lived by farming along the river valleys. Once they had horses they were able to abandon farming and live by hunting the abundant game, taking their homes and goods with them.

A tribe consisted of a group of related families, and there were many tribes living on the Plains. These included the

Arapaho, Assiniboine, Blackfeet, Plains Cree, Plains Ojibway (Chippewa), Cheyenne, Comanche, Crow, Ioway, Kaw, Missouria, Omaha, Osage, Otoe, Ponca, Quapaw, Kiowa, Tonkawa, Sarcee, and Sioux. In the late 18th century, before they were much affected by Europeans, each of the main tribes probably comprised about 50,000 people. Smaller tribes often joined one of the larger groups. A band of Apache joined the Kiowa, for example, to form the Kiowa-Apache and the Sarcee joined the Blackfeet. The Sioux comprised the Dakota, Lakota, and Nakota peoples.

Their dependency on the bison meant the peoples of the Plains had no choice but to live as nomads, because the bison were migratory. In the fall they split into small herds that spent the winter widely scattered, and the people reliant on them did the same, living in bands beside the rivers or wherever they could find shelter, wood for fuel, and game to hunt. Each band had a chief, and bands varied in size, depending on their success at hunting or war. Cheyenne bands had about 350 members, those of the Sioux had more, and Kiowa and Kiowa-Apache bands had fewer. In late spring, as the snows melted and the fresh grass began to appear, the bison herds merged to form much bigger herds. That is when the bison mated.

The Native American bands also merged at this time of year, the season of social activities and important religious observances. Cheyenne practices are a good example of these summer gatherings. A lodge was erected at the center of the camp to house important tribal symbols under the care of a keeper. Another lodge was built in which the chiefs met and made the political decisions affecting the life of the tribe. The Cheyenne had a particularly elaborate council. Every 10 years each of the 10 bands elected four chiefs. In addition to these 40 chiefs, the council retained four chiefs from the previous council. War societies also erected lodges from which they competed for military honors, and one society acted as the camp police force and organized the communal hunts that supplied all the food for the tribe. There was much dancing and many feasts were held. Women joined parallel societies concerned with making tepees and other items.

The nomadic life was necessarily simple, however. Lodges were made from earth and thatched with grass, but for most of the year people lived in tepees. These were conical tents made from three or four long poles covered with bison skins that were cut to shape and sewn together. There was a hearth at the center of the tepee and a vent at the top to release smoke. The vent opened to the side rather than vertically, and its direction was controlled by another pole. This structure allowed smoke to leave the tepee regardless of the wind direction. Everyone dressed in bison skins, often highly decorated with porcupine quills, elk teeth, and beads. Bedding was also made from skins. Personal possessions were kept in rawhide bags.

Life was more settled for the tribes of the eastern tallgrass prairie, such as the Mandan, Pawnee, Wichita, and Omaha. They lived in permanent lodges in villages, and as well as hunting game they grew corn. Their social life was more complex than that of the nomadic peoples.

Bison meat was the staple food for all the peoples of the Plains. They cut fresh meat into small pieces that they ate raw. They also placed pieces of meat into rawhide bags and cooked them by heating stones on a fire and then plunging them into the bags. They also preserved meat by cutting it into narrow strips that were dried in the Sun to make *jerky* and made *pemmican* by pounding the dried strips of meat to a paste, mixing the meat with melted fat and dried fruits, and forming it into small pemmican cakes.

## Homesteaders and the way the prairie was transformed

The so-called Wild West and the lifestyle of the "cowboys and Indians" who lived there in the 19th century ended abruptly in the 1880s. That way of life, depicted in so many stories and movies, centered on the cattle trails. Every year vast herds of Longhorn cattle—descendants of 16th-century Spanish cattle—were driven northward from Texas in search of better pasture. The drive did not last long, however. In 1865 Jesse Chisholm (ca. 1805–68), the son of a Scottish father and Cherokee mother, drove a wagon laden with goods from his base in Kansas to Texas and returned with buffalo hides. Other traders then began using the "Chisholm Trail," and then cattlemen drove their herds along it. Sometimes the animals walked hundreds of miles, and in the course of the trek herds belonging to different ranchers would mingle and become mixed. Once a year the animals had to be sorted, at a "roundup," when all the cattle in a wide area were driven to a central point. Calves were branded and animals to be sold were chosen and driven to markets. Texan ranchers had been raising cattle since the 1730s and drove cattle to Louisiana. Comanche bands frequently attacked in order to steal cattle, but the price of cattle was much higher in Louisiana than in Texas, so the trade was highly profitable.

It was not to last. The winters of 1885–86 and 1886–87 were hard, with terrible blizzards. Bison are adapted to the prairie climate. A bison can push the snow away with its huge head to find the grass below. Horses can also survive, by pawing the snow away. The Longhorns were helpless, and in those two winters approximately 84 percent of them perished. It was the end of the old way of life. If the ranchers were to survive economically they would have to supply food for their cattle in winter. This meant the ranges had to be fenced to control the movements of the herds. Fencing called for increased investment, and to make it worthwhile, the cattle ranchers needed more productive breeds. Once those were introduced, the Longhorns were unable to compete and their numbers declined.

The ranchers already had competition from settlers, who were enclosing the most fertile land and establishing farms. Once they had acquired a plot of land, the newly arrived farmers owned it and were entitled to the exclusive use of it. They were Europeans or recent descendants of Europeans, and they believed that their civilization was founded on the concept of property. Individuals had an absolute right to own land, and the ownership of land conferred social status and political influence. The idea is out of date now, but until quite recently English people talked of "the landed gentry" as a class of persons entitled to respect for the power they wielded through their ownership of land. The landed gentry were socially superior to those whose money was derived from industry or commerce. Wealthy industrialists bought themselves country estates as a means of gaining social acceptance. The power derived from land ownership was still very important in the 18th and 19th centuries, and many European emigrants dreamed of joining the landowning class. It would not have occurred to them that the idea of owning land was as incomprehensible to many Native American peoples as the idea of owning the air or the ocean is to us.

Politicians in the young United States were keen to encourage immigration. They, too, saw land as a commodity to be bought, sold, and owned. The land had to be put to good use, however. Nowadays people find mountains, natural forests, and areas of wilderness attractive. We seek to protect and preserve them, and for very good reasons, but that is not how people felt in the early 19th century. Europeans were familiar with famine, and to them an attractive countryside was one of weed-free fields filled with ripening crops. William Cobbett (1763–1835) expressed this attitude very clearly in his *Rural Rides,* published in 1830. Cobbett was an English author, journalist, and supporter of political reform, who served in the British army in North America. From 1817 to 1819 he lived on a rented farm at North Hempstead, Long Island, after fleeing England to escape imprisonment for his support of radical causes. *Rural Rides* is in the form of a journal describing a series of fact-finding journeys he undertook on horseback through southern England in the 1820s. On August 28, 1826, he saw what he and most people at that time considered an almost perfect countryside.

> *The shepherd showed me the way towards MILTON; and at the end of about a mile, from the top of a very high part of the down, with a steep slope towards the valley, I first saw this Valley of Avon; and a most beautiful sight it was! Villages, hamlets, large farms, towers, steeples, fields, meadows, orchards, and very fine timber-trees, scattered all over the valley.*

This was the ideal, a well-tended landscape producing food and timber to support a dense population living in peace and tranquility, and this is the kind of countryside the European settlers sought to create in North America. If what they saw as the vast prairie wasteland could be converted to productive farmland, towns and cities would spring up across the continent and markets would grow rapidly for goods manufactured in the East. Everyone would prosper.

Ever since the American Revolution, migrants from the East had been settling—"squatting"—on public land in the West. Although the government favored the sale of land to settlers, the processes of surveying plots, calculating their price, and organizing the sale were so slow that, illegal though it was, squatting was the only way the settlers could obtain land. Squatting in frontier regions was encouraged, and squatters were not considered to be breaking the law. Some politicians held the view that squatters should be allowed to buy the land they occupied without competition—meaning no one else could claim it or bid for it—as a reward for their contribution to the agricultural and economic development of the country. Eventually there was widespread agreement that settlers should be offered free land, and Abraham Lincoln supported this policy during the 1860 presidential campaign. Indeed, many commentators believe it was Republican support for the Homestead Bill that swung the election in Lincoln's favor.

Congress passed the Homestead Act overwhelmingly, and on May 20, 1862, President Lincoln signed it into law. That legislation transformed the prairie. The act stated that any person older than 21 years of age and head of a family, who was a citizen or had declared an intention to become a citizen, might acquire, free of charge, the title to not more than 160 acres (65 ha) of land (other than land used for mineral extraction) after living on it and making improvements on it for five years. Alternatively, such a person could buy the land for $1.25 per acre ($3.09/ha) after living on it for six months and improving it. In addition, citizens could buy unoccupied land for the regular market price any time after six months from the date of filing their application.

Many fraudulent claims were made under the Homestead Act, allowing mine owners, land speculators, and others to acquire cheaply land they might otherwise not have acquired at all. Despite this, the act gave grants of land to more than

1.6 million people. It contributed greatly to the agricultural development of the Plains and it established a pattern of family-sized farms—homesteads—where the family did most of the work. The farmers were immigrants, of course, or the descendants of immigrants. Most of those who moved west were ethnically English, Scottish, and German. There were also Dutch, Swiss, and Scandinavian farmers, but their numbers were smaller.

The prairie had not been vacant before their arrival, however. Although the Great Plains were then known among the immigrants as the "Great American Desert," the grasslands were home to many Native American tribes. Until their settlement under the Homestead Act the prairie had been considered uninhabitable for Europeans. Native American tribes had been driven onto the prairie from the better farmland in the East. Subsequently as more and more of the prairie was converted to farms, Native Americans were confined in ever-smaller areas.

The Dawes Severalty Act of 1887 aimed to redress this injustice. *Severalty* is the allotment of land, and the Dawes Act allotted land to Native Americans—partly in the hope that once they had received their allotments they would leave the reservations, thus releasing more land for the settlers. Unfortunately the Native Americans did not fully understand the European concept of land ownership. Many sold their allotments, and many more were cheated out of them. The Dawes Act allotted 138 million acres (55.8 million ha) of land to Native Americans. By 1934 they had lost 86 million acres (34.8 million ha) of this, and the proportion that remained was mostly desert or semidesert and useless for farming.

In January 1934 a number of associations and groups began campaigning for the repeal of the Dawes Act and the promotion of community ownership and control of land. President Franklin D. Roosevelt supported this policy and signed legislation implementing it in June 1934. Land was returned to Native Americans, and at least some of the wrongs they had suffered were remedied.

So far as the settlers were concerned, it was soon evident that the type of farming they learned in Europe would not succeed in the very different climate of the western prairie. The railroad companies owned large areas of land on each side of their tracks and sold much of it to homesteaders. The railroad companies urged the Department of Agriculture to establish a Bureau of Dry Land Agriculture. This opened in 1906 to promote dry farming, in which half of the land lies fallow each year to accumulate moisture, which is taken up by the crop grown on it the following year. To allow for this, the Enlarged Homestead Act of 1909 increased the permitted size of holdings in dry areas to 320 acres (129.5 ha) and required the farmer to cultivate only 80 acres (32 ha). Farming was often difficult, however, even in the less arid regions. There were periodic droughts, culminating in those of the 1930s (see "The Dust Bowl" on pages 55–57).

## Indians and gauchos: The peoples of the pampa

When the first Spanish colonists reached what is now Argentina in 1516, many Native American tribes inhabited the pampa, speaking a variety of languages. Those in the northwest spoke Quechua, the official language of the Inca Empire centered in Peru, and to some extent were under Inca control. They had learned the Inca skills of pottery making, metalworking, and farming. Guaraní tribes, living in the northeast, were farmers. In all the Native American population probably amounted to about 300,000.

The open grasslands were unsuitable for farming, however, and there the people were mainly nomadic. These people were called the Querandí, but little is known about them and no one knows what language they spoke, although they resembled other nomadic peoples of the South American plains. They lived by fishing, using nets to do so, and by hunting rheas (see "Grassland birds" on pages 130–135) and guanaco (*Lama guanicöe*), a member of the camel family closely related to the llama, but smaller. They used the *bolas* to take down game. This weapon consisted of three lengths of rope, joined at one end and weighted at the other. When thrown, it became entangled around the legs of the quarry, making the animal fall. Once they acquired horses—by domesticating animals that had escaped from Spanish estates—the Querandí were able to form much larger bands. They made war against other tribes and against the Spaniards. In 1541 attacks by the Querandí forced the Spanish settlers in Buenos Aires to abandon their homes and flee upstream to the town of Asunción. There is no record of the Querandí after 1678. They may have died out or have merged with other tribes, known collectively as "Pampa Indians."

Besides horses the Spanish settlers had European cattle and donkeys. Inevitably some of these escaped from the farms. Out on the pampa they found unlimited food, with no other large grazing animals to provide competition and no predators, because there were no large cats or dogs hunting on the South American grasslands. The escaped animals thrived and their numbers grew rapidly, providing the livestock that people called the Mapuche captured. The Mapuche, whose name means "land" (*mapu*) "people" (*che*) in their Araucanian language, are one of three major groups of Native Americans whose ancestors crossed the Andes from Chile and settled in eastern Chile and part of Argentina. The Picunche (*picun* means north) were defeated and assimilated by the Spanish. The Huilliche (*huilli* means south) were assimilated into the rural Hispanic population.

Once the Native Americans had horses, the Spaniards found them to be fierce opponents of colonization. The Mapuche fiercely defended their territories against European invaders until they were finally defeated in the war of 1880–82. That was one of several wars in which many Indians died. Other Indians died of European diseases to which they had no natural immunity. Today only three percent of the Argentine population are Native Americans and people of mixed European and American origin, called *mestizos*.

The Spanish farmers showed no interest in developing the pampa. In any case before they could enclose land for cultivation they would have to wrest control of it from Native Americans who were prepared to fight to defend it. Consequently, the grasslands became the home of free-spirited Spanish horsemen with no taste for the settled life of a farmer. Together the horsemen and the Indians herded and hunted the wild cattle and horses. They also intermarried, giving rise to the mestizo population.

These were the colorful figures who, early in the 19th century, became known as *gauchos*—a word of uncertain origin, but possibly derived from an Araucanian word. They soon became folk heroes, greatly admired for their skills and courage and perhaps envied for their apparently carefree way of life.

Times were changing, however. There were a growing European market for South American leather and a South American market for Argentine mules. By the latter part of the 18th century some of the herds of half-wild pampas cattle and mules were privately owned. The pampa was becoming commercialized, and by the end of the 19th century it was being plowed up and fenced to make vast *estancias* (cattle ranches) that were managed by European tenants.

The free world of the gaucho was ending and the gauchos had to abandon their nomadic life. They became employees working on the estancias, the South American equivalent of the North American cowboys. To this day, however, they proudly maintain their right to be called gauchos and to wear the traditional gaucho dress.

## Farmers of the pampa

Early in the 16th century Spanish immigrants established a settlement they called Buenos Aires in what is now Argentina. In 1541, however, attacks from the Querandí, the Native Americans who lived on the pampa, drove them out. The Spaniards returned to Buenos Aires in 1580, but the experience made them determined to keep open the trade route to the north linking them to Santa Fe, Asunción (just across the border in Paraguay), and Peru. Once this route was secure, settlers began establishing cattle ranches on the pampa to the northwest of Buenos Aires.

These ranches, the *estancias,* were huge, covering hundreds of square miles. Some were the size of a small country. During the 17th century the government granted or sold the tracts of land for establishing estancias to descendants of Spanish settlers. The owners, called *estancieros,* stocked their lands with half-wild cattle and horses and hired gauchos to manage them (see "Indians and gauchos: The peoples of the pampa" on pages 165–167). The estancieros lived in simple houses, called *ranchos,* and the gauchos in lean-to dwellings or huts. There were also inns, called *pulperías,* conveniently located and used for trading and banking, as restaurants, and for communal functions. Some of these later grew into villages.

The estancias became extremely important in Argentine economic, political, and cultural affairs, and gradually they spread outward from Buenos Aires to the west and the south. Times were changing, however, and from the middle of the 19th century rising world demand for agricultural products led to changes in the pampas farms. Sheep were introduced and more productive breeds of European cattle replaced the original breeds—just as new breeds largely replaced the Longhorn on the prairie (see "Homesteaders and the way the prairie was transformed" on pages 160–165).

There was a problem, however. Sheep and imported cattle could not subsist on the natural grasses of the pampa. Their diet had to be augmented with alfalfa, which is rich in protein. The alfalfa had to be grown, and there were not enough gauchos who were willing to cultivate the land. The estancieros had little choice but to allow European immigrants to farm areas of the estancias as tenants.

While this was happening, new estancias were being established farther to the south. Native Americans resisted the settlers, but their resistance was overcome and by 1880 tenant farmers were able to live safe from the risk of attack throughout the territory to the north of the Negro River, which marks the boundary between the pampa and Patagonia to the south. Europeans continued to arrive to work on the land, and little by little the estancias were divided into small tenant- and owner-occupied farms.

As the pampa became more densely populated, cities sprang up to serve the needs of the agricultural community. Meatpacking plants, called *frigoríficos,* for the export of beef and mutton opened late in the 19th century, and manufacturing industries also developed on what had been the grasslands. Today the farms and factories make the moist pampa the most prosperous and economically important part of Argentina.

## Peoples of the African savanna

Most of the African savanna is unsuitable for growing crops on a large scale. There are cattle ranches in some places, but the importance of the wild animals—to science and to tourism—means that development is prohibited over large areas, allowing the traditional ways of life to survive.

The savanna tribes are pastoralists—people who own herds of livestock that they drive between traditional grazing areas. They augment this way of life with some small-scale farming, partly to provide crops for trading, as well as fishing and hunting.

*Maasai tribesmen in East Africa are pastoralists, making their living by tending the herds of cattle that are their most valuable possession.* (Courtesy of Mitsuaki Iwago/ Minden Pictures)

There are several savanna tribes, of whom the Maasai are the best known. Tall, slim people, famous for covering their body in red ocher and wearing red robes and ornate decorations made from beads, the Maasai have resisted all attempts by governments to persuade them to settle in permanent villages. They go where they will, ignoring national frontiers, and have demanded—and received—the right to graze their cattle in several of the Kenyan and Tanzanian national parks.

Their refusal to compromise with the modern world and their colorful appearance have led to the romanticization of the Maasai way of life. In this respect they are something like an African equivalent of the cowboy and gaucho. Tourists enjoy meeting Maasai, watching Maasai dances, and hearing tales of their prowess as warriors who (it is said) can kill lions with their bare hands. Yet the reality is that nowadays many Maasai are employed on the ranches to herd cattle, where they abandon their tribal finery and dress in more workaday clothes, and an increasing number of Maasai children attend school.

Cattle are central to the traditional Maasai economy and culture. Men often decorate the horns of their favorite oxen, and a man and his ox may share the same name. Cattle represent wealth and men accumulate as many as they can. Consequently, Maasai herds are often very large. The animals are sold or traded to settle debts and given as bride wealth—the price a man must pay a bride's family in order to "buy" her for his son—but they are rarely killed for meat. The Maasai diet is based on milk and milk products, together with grain and, in the drier parts of the savanna, blood mixed with milk. Blood is taken from a live animal and the wound allowed to heal, so the animal suffers no serious harm. The Maasai enter towns and cities to sell cattle when they need to buy supplies. They also earn money by selling their beadwork to tourists.

Cattle are so important that the Maasai were once notorious cattle rustlers. According to Maasai myth, their god gave all cattle to them for safekeeping, and they believed there was nothing wrong with taking care of those of other tribes. Young men tend the herds. They often live in small camps, moving frequently in search of water and fresh pasture.

It is the young men who color their skin with ocher and spend hours, or even days, dressing their hair in elaborate styles. Their hairstyles and decoration identify the age set to which they belong. Maasai society grades boys and girls according to their age, and they live apart from the adult men and women. When a young man passes from one age grade to the next, he shaves his head and an animal is slaughtered as a religious offering—one of the few occasions when an animal is killed. When a girl reaches puberty she is usually married to an older man.

The Samburu are a tribe closely related to the Maasai. They live north of the equator, close to the region where the savanna merges with the Sahara. Their way of life revolves around the cattle, sheep, goats, and camels that they herd. Groups of five to 10 families live together, moving to fresh pastures whenever the grazing starts to deteriorate. The adult men look after the animals, while the women maintain the portable huts in which Samburu families live, gather firewood and water, and milk the cows. The huts are made from a frame of wooden poles covered with hides, grass mats, or plastered mud.

## Traditional life on the steppe of Central Asia

On average fewer than three people live in every square mile (1.1 persons/km$^2$) on the steppe of Central Asia. This makes the region one of the most sparsely populated in the world. Most of the inhabitants are Khalkha Mongols. There is some farming, but the arid climate makes farming difficult, and although cereals can be grown in some areas, harvests often fail as a result of drought. Most of the farmers are descendants of Chinese settlers, not ethnic Mongols. Mongols prefer a nomadic way of life. The Mongolian government has tried hard to persuade them to settle in the capital, Ulan Bator, or in the second city, Darhan, but most people still spend at least some of the year moving around.

Traditionally the nomadic Mongols spend the winter in campsites where their livestock can be fed and sheltered against the fierce icy winds and blizzards. At one time the herders had nothing more than a corral surrounded by stone walls to provide shelter for their sheep, goats, cattle, yaks (*Bos grunniens,* a type of long-haired cattle), and camels. Many of the animals died in the winter storms, but since the 1950s the winter campsites have provided better shelter and more nutritious food than the hay made during the summer, and livestock survival rates have improved.

The herding camp is the basic social unit. It comprises between two and six families, with their livestock and all their possessions. The families agree to travel together for one year. At the end of the year each family chooses whether to remain with the group or join another group. If the herding camp grows so large that managing the grazing becomes difficult, some of the families move out and start another camp.

Each family lives in a circular dwelling called a *ger,* also known as a *yurt* or *yurta.* It consists of a framework of wooden poles covered with skins, woven cloth, or most often felt. The dwelling is sufficiently strong and waterproof to withstand the weather, but light and easy to transport. There is a hearth near the center, and a hole in the roof vents out smoke. Sheep dung is the fuel used for cooking and heating. The only furnishings are brightly colored rugs.

Mongolian people are famous for their horsemanship, and children as young as four take part in horse races. Horses are the special responsibility of the men. Only men care for them, and at one time Mongolian men thought it undignified to undertake any work that could not be performed on horseback. It is hard to overstate the significance of the horse in Mongolian culture. In the Mongolian version of chess the most important piece is not the queen, but the horse; the national drink, called *airag,* is fermented mare's milk. Mines and factories maintain herds of horses to supply airag to the workers. People ride horses, but camels are more often used as pack animals. These are two-humped Bactrian camels (*Camelus bactrianus*). In addition to carrying loads, Bactrian camels produce milk and give wool that is woven to make clothes and blankets.

People drink tea as well as airag. Tea is made in a large bowl with added salt and milk. Sheep's milk is used to make a dish called *arul* from dried curds and cheese. The nomadic diet consists entirely of meat, dairy produce, and some flour made from wheat, barley, or millet. It includes no vegetables or fish. The nomads visit the towns from time to time to trade animal products for flour, tea imported from China, silk cloth, and metal cooking pots and tools.

Sheep are the most important animals economically. They provide meat, milk, wool, skins, and dung. A herding camp always has sheep, but it has herds of horses, goats, and cattle only if there are enough pasture for them and enough people to look after the herds and flocks. Each species has different needs, and so each herd or flock is managed separately. The families have to decide whether it is profitable to have one or more people working full time caring for each species.

In spring everyone sets out to find pasture for the animals. The group moves slowly across the plain, its livestock widely scattered and its camels laden, heading for the first of the traditional grazing grounds. Once they arrive, grazing is strictly controlled. All the sheep are managed as a single flock. The shepherds have ferocious dogs to protect the flock from predators such as wolves. The dogs will attack any animal (or person) who approaches too close, but they do not herd the sheep.

Every morning the sheep are taken out to graze, watched over by the shepherds and their dogs, and every evening they are led back to the camp. This is done partly to protect them overnight, but it also ensures the supply of dung; sheep feed during the day and defecate at night. Each day the flock grazes a little farther away from the camp, following a spiral path. This is the most efficient way to manage the pasture, ensuring that the sheep eat all of the grass, but with no risk of overgrazing. If the herding camp has other species, these are turned out onto the pasture most suitable for them. When the fresh pasture is so far from the camp that the sheep are spending too much time walking to and from it, the camels are loaded with homes and possessions and the herding camp moves on to the next site.

## Genghis Khan, the Golden Horde, and Mogul emperors

In about the year 1167 a Mongol chief called Yesugei Ba'atur killed a Tatar chief called Temujin. At that time the Mongols comprised a group of clans confined to the northeastern corner of what is now Mongolia. Turkish tribes occupied most of the western and some of the southern parts of Mongolia, and the Tatars held the remainder of the southern and eastern parts of the territory. A son was born to Yesugei at about the time he killed Temujin, and, as was the custom, the infant was given the fallen warrior's name.

When he was eight, Temujin was betrothed to Burte, a young woman of a different tribe, the Onggirat (or Konkirat). When a Mongol boy became betrothed, customarily he moved into his future father-in-law's camp, and Yesugei took Temujin to the Onggirat camp. On his way home, however, Yesugei was poisoned by Tatars, and as he lay dying he sent for Temujin to return. Yesugei died, leaving the tribe without a chief. The warriors and other subjects deserted Temujin and his mother, and relatives stripped them of their possessions. Temujin and his mother, together with Temujin's four brothers and two half brothers, were reduced to dire poverty.

Temujin grew up to be a skilled horseman and brave fighter. At age 15 he proved he was entitled to the status of warrior by recapturing some horses that had been stolen. With his new status he claimed Burte, his bride. Her father gave Temujin a cloak made from sable pelts as a dowry. Temujin gave this cloak to one of his father's former allies. The gift bought Temujin the protection of a powerful tribal chief and marked the start of Temujin's career. An astute politician, he won the loyalty of those around him and always rewarded that loyalty. Temujin made more friends than enemies, and over the following years he built an alliance of Mongol tribes. Once they were strong enough, his warriors conquered their tribes' traditional enemies, such as the Tatars, and in late 1206 or January 1207 their successes prompted the warriors to acclaim Temujin as their "wide-encompassing chief," or *Chinggis Khan* (also spelled Genghis Khan and Jenghis Khan).

Mongol warriors were mounted archers. Fast, highly maneuverable, and capable of a high rate of extremely accurate fire, they were more than a match for any army existing at that time. They wore a type of armor that was made from silk. When a warrior was struck by an arrow, the arrowhead carried part of the fabric into the wound. This allowed the arrow to be gently worked out of the wound, still wrapped in silk, thus minimizing the damage to the surrounding tissue and reducing the risk of infection.

The Mongols did not rely only on force, however. They made great use of spies to gather intelligence and used propaganda to persuade enemies to surrender. If the defenders submitted, the people were spared; if they did not, the entire population was killed or taken into slavery. The Mongols fought best on the open plains. If they needed to besiege a town or fight in the hills, they enlisted warriors from subject tribes to fight on their behalf.

Led by Chinggis Khan, the Mongols first attacked Hsi-Hsia, a kingdom in northwestern China, whose king then swore allegiance to the Mongols. Northern China was attacked next, leading to the fall of Beijing in 1215. Eastern Turkistan became part of the Mongol Empire in 1218, and when some of its Muslim subjects were killed by forces from western Turkistan the Mongols attacked and conquered them. Mongol troops raided cities in the Crimean Peninsula in 1223.

Chinggis Khan died in 1227. At that time the Mongol Empire stretched from the Caspian Sea to the East China Sea, and from the edge of the Siberian taiga to Tibet and the central plains of China.

Nobles assembled to elect Chinggis's third son, Ögödei, as their new khan, and fresh campaigns took the Mongol armies farther into Russia. Kiev fell in December 1240. Advance parties then reached Wrocław, Poland, and on April 9, 1241, Mongol troops inflicted a heavy defeat on a combined force of German and Polish knights. A Mongol army then turned south and attacked Hungary. They settled in Hungary, where the western edge of the steppe may have reminded them of their homeland.

This western portion of the empire came to be known as the Golden Horde, ruled by Batu, the son of Chinggis's eldest son, Jochi, who had died in 1227. Batu ruled until his death in 1255 and was succeeded by his brother, Berke, until Berke's death in 1266. Berke converted to Islam and forged an anti-Persian alliance with the rulers of Egypt, making the western empire extremely influential throughout eastern Europe and the Middle East.

Ögödei died in 1241. Batu claimed the succession, but Ögödei's widow, Töregene, secured it for her son, Güyük. War might have broken out between the rivals, but Güyük died in 1248 and in 1251 Mangu, a descendant of Chinggis's youngest son, Tolui, was elected khan. The two branches of the family remained hostile to each other.

Mangu Khan continued to expand the empire, assisted by his two brothers, Hülagü and Kublai, and it was Kublai whose generals led a campaign against China. When Mangu died in August 1259, Kublai was elected to succeed him. Kublai Khan (1215–94) became one of the greatest of all emperors of China.

In about 1300 the Mongol Empire extended from the Black Sea to the East China Sea, South China Sea, and Sea of Japan, and from north of Moscow to the Persian Gulf. It included Afghanistan and all of China, but not Tibet. Already, however, the great diversity of cultures was making itself felt. Kublai had thought of himself primarily as a Chinese emperor and had transferred the Mongol capital from Karakorum to Beijing in 1267. In other parts of the empire the local khans converted to Islam or Buddhism and the provinces developed their own identities, becoming progressively less Mongol. During the course of the 14th century the empire dwindled to nothing. Togon-temür, who ruled from 1333 until 1368, was the last Mongol emperor of China. He fled into the steppe in 1368 and died there in 1370. Shahin Girai, the last European ruler descended from Chinggis, ruled in the Crimea until he was deposed by the Russians in 1783.

India never formed part of the Mongol Empire, but on the death of his father in 1494 Bābur, or Zahīr-ud-Dīn Mohammad (1483–1530), inherited the struggle among his family for control of Fergana, a town and district in Uzbekistan. Eventually the ongoing conflict led his forces into northern India. In April 1526 they occupied Delhi and Agra, and in May 1529 they defeated the Afghan rulers of Bihar and Bengal. By the time of his death Bābur had established a military claim to an empire in India that his successors consolidated. Bābur was a Turk, descended on his father's side from Timur Lenk, or Tamerlane (1336–1405); on his mother's side he was a descendant of Chinggis Khan, and the rulers who followed him are known as the Mogul dynasty (*Mogul* is Arabic and Persian for Mongol). The Mogul dynasty ruled India until the middle of the 18th century.

## Aboriginal peoples of the Australian grasslands

People have lived in Australia for at least 40,000 years. Evidence from one archaeological site suggests that people lived there as much as 100,000 years ago, but this date is uncertain. Most probably the ancestors of the modern Aboriginal people landed about 50,000 years ago. They travelled there from the islands to the north of Australia at a time when vast ice sheets, covering much of Europe and North America, held so much accumulated water that the sea level was far lower than it is today. Travelers would have been able to walk from the Malay Peninsula in mainland Asia through Sumatra and Java, but the final part of their journey to Australia must have been made by sea. So the first Australians were good sailors.

As their numbers increased and they occupied more and more of the land, the people developed a way of life suited to the environment in which they found themselves. This lifestyle was quite unlike the situation of the Native American tribes of the prairie or the tribes living on the African savanna. The climate was too dry for farming, and there were no large mammals that could be domesticated and herded. Hunting was the only means of obtaining meat, and plant foods had to be gathered from the wild. The people were hunter-gatherers and had no choice but to go on living in that way.

They were also nomads. If a group remained long in one place, it would deplete the plant resources in the immediate vicinity. There would be less food both for the people to eat and for the animals that supplied them with meat. Hunting and foraging expeditions would have to travel farther and farther from the camp, and before long it would make more sense to move the camp than to undertake such long journeys.

The constraints imposed by the natural environment conditioned the development of Aboriginal culture. In areas where the vegetation was fairly abundant, people visited traditional camping places at particular times of year. These camps were close to water, and the land around them held great mythological significance. People would move out from the camps to find food, often returning later the same day but sometimes staying away for a few days. In drier areas smaller groups occupied much larger territories and spent their time on the move, traveling along well-defined routes from one water hole to another.

Fires were very important. The campfire was not allowed to go out while the camp was occupied, and when the group moved on, or when a hunting party left for more than a day, someone carried a smoldering brand from which a fresh fire could be lit.

Aboriginal people living in the north, where the summer monsoon brought heavy rain (see "Monsoons" on pages 57–61), made huts on stilts and shelters from tree bark to escape flooding and biting insects. If there were suitable dry caves they moved into those. People on the drier grasslands preferred to sleep in the open, with a windbreak for shelter and the fire and their dogs for warmth on cold nights.

Survival in these harsh surroundings depends on an intimate knowledge of the landscape and of all the plants and animals that inhabit it. Aboriginal people learned to navigate every inch of their territories. Several family groups constitute a tribe, and the tribe owns the territory in which it finds its food and water. Their ownership makes them responsible for the fertility of the plants and animals and gives them the ability to sustain the resources of the territory through the performance of religious rituals and obedience to religious law.

The first European settlers arrived in January 1788. At that time there were an estimated 750,000 Aboriginal Australians, speaking about 700 different languages and living throughout Australia. According to an Australian government estimate, in June 1996 the Aboriginal population was approximately 386,000 and had increased by more than 40,000 since 1991.

## CHAPTER 8

# USES FOR GRASSLAND

## Cereal farming

Most of the original prairie has vanished, as have the European steppe and much of the South American pampa. The wild grasses, along with the other plants that grew among them, have been cleared away to make room for wheat, rye, barley, and corn. These are also grasses, so what was once wild grassland has been transformed into domesticated grassland. All four crops—wheat, rye, barley, and corn—are grown in big fields where most of the farming operations are now mechanized, and so the open landscape that cereal farming produces is not unlike that of the original grassland. The American natural grasslands were cleared only recently, but the spread of cereal farming began thousands of years ago in the Middle East, where the ancestors of modern crop plants still grow wild (see the sidebar).

Wheat is one of the world's most important crops. It is a staple food, of course, but it is also the food commodity that is traded internationally more than any other. In 2004 the world as a whole produced 1,380 trillion tons (627 trillion tonnes) of wheat grain, compared with 1,333 trillion tons (606 trillion tonnes) of rice, but most rice is eaten close to where it is grown.

Wheat grain is ground (milled) into the flour from which we make bread and cakes. This type of grain is from *Triticum vulgare,* the bread-wheat plant. Grain from durum wheat (*T. durum*) is made into semolina, the flour used to make pasta and noodles.

The difference between types of wheat centers on their protein content. Wheat flour is rich in proteins, and a mixture of two wheat proteins, gliadin and glutenin, is known as *gluten.* When gluten is moistened and kneaded, it acquires an elastic, almost rubbery texture. That texture allows the flour

# The origin of cereals

In parts of southern Turkey and northern Syria and Iraq there are areas of natural grassland where the predominant plants include *Triticum boeoticum,* one of the ancestors of modern wheat. At one time *T. boeoticum* grew alongside other *Triticum* species, rye (*Secale vulgare*), and barley (*Hordeum vulgare*), and the grasslands extended through parts of what are now Lebanon, Israel, and Jordan as far south as the Nile Valley, in Egypt.

Thousands of years ago people living in this part of the world harvested the seeds of these and related grasses and ground them into a coarse meal or flour. They boiled the meal in water to make a type of porridge or thin gruel and made the flour into bread. These highly nutritious foods formed a major part of their diet.

About 13,000 B.C.E. the climate changed as the world emerged from the most recent ice age. Woodland expanded, but the changes also benefited the grasses and the wild cereals became more plentiful. People who lived by hunting game and gathering wild grass seeds were able to store enough grain to last from one harvest to the next, freeing them of the need to travel in search of late harvests or alternative plants. This abundance allowed them to give up their seminomadic lifestyle and settle in permanent villages. Their populations increased and after a time they found a way to regulate their food supply. They gathered seeds from the best-tasting and most productive plants, cleared the ground to remove competing plants, and scattered the seeds on the bare soil. These peo-

to be rolled or drawn into fine strips or strings without breaking. It also forms the bubbles filled with carbon dioxide from fermenting yeast that make bread soft and improve its keeping quality. The proportion of gluten it contains determines whether flour is best for making cakes, bread, or semolina. Flour that has only a small amount of gluten—known as "soft" flour—makes cakes and biscuits. Bread flour—"strong" flour—has more gluten. It makes bread. The flour with the highest gluten content, which is made from durum wheat, makes pasta.

Rye (*Secale vulgare*) may once have been a weed that grew among wheat crops. Farmers had no way to remove it, but eventually they began growing it as a crop in its own right. Rye flour is dark in color and has a strong flavor. It makes black bread and crispbread.

ple were the first farmers. They lived about 12,000 B.C.E. in the valley of the Jordan River and in the northern part of the Fertile Crescent, between the Euphrates and Tigris in what is now Iraq.

Wheat, rye, and barley were not the only crops they learned to cultivate. They also grew lentils, chickpeas, and peas, as well as flax, from which they made linen cloth. Agriculture then spread westward into Europe and eastward into northern India. Rice farming began independently in India and China, and corn (maize) farming began later in Central America.

Wild wheat plants shed their ripe seeds. That is how the plant reproduces, but the early farmers grew their crops from plants that held on to their seeds for a little longer than the others. Farmers could harvest all the seeds from these plants, and by the same means they also controlled the plants' reproduction. Over many generations this selective breeding produced wheat plants that retained their seeds, and gradually the cultivated cereals continued to change. The wheat that farmers grow commercially today has changed so much genetically that it is a different species from its wild ancestor.

The wild wheats were called emmer (*Triticum turgidum*) and einkorn (*T. monococcum*). Emmer was grown for making bread and is still grown on a small scale in some places, nowadays mainly to feed livestock. Spelt wheat (*T. spelta*) was an early cultivated species, grown extensively in Roman times. Modern bread wheat is *T. vulgare,* and durum wheat, used to make pasta, is *T. durum.*

Barley (*Hordeum vulgare* and *H. distichon*) is also ground into a meal or "pearl barley," which is added to soups. Most barley, however, is grown either to feed livestock or to make malt. If the grain contains a high proportion of protein, it is fed to livestock; if it contains little protein, it is sold—at a much higher price—for malting. In this process the grain is spread on a floor, moistened, and kept warm until the seeds sprout. After a few days the very young seedlings are dried. It is then malt and contains enzymes that convert starch in the barley grain into sugar that will ferment when yeast is added. Malt is used to brew beer.

Wheat needs a period of dry weather and warm sunshine to ripen the grain, but rye and barley will grow in climates that are too cold or wet for wheat. Consequently, rye and barley are cultivated mainly in the north and at high elevations.

All three crops are usually sown in spring and harvested in late summer, but some wheat is sown in the fall. This is known as winter wheat, in contrast to spring wheat. Its seeds germinate in the fall, and the young seedlings survive the winter ready to start growing rapidly in early spring. Winter wheat produces larger yields than spring wheat, but it can be grown only where the climate is suitable.

Corn (*Zea mays*) requires a long, warm summer to ripen the grain, and consequently it is not grown in northern regions. Its history is obscure, because the plant has changed so much that it is very different from its closest relative and probable ancestor, a grass called teosinte (*Z. mexicana*). There is no such thing as wild maize. Cultivated corn protects its seeds with overlapping husks. The husks are easily pealed away, but the plant is unable to release its seeds itself. It cannot survive without human assistance.

People were growing corn in Mexico 7,000 years ago. Columbus took specimens of the plant to Europe in the late 15th century; today it is grown wherever the climate is suitable, and vast quantities are produced. In 2004 the world produced 1,586 trillion tons (721 trillion tonnes) of corn.

## Cattle ranching

Grasslands thrive in a fairly dry climate and over large areas where conditions are too dry for crop growing. There cattle and sheep are allowed to move freely, finding food and water where they can. This is ranching, the type of farming practiced over much of western North America, from Mexico to Alberta, where the climate is too dry for cereal farming, or the soil too infertile, or the land too steep or rocky.

Ranching expanded rapidly through the 19th century. By the 1880s in the western United States there were "cattle kingdoms" claiming rights over as much as 6 million acres (2.4 million ha), and a ranch of 100,000 acres (40,000 ha) was considered small. As recently as the 1920s, the XIT Ranch in Texas covered 3 million acres (1.2 million ha), had 150,000 cattle, and employed 150 cowboys. By that time ranches were enclosed. The XIT was contained inside a fence 6,000 miles (9,654 km) long.

The land was open range. In the 19th century there were no fences to mark boundaries, and the cattlemen did not own the land but only had the right to use its pasture and water. In any case it would have been quite impossible for them to defend the borders or watercourses over such vast areas. An unwritten law, the "Code of the West," maintained peace among rival ranchers, but outsiders were subjected to considerable fraud. Eastern investors would be sold shares in nonexistent range rights or in herds of cattle that were much smaller than claimed—if they existed at all.

Open-range ranching was very different from most modern livestock farming. No one tended the animals. They wandered at will, feeding on the native grasses. Cowboys would round up the cattle at least once a year. That is when calves born since the last roundup were branded and those to be sold were driven to market.

Only Longhorn cattle, descended from imported European stock, were hardy enough to survive the harsh environment. Cattle replaced the American bison that had once roamed the prairie. Bison were well adapted to the conditions, but all attempts to domesticate them failed—and the European bison was just as impossible to domesticate. Instead, the American herds were descended from wild cattle that once roamed widely across Europe and northern Asia (see the sidebar).

Threats to the "Wild West" way of life increased as homesteaders, called "nesters," started farming more and more of the better land (see "Homesteaders and the way the prairie was transformed" on pages 160–165). At first the cattle kings held their own, taking the law into their own hands and allowing their cattle to destroy the crops, but in 1873 they suffered a fatal setback. That was the year when an Illinois farmer, J. F. Glidden, made and later patented barbed wire. In the following years sales rose and prices fell until by the turn of the century barbed wire was the cheapest form of fencing. Cattle could not push through barbed wire as they had pushed through smooth wire. The farms were safe.

By that time ranching was changing in other ways. Longhorn cattle were disappearing and more productive breeds taking their place. The new breeds were less hardy, however, so ranchers had to improve their living conditions. Ranchers also fenced areas of pasture to control the movement of livestock and allow the vegetation to recover after grazing. This fencing prevented overgrazing and improved the quality of the grassland. Salt and water were used to attract cattle into lightly grazed areas in order to utilize the range more efficiently. Brush, comprising plants such as cactus, mesquite, and sagebrush, grew alongside grasses in the natural grassland. These plants use large amounts of water, and in places they grow so densely as to form impenetrable stands.

## The origin of cattle

There are many breeds of farm cattle. Some are raised mainly for milk, others for meat, and some for both. All European and Amerian breeds are descended from an animal called the *aurochs* (plural *aurochsen*), also known as the giant ox. Herds of aurochsen (*Bos primigenius*) once roamed Eurasia between latitudes 30°N and 60°N. They lived mainly in the forests, feeding by browsing leaves on branches low enough for them to reach, but they also grazed in more open areas.

A s related species, *B. namadicus,* lived farther south in India. It may be the ancestor of the humped zebu cattle found in India and Africa.

The aurochs is now extinct. The last individual is believed to have been killed in Poland in 1627. We can no longer see an aurochs, but we can imagine what aurochsen looked like from cave paintings, especially those at Lascaux, France. These show bulls that were five to six and a half feet (1.5–2 m) tall at the shoulder, with long horns that curved forward. Most males were black, often with a white line along the center of the back. Cows were much smaller, had smaller horns that spread to the sides rather than forward, and were reddish in color, as were calves.

Clearly aurochsen were much bigger than domestic cattle. They were also dangerous. Aurochsen lived in herds and if threatened the bulls would defend the cows and calves.

People hunted these wild cattle and we can only guess at how they tamed such a big, aggressive beast. Possibly they exploited their one weakness: a craving for salt. There are people living today in the hills of Assam, India, who lure wild cattle (unrelated to domestic cattle) to their villages by leaving salt and water for them. While the animals are licking the salt people are able to approach them safely and even stroke them. This may be how early farmers began to tame the aurochs.

Ranchers now control them by burning, uprooting, or poisoning the shrubs with herbicides. The landscape still resembles open grassland, but nowadays it is managed grassland and very different from the natural grassland it has replaced.

Cattle ranching is not confined to North America. Very similar management systems have developed in South America, first on the open pampa and more recently in areas of tropical savanna established on land that was formerly forested. There are also cattle ranches in Australia and on the South African veld.

---

Partly tamed aurochsen would have been suspicious of people and much too nervous to allow themselves to be milked. Indeed it is unlikely that the cattle were used for food at all. They were probably taken into villages for religious purposes—as they are today in Assam—and used in religious rituals that involved decorating and venerating them, but not killing them. After a time they were used as draft animals, to haul wheeled carts and plows.

Cattle living close to the village would have changed the immediate environment. They would have destroyed the lower branches of trees and trampled the surface vegetation, enlarging the forest clearings in which people lived. They would also have destroyed crops, unless these were fenced for protection; fouled riverbanks and ponds used for drinking water; and attracted wolves, lions, and other unwelcome visitors. Every day people would have had to drive the cattle away from their crops and drinking water, and every evening they would have had to protect them by driving them into fenced enclosures or cattle sheds. Gradually the animals would have grown accustomed to humans and less fearful of them.

The earliest evidence of domesticated cattle has been found at the site of Çatal Hüyük, an ancient town in Turkey, where as well as bones there is a shrine where aurochsen horns are set in clay. The earliest bones date from about 6400 B.C.E.; the shrine dates from about 5950 B.C.E.

Over many generations the descendants of aurochsen became smaller and more docile. Although aurochsen and domestic cattle are sometimes classified as belonging to the same species, domestication created major physiological and temperamental changes, and many scientists consider them two species: *Bos primigenius* (aurochs) and *B. taurus* (domestic cattle).

## Sheep farms of Australia and New Zealand

No one is certain when the ancestors of today's Native Australians first landed in Australia. It may have been approximately 40,000 years ago or perhaps even earlier, and they must have migrated by moving from island to island across the Pacific Ocean—a process known as island-hopping. They traveled during the last ice age, when the vast ice sheets held so much water that the sea level was much lower than it is today. People who reached Australia later, between 8,000 and 6,000 years ago, took their dogs with them. Some of these later escaped, and their descendants are dingoes (*Canis dingo*)—Australian wild dogs.

These imported dogs were different from most of the animals their owners found in their new land. Apart from mice, rats, and bats, which drifted across the ocean on rafts of vegetation or arrived by island-hopping just as humans did, the Australian mammals were either marsupials or monotremes. Marsupials are animals such as kangaroos, koalas, possums, and wombats. Most of our familiar mammals, including rats, mice, and bats, are known as *placental mammals* (but American opossums are marsupials, although only distantly related to Australian possums). Pregnant females develop a *placenta*. This tissue secretes hormones regulating pregnancy and birth, carries nutrients to the embryo, and removes waste products, all while keeping the mother's and embryo's blood separate. Pregnancy is very different in marsupial mammals. Female marsupials have eggs rich in yolk, and the yolk nourishes the embryo until, at a very early stage in its development, it is big enough to leave its mother's body. The baby is tiny. A baby red kangaroo, for example, is then about the size of a honeybee. Its hind legs are merely buds, but its forelegs are strong enough for the newborn to drag itself across its mother's body to her pouch, or *marsupium,* where it attaches itself to a nipple and completes its growth feeding on her milk.

Monotremes are even more different. This group includes only three species: the platypus (*Ornithorhynchus anatinus*), long-beaked echidna (*Zaglossus bruijni*), and short-beaked echidna (*Tachyglossus aculeatus*). Echidnas are sometimes called spiny anteaters. Monotremes lay eggs with soft shells that hatch after about 10 days. The young then feeds on its mother's milk. The echidna develops inside a maternal pouch, and the young platypus clings to its mother's fur, licking up the milk she secretes from her skin—she has no nipples.

Native Australians lived by hunting the marsupials. Apart from their dogs, there were no placental mammals bigger than a rat until Europeans introduced farm livestock in the early 19th century. Although hunters kill some species of kangaroos for their meat and hides, no marsupial animal has ever been domesticated. European migrants who aimed to farm in Australia had no option but to take with them the cattle, sheep, goats, horses, pigs, and other domesticated animals with which they were familiar.

In addition to these they also introduced domestic dogs and cats, as well as foxes for hunting, and in 1787 Admiral Arthur Phillip (1738–1814), the first governor of New South Wales, imported a small number of rabbits. More rabbits arrived in 1791, and several additional batches arrived in subsequent years. None of these early arrivals escaped to establish themselves in the wild. All of the rabbits that now live throughout more than half of mainland Australia are descended from a batch of 54 animals that were sent from Britain to Barwon Park, near Geelong in the state of Victoria, in 1859. The ancestors of the rabbits now living in Tasmania arrived earlier, around 1830. Rabbits cause a great deal of damage to Australian crops and pasture.

The imported farm livestock thrived. There are now approximately 23 million cattle in Australia, but sheep were the animals that proved to be best adapted to Australian conditions. Australia has approximately 120 million sheep; that works out to six sheep for every human. Sheep farms, called stations, cover many thousands of acres and are comparable to American cattle ranches. The equivalent of the American cowboy is the drover, who rides on horseback and has sheepdogs to help with rounding up the vast flocks. Australian farms supply almost one-third of all the world's wool.

Farmers were raising domesticated sheep 5,000 years ago (see the sidebar), and over the long period since, farmers have developed many breeds, each suited to a particular type of landscape and climate. The most widespread sheep on Australian farms is the Merino, a breed that was known in Spain in the 12th century and that may have originated in North Africa. It thrives in the dry climate of Australia. Merino wool is fine textured and of high quality.

The Maori arrived in New Zealand in about C.E. 850 and found themselves in a land where birds took the place of mammals as grazers and also as hunters (see "The transformation of New Zealand" on pages 78–80). Apart from bats, New Zealand has no native mammals. Maori hunters and farmers cleared the forest covering much of the land, so when the first Europeans arrived, they found extensive grasslands that were ideal for raising sheep. Captain James Cook (1728–79) took the first sheep to New Zealand in 1773, and during the 19th century settlers, predominantly from Britain, took in more.

Romneys are the most popular breed. They originated in the Romney Marshes in southeastern England, where farmers had been raising them since the 13th century and possibly longer. They are big sheep with hard hooves that resist foot rot—a disease to which sheep living on wet ground are highly susceptible. Romney flocks also have a habit of spreading out while they are feeding so they make the best use of the pasture. Romneys thrived in the wet lowlands of New Zealand, and as new farms were established on the steep hillsides of North Island they quickly adapted to this very different environment. Eventually the hill sheep were so different from the original Romneys that they were recognized as a distinct breed: New Zealand Romneys. Their wool is used to make carpets, blankets, furnishing fabrics, and thick sweaters. New Zealand Romneys are farmed for meat as well as wool. The Romney is one of several sheep breeds developed in New Zealand and found on New Zealand farms.

Today there are about 46 million sheep in New Zealand—almost 12 sheep for every person—and New Zealand is the world's second-largest wool producer, after Australia. A typical New Zealand farm is 500–740 acres (200–300 ha) in area and carries approximately 2,500 sheep, together with some cattle. Some farms, owned by companies or Maori Trusts, are much bigger. They carry 6,000–10,000 sheep, together with cattle and often deer.

# The origin of sheep

Wild sheep inhabit most temperate regions of the world, and there are many species. This made it difficult to trace the ancestry of the domestic sheep until biologists were able to study their DNA (deoxyribonucleic acid). In fact, the biologists examined mitochondrial DNA (mtDNA), found in organelles called *mitochondria*. Mitochondria are present in every cell of the body except sperm cells but including ova (eggs), so they are passed from mothers to their offspring. Mitochondrial DNA changes as a result of mutations more rapidly than the DNA in cell nuclei; that fact makes mtDNA useful for measuring the closeness of relationships—the more similar the mtDNA in two individuals, the more closely they are related. These studies revealed that the most likely ancestor of the domestic sheep (*Ovis aries*) is the Asiatic mouflon (*O. orientalis*). At one time scientists suspected that the European mouflon (*O. musimon*) might be the ancestor of domestic sheep. It now appears that the Asiatic mouflon is the ancestor of both species and that the European mouflon is descended from a very early form of the domestic sheep.

Mouflons have dark coats, small bodies with long legs, short tails, and long horns marked with rings. They live in the mountains, the Asiatic species from the eastern Mediterranean to southern Iran. The European species has been introduced in several areas from a population that was formerly confined to Corsica and Sardinia.

There are also native North American sheep. The thinhorn sheep (*O. dalli*) lives in the mountains of Alaska and northern British Columbia, and the bighorn sheep (*O. canadensis*) inhabits western North America from Canada to northern Mexico. Neither species has ever been tamed, and all the sheep on American farms and ranches are descended from imported stock, as are the sheep on Australian and New Zealand farms.

Sheep are social animals. They thrive most when they live as groups with a leader, grazing within a well-defined range. This behavior made it fairly easy for people to control the flocks, and as they did so, they would have rescued orphaned lambs and raised them in their own homes. The flocks would have grown accustomed to people and the lambs would have grown into adults with no fear of humans. The earliest evidence of sheep that lived under human control is from a site in northeastern Iraq where the remains are about 10,870 years old. The first domesticated sheep were smaller than wild sheep, and the females of many domestic breeds often lack horns. Fully domesticated sheep were common in Asia 5,000 years ago.

Sheep were domesticated as a source of meat and skins. Wild sheep have an outer coat of long, stiff fibers over a woolly undercoat that grows in winter and is shed in spring. It was later that selective breeding produced domesticated sheep lacking the coarse outer coat and with a much thicker undercoat—the fleece.

## Upland sheep farming

Today there are many breeds of sheep, each possessing distinct characteristics of its wool, meat, or both. Breeds can sometimes be developed further. Romneys, for example, produce dense, curly wool, but a New Zealand scientist, Francis Dry, discovered that some Romney sheep had straight wool. During the 1930s and 1940s Dr. Dry selected these individuals and developed a new breed from them. Called the Drysdale, this is now a popular New Zealand breed, producing wool that is so long—eight to 12 inches (20–30 cm)—that the sheep are often shorn twice a year to prevent the fibers from becoming damaged. Established breeds can also be crossed to produce a new breed, known as a crossbreed, that shares some of the characteristics of the original breeds. The Corriedale crossbreed is popular in the United States, Australia, and New Zealand. It thrives both on farms and on the open range, and its wool and meat are of high quality. It was produced in New Zealand in the 1880s by crossing Lincoln Longwool rams with Merino ewes.

Wool that is spun into wool for knitting is of a different quality from wool that is woven into the cloth used to make suits and dresses, and both are different from the wool used to weave blankets or to make carpets. Each sheep breed produces wool for particular uses, and breeders also aim to produce animals that will thrive in particular environments.

Lowland regions often have fertile soils, level ground, and a climate suitable for growing crops. Meat and wool from sheep raised on a lowland farm must sell for at least as high a price as crops grown on the same area of land. In order to make sheep farming economically possible, lowland farmers grow grass as a crop, plowing up and reseeding the fields every few years to ensure pasture of the highest nutritional value. Doing so is expensive, and to cover the cost and make the best use of the pasture the farmer must stock as many sheep as possible and control their movement. As soon as a flock has finished grazing in one field it is moved to the next. Certain breeds grow well on this rich diet and accept the intensive management.

Upland conditions are very different. There the climate is cooler, wetter, and windier. The pasture is much poorer than lowland pasture and farmers cannot cultivate the steep hill-sides and high, bleak moors. Land of this type is usually rich in wildlife but of little agricultural value. It is not quite value-less, however: Sheep are descended from animals that live in just this type of country, and they can thrive in the hills.

Sheep that can survive on a poor diet in the harsh upland climate must be hardier than lowland sheep. They must also be more active, because they need to walk long distances in search of food, crossing streams and climbing or jumping over obstacles. Not surprisingly, hill sheep are agile and very difficult to raise in the lowlands because they wander where they will and almost no wall or fence can contain them.

Hill sheep range over large areas. They are not wandering randomly, however, and farmers have no difficulty distin-guishing their own sheep from those of their neighbors. This is because most hill breeds are *hefted:* They occupy a particu-lar range enclosed by a boundary that the sheep recognize and do not cross.

Given the tough living conditions of hill sheep, it would be natural to assume that they produce tough, coarse wool suitable for making hard-wearing carpets. Some breeds, but by no means all, do produce wool of this type. Wool from Rough Fell sheep is used to make carpets, but wool from Cheviot sheep is made into lightweight suits and dresses, and that from Welsh Mountain sheep is so soft it can be made into scarves and flannel. All three of these are hill breeds.

Hill sheep that are raised mainly for meat are often sold to lowland farmers, who fatten them for market on their more nutritious pasture. Lowland farmers also buy ewes when they reach the end of their reproductive life in the hills. Under the gentler conditions of the lowlands they are still capable of breeding to produce healthy lambs.

## Forestry

As the ice sheets retreated northward at the end of the last ice age, plants slowly recolonized the land until eventually most of lowland Europe and much of North America were blanket-ed in forest. At first the people living in the forested land-scapes obtained food by hunting game and gathering edible wild plants, but when knowledge of farming reached them, they began to clear away the forest in order to cultivate the land. Farming has spread into parts of the natural prairie, pampa, and steppe grasslands, but the best farms are located in areas that were once forest. Forest timber was also useful, of course, for building and making of furniture and other items, and as fuel.

During the 19th century naturalists began to notice harmful effects that they associated with forest clearance in southern Europe, Africa, and Asia. Soil erosion often followed the clearance of forests on hillsides, and the eroded soil washed into rivers, making the water cloudy and harming fish. Removing trees was linked to local climate change—weather became windier, cooler, and often drier. In the United States people not only began to fear these adverse environmental consequences of forest clearance, but also worried that if the forest area continued to decrease at the same rate the nation would one day have to import timber. Britain was in that position; its forests were cleared centuries ago, and Britain had long relied on imports of timber. The dangers of that reliance became very apparent during World War I, when German attacks on shipping left the country short of timber for construction and for the manufacture of such essential items as pit props, used to support the roofs of galleries in coal mines.

Many writers commented on the need to conserve existing forests and to plant new ones, but none challenged the wastefulness of current forest use more forcefully or influentially than George Perkins Marsh (1801–82). A lawyer, politician, and diplomat, Marsh spoke 20 languages, specializing in Scandinavian languages. He was the U.S. ambassador to Turkey from 1849 to 1854 and ambassador to Italy from 1862 until his death. While living in the Mediterranean region he saw for himself the once forested but now eroded hillsides around the sea's northern shores. While in Italy he wrote a book called *Man and Nature,* published first in 1864 and in a second edition, retitled *The Earth as Modified by Human Action: Man and Nature,* in 1874. Marsh wrote that although people need to control natural plants and animals in order to grow food, there is an acceptable limit to this control. "This measure man has unfortunately exceeded," he wrote. "He has felled the forests whose network of fibrous roots bound the mold to the rocky skeleton of the earth; but had he allowed here and there a belt of woodland to reproduce itself by spontaneous propagation, most of the mischiefs which his reckless destruction of the natural protection of the soil has occasioned would have been averted."

*Man and Nature* captured the public imagination and led to the establishment of federal forest reserves in the United States and to similar measures in other countries. It also reinforced the need to plant new forests. In 1919 the British government established the Forestry Commission to manage the state-owned forests and to grow a stock of timber extensive enough to prevent shortages during any future war. After centuries of forest clearance trees were being planted on grassland and new forests began to appear.

These were not natural forests, however, but plantations in which trees were a crop no different from any other plant crop except in the time they needed to grow to marketable size. As a crop the trees had to compete economically with other uses for the land on which they grew. This confined them to the poorer farmland in the uplands and required that the tree species chosen grow fast and straight. The new plantation forests consisted of conifers, such as spruces, hemlocks, and pines, planted close together to provide mutual shelter and to discourage the growth of side branches. The new forests grew tall and dark. Conservationists disliked them, because they supported much less wildlife than more open broad-leaved forests and because their straight, sharp edges on open hillsides made them visually unappealing.

Forestry policies have evolved over the years, and now as the original forests mature and are harvested, the plantations replacing them contain a wider range of species, including broad-leaved trees, and natural regeneration is encouraged. Forests are also being planted in the lowlands as public amenities, for recreational use. As the new forests continue to expand, more of the upland grassland and lowland farmland will be transformed into something approximating its original state.

## Biofuel production

Where the climate is suitable, farmers can plow up grassland and sow crops other than grass. Traditionally farm crops were grown to supply food, fiber, or certain industrial raw materials such as oils and waxes. Nowadays farm crops may also be grown to produce fuel. Fuel obtained from crops grown for the purpose is known as *biofuel.*

There is nothing new in this, of course. Until coal and more recently oil and gas displaced it, wood was the fuel everyone used for heating and cooking, and it was processed into the fuel for such industrial processes as firing pottery and smelting and forging metals. Wood is still the most widely used fuel in many parts of the world, and it is obtained from living forests. It is a biofuel.

Wood can be burned on open fires or in kilns or furnaces. It can raise steam to generate electricity and drive steam locomotives, but its usefulness is very limited. Wood is a solid, and many modern machines and processes demand fuel that is in liquid or gaseous form. Wood also contains a large amount of water. Water accounts for up to two-thirds of the weight of green wood, and even when wood has been dried, the water content is seldom less than one-sixth by weight. Wood's high water content makes it burn at a low temperature and makes it bulky. A wood-fired furnace will not produce a temperature high enough to smelt metal. In the days when wood was used for smelting and forging, it was first converted into charcoal by a process that drives off the water to leave a much more concentrated form of carbon.

Modern biofuels are much more advanced. Wood can still be used to generate electricity or heat for industrial processes that do not require very high temperatures, but forest trees grow much too slowly to be practicable as fuel. Instead, the fuel is harvested from plantations of fast-growing species such as willows (*Salix*).

Liquid fuels can also be obtained from conventional farm crops. Potatoes and corn (maize) are rich in starch, which can be converted to sugar. Sugar beet and sugarcane produce sugar directly. Add yeast to a sugar solution and the resulting fermentation yields *ethanol,* the alcohol present in alcoholic drinks. With minor modification automobile engines will

# Biofuels and the greenhouse effect

Air is transparent to sunshine. As the Sun's rays pass through the atmosphere some of their energy is reflected by clouds and pale surfaces, such as snow and desert sand, and some is scattered by collisions with particles and flies back into space, but approximately 51 percent of the energy is absorbed by the land and sea surfaces. Most of the solar energy is in the form of visible light, but when it is absorbed, the energy is converted to heat.

Any object that is warmer than its surroundings radiates energy, and it continues to do so until it has cooled to the same temperature as its surroundings. Absorbing solar energy makes the Earth's surface warmer than the space surrounding the Earth, and consequently the surface radiates energy into space. When objects radiate in this way, the wavelength of their radiation is inversely proportional to their temperature. The Sun is very hot, so it radiates mainly at short wavelengths. The Earth's surface is much cooler, so it radiates at long wavelengths.

Air is transparent to short-wave solar radiation; it is less so to long-wave radiation because certain gases—principally water vapor, carbon dioxide, and methane—absorb radiation at these wavelengths. This absorption of energy warms the air. It is called the greenhouse effect because, in a similar fashion, the glass of a greenhouse allows the sunshine to enter and the warm air inside the greenhouse is unable to escape, so the air inside the greenhouse becomes much warmer than the air outside.

The greenhouse effect is entirely natural, but at present human activities are enhancing it by releasing carbon dioxide, an important "greenhouse gas," into the air. We release carbon dioxide ($CO_2$) whenever we burn a carbon-based fuel such as coal, oil, or gas. Combustion (burning) is a chemical reaction in which carbon (C) is oxidized (combined with oxygen, O), releasing energy and yielding carbon dioxide as a by-product:

$$C + O_2 \rightarrow CO_2 + heat$$

Biofuels are also based on carbon, so burning biofuel also releases $CO_2$. This $CO_2$ does not contribute to the greenhouse effect, however, because unlike coal, oil, and gas, biofuels are obtained from plants that lived very recently. Coal, oil, and gas are often called *fossil* fuels, partly because they are taken from the ground (originally a "fossil" was any object discovered below ground) and partly because they are the remains of organisms that lived many millions of years ago. Fossil fuels contain carbon that was removed from the air long ago and has been stored; biofuels contain carbon that was taken from the air recently by the process of photosynthesis and that would otherwise have returned to the air when the plants died and decomposed. Consequently, burning fossil fuels increases the atmospheric concentration of $CO_2$, but burning biofuels does not.

run on ethanol. If the ethanol is distilled to remove the water mixed with it and then mixed with gasoline, usually with 20 parts of ethanol to 80 parts of gasoline, unmodified engines will run on it.

*Methanol* is another type of alcohol. It is such a clean, efficient, and safe fuel that many racing cars use it: If the car should crash and rupture the fuel tank, methanol will not explode in a fireball, unlike gasoline. Methanol or a substance derived from it is added to most unleaded gasoline. Nowadays methanol is produced industrially from natural gas, but it was formerly made by heating wood chips, a process that gave it its other name—wood alcohol. It can still be made from wood grown on former grassland.

Canola, also called rape, is grown for its oil, mainly for human consumption, but it also has industrial uses in soap and synthetic rubber manufacture and as a lubricant. Soybeans also provide oil, as well as a range of human and livestock foods. These oils can be burned as fuel and processed to make rape methyl ester (RME) or soy methyl ester (SME). RME and SME are alternatives to diesel oil, known as "biodiesel" fuel. Sunflower oil is also used. Biodiesel emits fewer pollutants than diesel oil when it is burned, and in the event of an accidental spill it breaks down harmlessly.

Biofuels are already in use. Biogas—ethanol or a gasoline–ethanol mixture—is used widely in Brazil and to a small extent in the United States. Biodiesel is used on a small scale, mainly to power buses and taxis. At present all of these fuels are much more expensive than coal, oil, or gas, but this could change in the future. If the price of conventional fuels were to rise high enough to make biofuels competitive, biofuel production might increase rapidly. Increasing production might then reduce the costs of processing, transport, and marketing biofuels, reducing their price still more. Biofuels could also help reduce diesel and gasoline consumption if people chose to take advantage of the fact that biofuels do not contribute to the greenhouse effect.

Burning biofuels releases energy through the oxidation of carbon, a reaction that releases carbon dioxide as the final product of combustion. Carbon dioxide is a so-called greenhouse gas—a gas that absorbs long-wave radiation—and climate scientists agree that releasing it into the air causes climatic warming through the greenhouse effect. Burning biofuels does not contribute to the greenhouse effect, however, because the carbon dioxide it releases is part of the natural cycling of carbon (see the sidebar).

## CHAPTER 9

# BIODIVERSITY AND GRASSLANDS

## What is biodiversity?

*Prairie, pampa,* and *steppe* are evocative names. They conjure images of endless tracts of grasses waving before the whispering wind beneath a clear blue sky. Grasses are the predominant plants—obviously, since these are grasslands—but natural grassland contains many species of grasses, and by no means are grasses the only plants. At certain times of year the grassland is ablaze with the color of countless flowers, blooming between the grass plants. Colorful flowers attract pollinating insects, and the air hums with their buzzing flight. Many birds feed on insects and they, too, can be seen patrolling in search of food. Mice and other small mammals scurry about on the ground, feeding on fallen seeds, while predatory mammals and snakes hunt them. In fact, the grassland harbors countless species of plants and animals, not to mention the even greater variety of microscopic organisms that inhabit the soil (see chapter 5, "Life on the Grasslands," on pages 81–142).

Such an abundant variety of living organisms is nowadays described as an example of *biodiversity*—a contraction of *biological diversity.* It is easy to see what it means—or is it?

In 1987 the U.S. Congress Office of Technology Assessment (OTA) proposed:

> *Biological diversity refers to the variety and variability among living organisms and the ecological complexes in which they occur. Diversity can be defined as the number of different items and their relative frequency. For biological diversity, these items are organized at many levels, ranging from complete ecosystems to the chemical structures that are the molecular basis of heredity. Thus, the term encompasses different ecosystems, species, genes, and their relative abundance.* (Technologies to Maintain Biological

Diversity. *Washington, D.C.: U.S. Government Printing Office, 1987*)

This remains the most widely quoted definition of biodiversity, but the term remains difficult to pin down precisely. Does it mean the whole of life? In *The Diversity of Life* (Cambridge, Mass.: Harvard University Press, 1992), the eminent biologist E. O. Wilson extends the definition to include the habitats and physical conditions under which organisms live.

At the smallest level, the OTA definition refers to "the chemical structures that are the molecular basis of heredity." These structures are genes and since every individual is genetically distinct, this would seem to suggest that biodiversity means the sum of all the genes in all the individual organisms. If that is so, then preserving biodiversity may be impossible unless we can find a way to prevent individuals from dying.

Most people would accept that the term refers to the number of species, either in the world as a whole or in a particular area. But even that is difficult, because biologists are uncertain of the best way to define a species and there are several competing definitions. Biologists do not equate biodiversity with the number of species. In the end although everyone has an idea of what the term means, the concept of biodiversity is so wide and so complex as to be almost undefinable.

Despite the problems, however, scientists are developing ways to measure biodiversity. Diversity arises from genetic differences, which can be measured very precisely within and between populations. Measuring differences allows biologists to arrange organisms into groups that reflect the variety among them. If we wish to maintain the greatest possible biodiversity, then those differences are what we need to preserve.

## Why it matters

It seems obvious that we should protect wild plants and animals and that preventing damage to the areas in which they live is the only practical way to do so. When the idea is expressed in this very general way, few people could disagree that conservation is desirable. Unfortunately this is not the way issues arise in real life. Suppose, for example, that many people live in crowded, unhealthy conditions because of a shortage of housing, and the community decides to help them by building more homes. The only place where new houses can be built is on the edge of town, on an area of natural grassland that is rich in wildflowers and insects, including a rare butterfly. Do we build the homes or protect the wildlife?

Planning departments and committees face conflicts of this kind almost every day, and they cannot deny people the right to a decent home simply because it is pleasant to have that area of natural habitat nearby. They must find a more substantial reason, not least because house building is only one of the demands they have to resolve. What can they say to the company that wishes to build a factory employing local people who need jobs, or a power plant to meet predicted demand, or a bypass road to relieve congestion downtown? It is more difficult than it seems.

Conservationists might argue that the natural grassland is beautiful and the species inhabiting it have a right to live undisturbed. But new houses look beautiful to people who need homes, and people have a right to homes. Someone might also point out that while grassland and butterflies are clearly attractive, extending this case for protection to rats, slugs, slimes, biting insects, and venomous snakes is difficult, yet these have the same right to live.

Each case has to be decided on its merits, but there are more compelling arguments for protecting natural grassland against which competing demands should be weighed. Among the wild plants and animals there may be some that could be useful. Perhaps scientists will discover that one of the grass species is resistant to a disease that affects wheat or corn and will find a way to transfer that resistance to crop plants. Maybe an insect living in obscurity among the plants has an insatiable appetite for another insect that is a devastating crop pest and could be recruited to control that pest as an alternative to spraying pesticide. There might be plants that manufacture compounds chemists could convert into medicines. Aspirin was originally obtained from willow bark, and digitalis, used as a treatment for heart disease and as a diuretic (to stimulate urination), was extracted from the leaves of foxgloves. There are countless other examples. Might a cure for some dreadful disease be awaiting discovery among the grassland plants? Or perhaps there are plants that might be cultivated as a source of industrial raw materials, such as fiber. Paper made from hemp (*Cannabis sativa*) fibers is greatly superior to paper made from wood pulp, and there may be other fibers that are just as useful.

Planners also need to bear in mind that ecologists still have much to learn about the way an ecosystem, such as an area of grassland, functions and how it relates to the other ecosystems around it. Clearing the grassland will probably have no adverse effect whatever, but it is difficult to be certain. Transforming parts of the prairie into farmland was highly successful until the drought that destroyed the farms and produced the Dust Bowl occurred (see "The Dust Bowl" on pages 55–57 and "Lessons from the Dust Bowl" on pages 218–220). One day scientists may be in a position to make reliable predictions about the consequences of clearing natural habitat, but they will be able to do so only if those habitats survive long enough to be studied. The need to acquire this knowledge is another reason for preserving natural habitats.

Scientists have succeeded in persuading governments of the importance of biodiversity and its protection. This was one of the principal topics discussed in 1992 at a conference in Rio de Janeiro held under the auspices of the United Nations (UN). The UN Conference on Environment and Development, also called the Earth Summit and the Rio Summit, was the largest meeting of heads of government ever held. One outcome was the Convention on Biological Diversity, also known as the Biodiversity Convention, which commits governments to the protection of natural habitats and sets out practical measures that will help them achieve it (see the sidebar).

## Protecting grassland species

Wildlife documentaries have allowed television viewers across the world to watch the animals of the Serengeti and

# The Biodiversity Convention

In June 1972 the United Nations sponsored the largest international conference held until that date. Called the UN Conference on the Human Environment, it was held in Stockholm, Sweden, and was known informally as the Stockholm Conference. Delegates to the conference resolved to establish a new United Nations agency, to be called the UN Environment Program (UNEP). UNEP came into being in 1973. Its tasks are to collect and circulate information about the state of the global environment and to encourage and coordinate international efforts to reduce pollution and protect wildlife.

UNEP sponsored several major conferences over the years, and in 1992, 20 years after the Stockholm Conference, it organized the UN Conference on Environment and Development, also known as the Earth Summit and the Rio Summit because it took place in Rio de Janeiro, Brazil. It was the largest meeting of world leaders ever held. The aim of the 1992 conference was to relate environmental protection to economic development, and to this end the delegates agreed on the provisions that were set down in the Convention on Climate Change and the Convention on Biological Diversity—also known as the Biodiversity Convention.

A convention is a binding agreement between governments. Government representatives sign the convention, and when their own legislatures have accepted it, the governments ratify it by signing it again, confirming their willingness to abide by its terms. The lawmakers must then translate those terms into national law. When a majority of signatory governments have ratified the convention, it becomes part of international law and is known as a treaty. By the summer of 2005 157 countries had ratified the Biodiversity Convention.

The Biodiversity Convention reminds governments that natural resources are not infinite and promotes the principle of using resources in sustainable ways that ensure future generations will also be able to enjoy them. The convention requires governments to develop national strategies and plans of action to measure, conserve, and promote the sustainable use of natural resources. National plans for environmental protection and economic development should incorporate these strategies and plans, especially in respect of forestry, agriculture, fisheries, energy, transportation, and city planning. As well as protecting existing areas of high biodiversity, governments should restore degraded areas. The convention strongly emphasizes the need to involve local communities in its projects and to raise public awareness of the value of a diverse natural environment.

Many countries have now taken positive steps to implement the Biodiversity Convention.

Masai Mara national parks. The Serengeti National Park covers approximately 5,000 square miles (12,950 km²) in Tanzania, and in neighboring Kenya the Masai Mara National Reserve covers about 700 square miles (1,813 km²). These are the most famous of the national parks located in savanna grassland, but there are many more across the semiarid regions of Africa. The United Nations has recognized the importance of Kruger National Park to the Canyons Biosphere Reserve in South Africa; it is included in the Man and Biosphere (MAB) Biosphere Reserves Directory maintained by the UN Educational, Scientific and Cultural Organization (UNESCO). The reserve covers 9,550 square miles (24,747 km²) of tropical savanna grassland, temperate grassland, and forest.

Savanna grassland is also preserved in Asia. The Baluran National Park, for example, extends over 96 square miles (250 km²) in the driest part of Java, Indonesia. Nature reserves in South America also protect small patches of savanna grassland located there. Overall, however, tropical grasslands are afforded little protection outside Africa.

Temperate grasslands have fared somewhat better. The Pampa Galeras Barbara D'Achille National Reserve, established in 1993, encloses 25 square miles (65 km²) of pampa in Peru; the reserve was established to protect the vicuña (*Vicugna vicugna*) living there and to improve the living standard of the local people, however, rather than to preserve the grassland as such. Much larger areas of pampa survive in Argentina, lying to the west and south of the capital, Buenos Aires, and extending southward deep into Patagonia. The Argentine pampas are not designated as national parks or nature reserves, and most have been modified as a result of cattle ranching, but some areas of the original grassland remain.

Large areas of the Asian steppe are still in their natural state, but even they benefit from protection. Another MAB Biosphere Reserve, designated in 2002, centers on Dalai Lake, close to the Russian border in the Inner Mongolian Autonomous Region of China (between 47.76°N and 49.34°N, and 116.84°E and 118.17°E). The lake has a surface area of 903 square miles (2,339 km²)—*dalai* is the Mongolian word for "sea"—and the reserve is internationally important for the migrating birds that stop over there. The lake is surrounded by steppe, raising the total area of the reserve to 2,856 square miles (7,400 km$^2$). The grassland soil is thin and the climate is dry, with an average annual rainfall of less than 14 inches (350 mm). Consequently the plants are at risk from overgrazing by the livestock of the 11,380 people living inside the reserve. In addition to the rare plants it contains the reserve is home to the Mongolian gazelle (*Procapra gutturosa*) and great bustard (*Otis tarda*). It is also important historically as the region where Mongolian culture originated and where Chinggis Khan united the tribes in the 12th century.

Little of the European steppe survives, but all those areas of steppe that escaped conversion to farmland in European Russia and Ukraine are protected in nature reserves. The Askania-Nova Reserve in Ukraine is one of the most important of these. It occupies 43 square miles (111 km$^2$) near the mouth of the Dniepr River on the northern shore of the Black Sea, and only six square miles (15 km$^2$) of it has ever been plowed. It was established in 1874 as a privately owned nature reserve and became a state reserve in 1921.

Most of the North American prairie has been converted to farmland, but scattered areas survived because for one reason or another farmers had no use for them. Tallgrass prairie once covered approximately 375,000 square miles (971,000 km$^2$). Today only about 3 percent of this area remains, much of it in the Flint Hills of Kansas. That is where, in November 1996, 17 square miles (44 km$^2$) was designated as the Tallgrass Prairie National Preserve. The Konza Prairie reserve, covering 13.5 square miles (35 km$^2$) also in the Flint Hills, is a UNESCO Biosphere Reserve managed by Kansas State University. Other states have also taken steps to protect the remaining areas of natural prairie within their borders.

In collaboration with the World Wildlife Fund in 1988 the Canadian Prairie Provinces of Manitoba, Saskatchewan, and Alberta produced a Prairie Conservation Plan. This has since been updated and each province has developed its own plan aimed at preserving the remaining natural prairie. The original prairie also extended into western Ontario, and some patches still remain. These are also protected, often inside larger parks or reserves that mainly comprise forest.

## CHAPTER 10

# THREATS TO GRASSLAND

## Conversion to farmland

Grassland is the most vulnerable of biomes. Forest land can be put to other uses, but first the trees must be felled and removed and the undergrowth cleared away. Clearance takes time and is expensive. Their harsh climates mean deserts and tundra regions cannot be converted to other uses economically—or at all. Grassland is very different. It is much more easily converted to farmland.

Settlers began farming the tallgrass prairie in eastern Ohio in about 1825, and farming expanded into the prairie rapidly between 1830 and 1880. The last of the wet prairie in Iowa was drained and plowed in about 1920. Tallgrass prairie once covered approximately 375,000 square miles (971,000 km$^2$). It disappeared in less than one century and today only about 3 percent of it remains (see "Protecting grassland species" on pages 201–204).

Most of the European steppe was converted to farmland centuries ago. Starting in the 13th century, Russian peasants—families farming just enough land to feed themselves—were gradually transformed into *serfs*—people who are not allowed to leave the farm and who must work part of the time for the landowner. Serfdom was abolished in 1861, but the former serfs were still not allowed to own land. They were made into tenants, but they had to pay such high rents to the landowners that many were forced out of farming altogether.

Substantial areas of steppe remained uncultivated by the first half of the 20th century, but Russia—by then the Union of Soviet Socialist Republics (USSR, also known as the Soviet Union)—remained short of food. Despite its vast size, only about one-quarter of the area of Russia is suitable for agriculture. The remaining lands are tundra (8 percent), desert or semidesert (13.7 percent), or too mountainous (30 percent) or too infertile (22.3 percent) to be cultivated. By contrast, 45 percent of the land area of the United States is used for agriculture.

The rapid mechanization of Soviet agriculture during the 1930s and 1940s opened the possibility of expanding cultivation onto lands that had never before been plowed, and in 1954 Nikita Khrushchev (1894–1971) launched the Virgin and Idle Lands Program. At the time Khrushchev was first secretary of the Communist Party (he became Soviet prime minister in 1958). His aim was to increase the area of farmland by cultivating steppe grassland in the northern Kazakh Soviet Socialist Republic (now Kazakhstan) and the Altai district of the Russian Soviet Federal Socialist Republic (now the Russian Federation), bordering it to the east.

At the end of the first year 73,340 square miles of the steppe (190,000 km²) had met the plow, and an additional 5.4 million square miles (14 million km²) was plowed in the second year. More than 300,000 people moved into the area, most of them from Ukraine, to work on the new farms. Soldiers, students, and machinery operators were drafted to help with the harvest. The program increased the area of cropland by 25 percent and the first harvest, gathered in 1956, was huge. For the first time the Soviet Union was producing twice as much wheat per head of population as any Western country, and the program was acclaimed as a great success.

Then problems began to emerge. The first was a lack of storage facilities for the grain, much of which was wasted for want of anywhere to keep it. The climate was very variable and droughts were frequent. This meant that the harvests were also variable. Wheat was almost the only crop grown, and after a few years the soil was depleted of the nutrients wheat needs. Yields fell, crops began to fail, and when the plants died the bare soil began to blow away in the dry wind. Erosion became severe. By 1960 the program had clearly failed and it was quietly abandoned. The Soviet Union was reduced to importing wheat from Canada—where, ironically, it had been grown on the prairie.

Most of the grassland in the lowlands of Europe is seminatural, in the sense that it grows on land that was originally forested. If the grassland is used only to graze animals and to make hay, and the land is never plowed, many other herbs will colonize it, growing among the grasses to make a meadow rich in wildflowers. Although they were once widespread, few such meadows have survived. During the latter half of the 19th century farmers were learning that dairy cattle produce more milk if they eat young grass. They began plowing up the meadows and sowing the land with grass seed. The farmers also found that the land will grow a good cereal crop if the new grassland is plowed again after three or four years. By the early 20th century it was becoming fashionable to grow grass as a crop. This was called *ley farming* and eventually it claimed almost all of the original meadows.

Without special protection, grassland is clearly at risk of being plowed up and converted to arable farmland. Even the seminatural grassland originally made by farmers is vulnerable, and as a result of changing agricultural methods most has already been replaced by temporary grassland, supporting far fewer plant species.

## Conversion to forest

Throughout most of human history people have lived with the knowledge that a failed harvest might herald famine. It is hardly surprising, therefore, that every corner of land capable of producing food was pressed into service. Where starvation was a very real risk, people regarded as beautiful a landscape of well-tended, weed-free fields growing healthy crops (see "Homesteaders and the way the prairie was transformed" on pages 160–165).

Modern agricultural technology, backed by scientific research into soils and plant growth, has eliminated the fear of famine from many parts of the world—although not yet from Africa. Crop yields have risen to such an extent that farmers in the United States and European Union are encouraged to take land out of production and devote it to other uses, such as wildlife conservation and public recreational amenities, often in the form of forests. In many parts of Europe and the eastern United States, where farmland was created by clearing forests, trees are the most natural alternative to farm crops.

Indeed abandoned fields will revert to forest without any need to plant trees. Petersham, Massachusetts, is a town set among trees and surrounded by forest, but 150 years ago it looked very different. Settlers first reached the area in 1733 and during the second half of the 18th century most of the forest was cleared to provide farmland. By 1860 only 15 percent of the original forest remained. Country lanes bordered by stone walls linked the farms and the town. But while the Petersham farmers had been tilling their fields, other settlers had begun farming the Midwest, where land was cheaper, and the expansion of the cities attracted the farmers' children to better-paid and more interesting jobs. The Petersham farms failed and were abandoned, and within a few years the forest had returned. The stone walls remain, broken down but still recognizable, as the only reminder of the farms that once occupied the land.

Where farms—artificial grassland—occupy land that was once forested, the forest will usually return if the farmers abandon their holdings, especially if there are natural forests growing not too far away. Tree seeds from the forest fall onto the abandoned fields and some of the seeds germinate. This always happened, but plowing destroyed the seedlings on arable fields and livestock nibbled or trampled them on pasture. The cessation of farming operations allows the seedlings to survive. Each year a few more young trees appear and in time the neighboring forest claims the land.

Nowadays local communities welcome this transformation. People cleared the forests because at that time farmland was more valuable than forest. That remains true economically, but not socially. Farm crops are more commercially profitable than timber, but forests harbor more wildlife and provide more leisure opportunities than farmland, making them more popular and therefore more socially valuable.

Between 1987 and 1997 the area of forest in the United States increased by 1.2 percent, from 737.7 million acres (298.5 million ha) to 747.0 million acres (302.3 million ha). Forests expanded in most parts of the country, except the Pacific coast, Alaska, and Hawaii, but including the Great

Plains, where the forested area expanded by 14.3 percent, from 4.2 million acres (1.7 million ha) to 4.8 million acres (1.9 million ha).

Forests once covered almost 80 percent of Britain. Farmers began clearing them approximately 8,000 years ago and today only about 4 percent of the British landscape is forested. It is a very small area, but it is increasing. Between 1990 and 2000 the area of British forest expanded by 6 percent, from 6.5 million acres (2.6 million ha) to 6.9 million acres (2.8 million ha). All of this expansion was of natural forest; the total area of plantation forest did not change. Forests are now growing on former farmland.

## Overgrazing and soil erosion

Grasses benefit from grazing, but if livestock trample or uproot the plants, they will destroy them, and if they nibble grass down to below the lowest node on the culm (see "How grasses work" on pages 84–89) the grass will die. These are the effects of *overgrazing,* and they occur when a traditional management system proves unable to cope with the demands made on it.

Stock farmers allow their animals to graze until they have eaten the most nutritious parts of the pasture then move them to a different area, leaving the grazed pasture to regenerate. The animals then feed in several other places before returning to the first, and they always graze areas in the same sequence. This system makes the best use of the plants and allows the pasture to recover between visits. It can be sustained indefinitely.

But a system of this type will become unstable if too many additional herds and flocks are added to it. This can happen when war or other disturbances drive people from their homes, or when drought forces people to move in search of food for their animals. The refugees arrive with their livestock, which begin to feed on the pasture, reducing the time required to graze each area. The animals have to be moved more frequently, and this increasing intensification of the farming system may reach the point at which pasture has too little time to recover between one grazing and the next. That is when the plants may be destroyed and the pasture begins to deteriorate. On the dry grasslands bordering the Sahara, the pasture begins to fail when the human population exceeds 50–100 people per square mile (20–40/km$^2$).

When the displaced people arrive with their herds and flocks the residents cannot refuse them access to the pasture, because the grasslands belong to everyone and to no one. The animals, on the other hand, have owners and are therefore valued. Each owner benefits from grazing stock on the land, but the cost of the deterioration of the pasture is shared among all the livestock owners. At first this cost is too small to concern anyone, or even to be noticed. By the time the damage becomes obvious it is too late and the pasture has been destroyed. William Forster Lloyd (1795–1852), a British political economist, described this process in 1833 in the form of a parable he called "The Tragedy of the Commons." The American biologist Garrett Hardin (1915–2003) used the same title for his updated interpretation of Lloyd's essay, published in 1968 in the journal *Science*.

Overgrazing leaves the land bare and exposed to the wind and rain, with nothing to prevent the soil from being blown and washed away. This is soil erosion, the most serious consequence of overgrazing. The Food and Agriculture Organization (FAO) of the United Nations estimates that soil erosion destroys 12–17 million acres (5–7 million ha) of farmland each year. Overgrazing is the cause of 67 percent of all erosion by water and 46 percent of all wind erosion. This amounts to more than one-third of all soil erosion—exceeding the 30 percent due to deforestation, which many people suppose to be the principal cause of erosion.

Overgrazing and subsequent erosion produce effects that are felt far from their source. Grasslands are often located on high ground, around the upper reaches of rivers that water more fertile lands downstream. Water erodes soil when heavy rain washes away the surface soil, carrying it into rivers, where it pollutes the water, killing fish and other aquatic organisms and thus reducing the quality of the water reaching downstream users. The river then flows more slowly across the cultivated plains, and the soil it carries settles onto the bottom, making the river shallower and less easy for boats to navigate. A shallower river is also more likely to overflow its banks, flooding the surrounding fields and buildings.

These problems are widespread and attract much attention, but they are far from new. Overgrazing and soil erosion have affected agricultural populations for thousands of years, yet farming has survived because when problems become too severe to be ignored, people solve them. European populations increased rapidly in the Middle Ages, forcing farmers to curtail the traditional practice of leaving land fallow (uncultivated) between crops long enough to allow its store of nutrients to replenish themselves. As the soil deteriorated and yields declined, communities devised new farming methods. They allowed cattle and sheep to graze land before it was plowed, so their dung would help restore the soil's fertility, and to assist in this they divided what had been open countryside into small fields and meadows enclosed by hedges. Instead of falling, crop yields increased. There is reason to hope, therefore, that the world's grasslands can be utilized sustainably and that in years to come modifications in farming methods will bring that about.

## Climate change

Climates are constantly changing and plant and animal communities change with them (see "Grasslands and past climate changes" on pages 73–76). Grasslands grow where the climate is warm enough for herbs to flower and ripen their seeds but too dry for trees to form forests. If the prairie, pampa, or steppe climate were to become wetter, the grassland would gradually be replaced by forest (unless people removed the trees to prevent this). If the grassland climate became drier the land would be transformed into desert.

Such changes are entirely natural. Today, however, many scientists fear that we may be altering the climate on a global scale by releasing into the air gases that enhance the natural *greenhouse effect* (see the sidebar).

It might seem that a rise in temperature leads simply to warmer weather, but the effects are more complicated. In the first place much depends on the way the warming occurs. At

# The greenhouse effect

When any object is warmer than its surroundings, it emits electromagnetic radiation, such as light or heat. The wavelength of that radiation is inversely proportional to the temperature of the object emitting it: The hotter the body, the shorter the wavelength of its radiation. This is because the amount of energy carried by electromagnetic radiation is greatest when the wavelength is shortest, meaning that more wave crests and troughs pass a stationary point in the same interval of time. Astronomical bodies such as stars and planets are surrounded by space, which is very cold. The Sun is hot and radiates most intensely at short wavelengths. Its radiation warms the surface of the Earth, which then emits radiation at a much longer wavelength because it is relatively cool.

Some of the sunshine falling on the Earth is reflected into space by clouds and pale-colored surfaces such as snow and desert sand. Some is scattered by particles and tiny droplets in the air and returns to space without reaching the surface. The surface of land and sea absorbs approximately 51 percent of the solar radiation reaching Earth. The absorbed energy warms the material that absorbs it.

During the day the Earth absorbs solar radiation—sunshine—faster than it loses heat by radiating it away, and so its temperature rises. By late afternoon the surface is radiating heat at about the same rate as it is absorbing it; during the night it continues to radiate, but because the Sun is no longer shining, the Earth's surface temperature falls. It continues to fall until about one hour before dawn, when the first light appears in the sky.

While air is transparent to incoming short-wave solar radiation, it is less so to outgoing long-wave radiation because certain gases—principally water vapor, carbon dioxide, and

present two-thirds of the warming is taking place in winter and especially at night. Maximal temperatures are rising, but most of the warming has the effect of reducing the difference between maximal and minimal temperatures. Winters are becoming shorter and the growing season for plants is longer because nighttime frosts end earlier in spring and commence later in the fall. The warming is not occurring evenly. Northwestern North America—Alaska and the Yukon—and northeastern Siberia are the regions most strongly affected, and the Antarctic Peninsula is also becoming much warmer, although much of the interior of Antarctica is growing colder.

methane—absorb radiation at these wavelengths. This absorption of energy warms the air. It is called the greenhouse effect because, in a similar fashion, the glass of a greenhouse allows the sunshine to enter but the warm air inside the greenhouse is unable to escape, so the air inside the greenhouse becomes much warmer than the air outside.

The greenhouse effect is entirely natural. The absorbed radiation warms the air, which radiates at longer wavelengths, and energy escapes into space each time it is radiated at a wavelength no gas absorbs, 8.5–13.0 µm, known as the *atmospheric window*. The departure of the outgoing energy is delayed but not prevented. Without the greenhouse effect the average air temperature at ground level would be approximately 34°F (1°C); in fact, the average surface temperature is 59°F (15°C).

At present, human activities are enhancing the greenhouse effect by releasing certain "greenhouse gases," especially carbon dioxide, into the air. We release carbon dioxide ($CO_2$) whenever we burn a carbon-based fuel such as coal, oil, or gas. Combustion (burning) is a chemical reaction in which carbon (C) is oxidized (combined with oxygen, O), releasing energy and creating carbon dioxide as a by-product:

$$C + O_2 \rightarrow CO_2 + heat$$

Most climate scientists agree that the accumulation of greenhouse gases is producing a rise in the average temperature over many parts of the world. They disagree over the extent to which this presents a serious problem. At present the average temperature is increasing at about 2.3°F–3.2°F (1.3°C–1.8°C) per century. It seems probable that the average temperature in the early 22nd century will be 1.8°F–3.6°F (1°C–2°C) higher than it is today.

When the air temperature rises, the rate of evaporation increases, more cloud forms, and precipitation increases. A warmer climate is usually a wetter one. If the grassland climates grow warmer, climate scientists predict they will also become wetter. It does not follow, however, that grassland soils will become more moist. Whether or not the soil becomes more moist depends on the way the increase in temperature affects the balance between precipitation and *potential evaporation,* which is the amount of water that would evaporate over a given time if the supply of water were unlimited. This is determined by measuring the rate at which water evaporates from a large container of water called an *evaporation pan* that is left standing in the open. Obviously the amount of water lost from the ground by evaporation cannot exceed the amount that falls as precipitation, but the potential evaporation can exceed the precipitation. It is possible, therefore, for precipitation to increase but for the ground to become drier.

If the average temperature rises by less than about 3.6°F (2°C), precipitation will increase more than the potential evaporation and so the ground will become more moist. This might allow some plant species to grow more vigorously at the expense of others, altering the balance of species in the natural grassland community, and it might encourage the growth of more trees. Where grassland has been converted to arable farmland, soil that is moister might increase crop yields, although crops could be damaged if some of the increased precipitation arrives in the form of violent hailstorms.

If the average temperature rises by more than about 3.6°F (2°C), potential evaporation will increase faster than precipitation and the ground will become drier. This would be a more serious situation. Crops would need more irrigation to make good the shortfall, and in time natural grassland would become dominated by plants that tolerate drought while less tolerant plants would disappear.

At present the evidence suggests that the rise in temperature will be modest and grasslands will not suffer, although their composition may change. It is possible that forest might expand into moister areas of what is now grassland. If the rate of warming were to increase substantially, however, grasslands would be confined to the moister regions while other areas turned to semidesert or desert.

## Expansion of towns and roads

Nowadays most Americans and Europeans live in cities. In the United States 79 percent of the population lives in urban areas. In the United Kingdom 89.5 percent of people are city dwellers, in France the proportion is 75.5 percent, and in Germany it is 87.7 percent. More Italians live in the countryside, but even in Italy 67.1 percent of the population is urban. Russia is vast, but 73.3 percent of Russians live in cities.

The move into the cities is fairly recent. Many city dwellers were born and raised in rural areas, and even more of them have parents or grandparents who lived in the countryside. Urban expansion is a process that accompanies the industrialization of economies. Britain is one of the most highly urbanized countries in the world, but in about 1800 almost 75 percent of the population lived in villages and hamlets, and most of the towns outside London had fewer than 1,000 inhabitants. In 1851 approximately 25.5 percent of the population lived in urban areas, but by 1931, only 80 years later, this proportion had risen to 76.7 percent. Industrialization and the associated urbanization occurred earlier in Britain than in most other countries, but even there many people still feel they have family links to the countryside. In other parts of the world the links are closer.

People moved into the cities—and still do—in search of a better life. Employment opportunities were greater and wages were higher than those paid by farmers. Despite the overcrowding, poor sanitation, and appalling working conditions in the industrializing cities of the 19th and early 20th centuries, urban life promised better prospects of improved living standards. They offered hope—dreams of streets paved with gold. But as the unrealized dreams faded, the new city dwellers began to recall their former rural lives more fondly. Memories of clear blue skies, green fields, trees, rivers of clean water, and sweet-smelling air seemed very attractive amid the smoke and grime of the city streets. The long hours of hard labor in the cold, rain, and mud were forgotten, along with the hunger, grinding poverty, and insecurity that were the lot of most farmworkers.

As a consequence, many modern city dwellers value the countryside highly. Some dream of moving there to live, and others content themselves with occasional visits, but even people who never leave the city find reassurance in the knowledge that the countryside exists and that they could visit it if an opportunity arose and they chose to do so. Many do visit the countryside, of course. When the railroads opened in the course of the 19th century one of their first tasks was to run excursions from the cities into the countryside, and the number of visitors increased still more rapidly when affordable mass-produced automobiles became available.

The countryside has come to be valued both as an amenity and as the historic background to the lives of our own families. Not surprisingly people guard it jealously and are strenuous in their opposition to any development that would diminish it.

People object to the expansion of urban areas into the countryside, both because this reduces the area of countryside and because expansion that takes place on the edge of an existing city moves the countryside farther away from those living near the urban center. Roads provide access to the countryside, but to do so they remove ribbons of countryside. They are also visually intrusive and noisy, and vehicle exhausts from them pollute the air.

Each year in the United States 1 million new homes and approximately 10,000 miles (16,000 km) of new roads are built in the 48 contiguous states and District of Columbia. Buildings and roads now cover 43,480 square miles (112,610 km$^2$). That is an area almost as large as the state of Ohio. It sounds immense, and the rate of expansion sounds alarming because of our high regard for the countryside across which these homes and roads are spreading. How can anyone doubt that urban expansion is gobbling up the countryside? Surely the scale of the problem is clear. At this rate it cannot be long before the few remaining patches of natural grassland vanish beneath the asphalt and concrete.

Indeed the total urban area of the United States is large, but many of the new houses are built to replace old houses that have been demolished. Even if all of them were being built in open countryside, however, the United States is a big country and buildings and roads cover only a tiny proportion of it—no more than 1.4 percent. This makes the United States more highly urbanized than the world average, of 0.2 percent of the total land area, but less so than some countries. In Britain buildings and roads cover 3.9 percent of the land.

This is not the way it appears to people traveling out from the cities. They see the road or rail track lined by buildings that extend far from the city center, with other groups of buildings in the distance, separated by fields and trees, giving them the impression that countryside survives only in pockets. It is not so, and the view from the air quickly dispels this false impression. Very little of the countryside has been sacrificed to urban development even in the most densely populated and highly urbanized countries, and there is no reason to suppose the urban area will increase greatly in years to come. Buildings and roads are unlikely to spread across the world's grasslands.

## CHAPTER 11

# MANAGING THE GRASSLANDS

## Lessons from the Dust Bowl

Grasslands grow in those parts of the world where the climate is too dry to sustain forests but not so dry as to prevent all plant growth. In a climate of this type droughts are likely to occur at intervals, and the fact that the grassland plants survive shows they are adapted to periodic drought. The Great Plains of North America are no exception, and the drought that caused the Dust Bowl (see "The Dust Bowl" on pages 55–57) was not unique. It led to tragedy—for the land as well as for the families it ruined—because farmers had been lulled into a false sense of security by several years of good weather and because they failed to take measures that would have reduced the amount of soil erosion.

Two lessons emerged from the Dust Bowl disaster. The first was that the native prairie grasses were able to survive prolonged drought. The second was that soil erosion can be minimized and that farmers needed to be educated in the techniques of soil conservation.

Grassland ecologists in Nebraska, Iowa, and Kansas studied the effects of the drought as it developed. In the years prior to the drought, vegetation covered 85 percent of the surface on the short-grass prairie where no livestock grazed. As the drought progressed, the grasses began to die back and new growth failed to appear in the spring, until by 1940 plants covered only 20 percent of the surface. The composition of the grassland also changed. As some plants—other flowering herbs (forbs) as well as grasses—died back, others spread. Nevertheless, the ground was almost bare and its surface soil blew in the wind.

When the drought ended with the return of the rain in the winter of 1941–42, grasses and forbs that had not been seen for several years began to emerge above ground. Their roots or underground stems had survived in a dormant state, needing only a generous soaking to stimulate them into producing new shoots. Moreover even while dormant, those roots and underground stems (rhizomes) bound soil particles together. Soil blew from the natural prairie and produced dust storms, but much more soil blew from land where the native grasses had been removed.

Soil scientists and ecologists recognized that certain parts of the short-grass prairie should not be cultivated because of the high risk of soil erosion during the inevitable periodic droughts. These areas were left as natural prairie or sown with native species where these had been removed.

The need to improve farming practices was obvious, and in 1935 the Soil Conservation Act established the Soil Conservation Service (SCS) as a bureau of the U.S. Department of Agriculture (USDA). Hugh Hammond Bennett (1881–1960), one of the world's leading authorities on soil conservation, was the first head of the SCS. The new service directed its help and advice beyond the Great Plains to farmers throughout the nation.

Under Bennett's direction SCS advisers promoted soil conservation techniques that were traditional in Europe. Bernard Eduard Fernow (1851–1923), a German immigrant who went on to head the USDA Division of Forestry, had demonstrated them at the Cotton States International Exposition held at Atlanta, Georgia, in 1895. Fernow showed three large models that had been made according to his instructions to show the same farm under different conditions. The first model showed the erosion that followed when deforested land was farmed badly; the second showed the same land being reclaimed; and the third showed the land fully recovered and productive. Techniques to prevent soil erosion clearly existed, and Fernow published photographs of his models in the 1895 edition of the *Year Book of the United States Department of Agriculture* (now called the *Yearbook of Agriculture*). Experts also encouraged farmers to adopt dry farming methods (see the sidebar "Dry farming" on page 224).

The SCS divides the country into "soil conservation districts," and in 1956 Congress designed the Great Plains Conservation Program to help farmers and ranchers devise and apply conservation measures to reduce the risk of erosion on their own land. Under the program landowners planted rows of trees and shrubs as windbreaks to shelter land from the wind. The program also improved the efficiency of irrigation systems and the reliability of water supplies to livestock. Many of the ponds built to conserve water also contain fish. Such measures as these have enhanced the beauty of the countryside, while increasing the productivity of the land.

The drought that drove countless families from their farms generated dust clouds that filled the sky over vast areas, and created the Dust Bowl was a catastrophe of epic proportions. It demanded an effective response, and it received one. Droughts continue to occur at intervals—they are natural phenomena and inevitable—but even though they continue to generate dust storms, the damage can now be limited.

## Ranching on equatorial grasslands

Cattle ranching is widespread on land that was formerly forested in tropical South America. Ranching accounts for an estimated 44 percent of all the deforestation that occurs in the whole of the South American tropical forest and for 70 percent of the deforestation in Brazil. Since the mid-1960s approximately 58,000 square miles (150,000 km²) of Amazonian forest has been converted to grassland, mainly in southern Pará and northern Mato Grosso states.

The ranchers are descended from Spanish and Portuguese settlers, and the first cattle ranch was established in 1692, on Marajó Island, near Belém, Brazil. Far from being a recent phenomenon, ranching is deeply rooted in Hispanic culture, and there have been cattle ranches in the South American Tropics for more than three centuries.

Nor is it true that the conversion of tropical forest to cattle ranches is driven by the "hamburger connection"—the demand for cheap beef in the United States. International beef prices were high in the 1960s and early 1970s, and the United States was an important export market for South American beef during those years, but almost none of the beef was raised on deforested land. In 1982 the Amazon supplied a mere 0.0007 percent of the beef consumed in the United States, and the Amazon region never produced more than five percent of Brazilian beef. The region has been a net importer of beef in most years. Most Brazilian beef is processed before export into such products as corned beef and sausages. Beef prices fell during the 1980s, and the U.S. market became more dependent on domestic production and imports from other North American Free Trade Agreement (NAFTA) members, with the result that U.S. beef imports from the whole of Latin America have declined greatly since then.

Ranching expanded for several reasons. Land prices rose steadily for several decades in tropical Latin America, making land acquisition a sound investment, and when governments introduced settlement programs and designated particular forest areas as reserves for conservation, prices rose even faster. Buyers acquired their land from governments, and several governments made it a condition of ownership that the buyer occupy the land. This policy made deforestation a condition of land ownership. Since it was easier and cheaper to convert forest to ranch land than to plow it and grow crops, ranching became the simplest way to meet the requirement. Some governments paid subsidies for clearing forest and introducing livestock. These incentives have now ended in most countries.

Ranchers also raise dairy cattle. The smaller stock farms generally specialize in dairying and the bigger ranches in beef production.

Cleared forest was sown with pasture grasses and stocked with about one head of cattle on every two acres (1.5/ha), but after about five years there were some places where the pasture would support no more than one animal to every six acres (0.5/ha). Weeds had sprung up among the sown grass, sprouts were growing from tree stumps, and trampling by cattle had compacted the soil. Insect pests attacked the grasses, termites thrived, and birds and mammals continued to deposit weed seeds. Ranchers responded by sowing different grass species and experimenting with different stocking densities. They found that if stocking is too sparse, the weeds will proliferate, and if it is too dense, the pasture will be overgrazed and the soil damaged by trampling—also encouraging weeds. Ranchers and farmers control weeds mainly by clearing them manually and by planting braquiarao, also called brizantão (*Brachiaria brizantha*), a pasture grass that grows vigorously and suppresses weeds. Herbicides are too costly to be used extensively.

Demand for beef and dairy products is rising, and pastures must be improved if the demand is to be met with the least harm to the environment. This will require more research into the most suitable species of pasture grasses and the most efficient management techniques. Increasing the productivity of existing farms and ranches will ease the pressure on the forest. There will be less need to clear the forest to provide more land, and landowners may find they have surplus land on which they can grow crops. This process will not remove the threat of deforestation, but it will reduce it.

## Farming tropical grasslands

Tropical grasslands support large herds of grazing mammals such as buffalo, antelope, elephants, and gazelles. The Serengeti and Masai Mara are world famous for their herds of grazers and for the lions, cheetahs, hyenas, and dogs that pursue them (see "Protecting grassland species" on pages 201–204). Local people have hunted game animals throughout history, and in Africa they also graze domestic livestock—humped (zebu) cattle, sheep, and goats—on the savanna grassland.

Savanna grasslands cover two-thirds of the land area of the African continent, and although the wildlife is protected in reserves such as the Serengeti and Masai Mara, grasslands outside the reserves are under threat. The human population is increasing, and some African countries encourage people to settle on the grasslands to relieve pressure on the much smaller areas of arable farmland. The people who live on the grassland and graze their livestock there depend on their domestic animals for food and income, and they rely on the natural vegetation for plant foods, fuel, and raw materials for building and for making household items such as furniture.

The average annual rainfall is 12–28 inches (300–700 mm), making the area too dry for conventional arable farming, and most people of the African savanna lead a pastoral life. Depending on local conditions, some live as nomads, moving their livestock from one seasonal pasture to the next. Others live a more settled life, moving between winter and summer pastures. There are also ranches on the savanna, where the people have permanent homes and allow their cattle to range over a wide area. Some people grow a few crops as well as tending livestock. These ways of life are traditional, but as pressure on the grasslands has intensified, overgrazing has become a serious problem (see "Overgrazing and soil erosion" on pages 209–211).

Savanna grasslands are so extensive and so many people depend on them that ways must be found to manage them more efficiently. At present grasslands are undervalued. The fate of tropical forests is a matter of great international concern, but grasslands are largely neglected. They belong to no one and are therefore vulnerable to the "tragedy of the commons."

A development program in the Darwin-Kakadu region of northern Australia is supporting farmers as they rapidly convert the grasslands to farmland. At the time the program began in 1979 buffalo were overgrazing and causing considerable damage. Agents removed more than 100,000 buffalo from the area between 1979 and 1990, but they were not eliminated entirely. A herd of domesticated buffalo was allowed to remain, but feral buffalo entering the farmed area from outside are removed whenever they are found. Most of the area comprises small-scale beef farms; there are larger properties to the south and west. Farmers have improved the pasture and the farms now produce cattle and buffalo. They also export hay, some of which is made into pelleted feed; increasing amounts of hay go to supply the needs of those raising recreational horses, a lucrative market.

Northern Australian grasslands enjoy a moister climate than the African savanna, with rainfall averaging more than 33 inches (840 mm) a year, but it is possible to improve pasture and even to grow crops in regions with low rainfall. "Dry

# Dry farming

In the 1860s a group of Scandinavian settlers plowed the land close to what is now Bear River City, Utah, but the water they used to irrigate their crops was alkaline and their crops failed. With only poisonous water available to them, the farmers could think of only one solution: Sagebrush was growing on the land around their farms. They plowed this land, mixing the sagebrush plants into the soil as they did so; sowed their seeds; and hoped for the best. The experiment succeeded and they harvested a good crop. The settlers had devised their own version of what is now known as *dry farming.*

Researchers explored the possibilities of dry farming in greater depth at the agricultural colleges that were being established across America during the 19th century, and techniques were developed independently in Utah, California, Washington, and Colorado. After the Dust Bowl years dry farming techniques were adopted over an even wider area. Today dry farming is practiced widely in regions where rainfall is sparse and unreliable. It makes farming without irrigation possible in climates that receive less than about 12 inches (305 mm) of rain a year.

The first aim of dry farming is to conserve moisture by tilling the soil thoroughly and including a period during which the land lies fallow. Where possible the land is plowed in the fall and the seed is sown as soon as the soil has been prepared. The crop grown must tolerate dry conditions—wheat, for example, rather than potatoes. Once the crop has been harvested, the land is left fallow, commonly for three years.

An entire field may be left uncultivated, or crops may be grown in widely spaced strips separated by uncultivated strips, and cropped strips created in different locations each year. Wild plants grow on the fallow land, and from time to time these are plowed into the soil. The plants gather moisture, and plowing buries their moist tissues before they have time to lose water by transpiration. By the end of the fallow period the partly decomposed wild plants will have released sufficient moisture into the soil to sustain the next crop.

Dry farming is not unique to North America. Farmers in many parts of the world have found ways to grow crops in dry climates without irrigation.

farming" was developed on the short-grass prairie of North America (see the sidebar).

Tropical grasslands can be exploited efficiently and sustainably. Herds of wild animals use the pasture efficiently, by moving on as soon as they have eaten the most nutritious plants. Domestic livestock can be managed in the same way.

Farmers can fence off areas once they have been grazed to allow them time to recover. This practice will prevent overgrazing and the deterioration of the pasture, and it may also make it possible to improve the pasture by sowing better grasses.

American dry farming was developed on temperate grassland, but its techniques can be adapted to tropical grassland. Its disadvantage is that land must be left fallow and during its fallow period it produces nothing.

There is an alternative. This begins with planting rows of trees; on sloping ground the rows should run parallel to the contours. Acacia trees are especially suitable: They grow naturally in the semiarid tropics, surviving drought well, and they are legumes, which are plants that contribute nitrogen, an essential plant nutrient, to the soil. Once the trees are established, annual crops such as millet or corn (maize) are sown in the ground between the rows. These crops grow through the rainy season and are harvested when they ripen. The following year at the end of the dry season the farmer cuts the trees down to about three feet (1 m) above ground level. The trimmed pieces themselves are useful; small, leafy twigs can be fed to livestock and the wood provides fuel. In addition cutting the trees in this way makes them grow into small, leafy bushes and leaves room for the next annual crop, which is then sown between the rows. This farming technique, called *alley cropping* or *corridor farming,* can be sustained indefinitely. Alley cropping is not practiced everywhere, but it is becoming more popular. Its success demonstrates that farming is feasible in the semiarid Tropics.

## Grassland restoration and conservation

During the Great Depression of the 1930s, the federal government formed the Civilian Conservation Corps as one of its projects to provide employment. In 1936 the University of Wisconsin hired workers from the corps to plant prairie grasses and forbs in the University Arboretum. That was the first recorded attempt to reconstruct prairie vegetation. In 1949 workers sowed 20 acres (8 ha) of prairie plants in the Brownfields Wood Preserve of the University of Illinois, under the supervision of the eminent ecologists Victor Ernest Shelford (1877–1968) and Samuel Charles Kendeigh (1904–86). There were further plantings at the Morton Arboretum, at Lisle, Illinois, in 1963.

Almost all the original North American prairie has disappeared, but the prairie plants have survived. They grow along the sides of roads and railroads, and in graveyards. The pioneers who died on the prairie were buried in cemeteries on the prairie. Prairie grasses and flowers covered the graves, and the cemeteries, enclosed to keep out large animals, have remained undisturbed ever since. They are tiny patches of the original prairie.

The task of restoring the prairie vegetation begins by marking out the restoration site and clearing it of nonprairie plants. This process requires at least a year and often longer, because seeds present in the soil must be allowed to germinate. Meanwhile workers collect seeds from an area of surviving prairie, usually by removing a small patch of soil together with all the plants growing on it. The soil contains seeds that are lying dormant, and the bare patch left behind soon disappears as seeds from surrounding plants fall onto it and germinate. The collected seeds are stored in a refrigerator—a process called *vernalization* that breaks their dormancy.

The seeds are then sown. Sometimes the scientists raise the forbs in a greenhouse and plant them out once they are big and hardy enough to survive in the open. Weeds have to be removed by hand or cut down, usually for about the first two years, by which time the sown plants are fully established.

Fires sweep across natural grassland whenever enough dead and dry plant material has accumulated to supply fuel, and once the vegetation is growing strongly, the managers of the restoration site imitate this by firing the vegetation each spring. After a few years the vegetation is burned less frequently.

Decades later the restored vegetation closely resembles natural prairie grassland. There are many restoration sites across the prairie states and provinces, with both short-grass and tallgrass types represented. The restorations are not perfect, however. Gradually certain of the introduced plants increase in number while others decrease, but the original planting proportions can still be detected for a very long time, and in many patches of restored prairie the proportions of species are markedly different from those seen on natural prairie.

There are also fewer animals. Animals will enter of their own accord if the area is accessible to them and supplies their needs, but restored sites are like islands surrounded by oceans of entirely different vegetation types. Few prairie animals are close enough to take advantage of such opportunities as the site may offer, and the sites are too small to support any but the smaller animals.

Restoration is valuable, but it is no substitute for the "real thing." Where areas of undisturbed grassland remain, it is important to conserve them, and there are prairie reserves throughout the United States and Canada. They vary in size from the 10 acres (4 ha) of the Searles Prairie Natural Area in Benton County, Arkansas, to the 13.5 square miles (35 km$^2$) of the Konza Prairie Biosphere Reserve and 17 square miles (44 km$^2$) of the Tallgrass Prairie National Preserve, both in Flint Hills, Kansas.

Areas of natural pampa, steppe, and tropical grassland are similarly protected in reserves wherever they have escaped being plowed or heavily grazed by farm livestock. Their value is recognized. It will never be possible—or desirable—to restore the vast grasslands that once existed, but the reserves will ensure that so far as possible the grassland plants and animals survive. Some reserves achieve more, allowing visitors to imagine what it must have been like when grasslands blanketed so much of the world.

# CONCLUSION

## What future for the grasslands?

Grasslands are places of romance. The Eurasian steppe that once stretched from the Danube to the Pacific is home to Mongolian nomads and Russian Cossacks. The South American pampa is where the defiant gauchos used to ride; tribes of proud hunters once stalked the North American prairie, and cowboys rode the plains. The African savanna is the land of antelope, gazelles, elephants, and rhinoceroses and of the predators that pursue them—the lions, cheetahs, hyenas, and hunting dogs.

With their wide skies and distant horizons the grasslands appeal to our love of freedom, of space, of travel. They also remind us of the animals and grasses we depend on for food. Grasslands can be cleared and plowed much more easily than forests, and although they are found in the interior of continents where climates are fairly dry, grassland soils can be cultivated. Grasslands may border deserts, but they are not deserts. Their suitability for cultivation has caused large areas—especially of the prairie and the European steppe—to be converted to farmland. We worry about the rate at which tropical forests are being cleared, but vast expanses of grasslands were cleared much faster and long ago.

This book has described where grasslands are to be found and how, over many millions of years, the movements of continents and raising and wearing away of mountain chains have produced the grassland landscapes and soils. It explains why grassland climates are dry and why sometimes they are violent, and it outlines the way grasslands have developed.

Grass is so commonplace, so ordinary, that we tend to take it for granted and look instead at the plants that bear brightly colored and sweetly perfumed flowers. "My love is like a red, red rose," wrote Robert Burns, the Scottish national poet.

He did not write, "My love is like a blade of grass." Yet the apparent simplicity of grass is misleading. It is a highly evolved, complex plant that belongs to a family (Poaceae) of some 9,000 species that thrive everywhere from the equator to inside the Arctic Circle and from the edge of the desert to the edge of the ocean. Among them the grasses harbor many other flowering plants, and together the plants support a diverse population of animals. Grasslands teem with life, including human life, for they support human populations and the livestock on which they depend.

The cereals that are our staple foods are grasses. Bread, the "staff of life," is made from the modern cultivated descendant of grasses that to this day grow wild in parts of Turkey and Iraq. Rice, domesticated in India and China, is also a grass, and so is corn, domesticated in Central America. It is no wonder that our ancestors plowed up so much of the natural grassland in order to grow grasses that produce edible seeds.

Farmers took over large areas of grassland, but they also cleared forests to make farmland, especially in western Europe and the eastern United States, using some of the land they cleared to grow cereals and some to grow pasture grasses for their livestock. In doing this they were converting forest to a type of artificial grassland.

Modern farming is highly productive. Farmers are now capable of growing such an abundance of food that politicians worry about the cost of storing the surpluses. But high productivity reduces the pressure on farmland, and that means some land can be taken out of farming and used for other purposes, such as conservation. Where the landscape was originally grassland, fields that are no longer required to grow food may be restored to something approaching their original state.

Restoring natural grassland is possible, but it is not a simple operation and it takes a long time. Fortunately the original plants have survived even where the land has been cultivated for generations. They cling to life as "weeds" growing on untended ground beside roads and railroads, and in other places where they are left undisturbed, providing a reservoir of plants and seeds from which the natural grassland can be slowly reconstructed. Larger areas of natural grassland are now protected in reserves. Much has gone, but not all.

We depend on grassland. It feeds us. It also inspires us. We must guard jealously those areas that remain and restore the wild grasslands where we can. We must make sure that into the far distant future people will still be able to gaze upon it and experience something of the world their ancestors once knew.

# SI UNITS AND CONVERSIONS

| UNIT | QUANTITY | SYMBOL | CONVERSION |
|------|----------|--------|------------|
| **Base units** | | | |
| meter | length | m | 1 m = 3.2808 feet |
| kilogram | mass | kg | 1 kg = 2.205 pounds |
| second | time | s | |
| ampere | electric current | A | |
| kelvin | thermodynamic temperature | K | 1 K = 1°C = 1.8°F |
| candela | luminous intensity | | |
| mole | amount of substance | cd | mol |
| **Supplementary units** | | | |
| radian | plane angle | rad | π/2 rad = 90° |
| steradian | solid angle | sr | |
| **Derived units** | | | |
| coulomb | quantity of electricity | C | |
| cubic meter | volume | m$^3$ | 1 m$^3$ = 1.308 yards$^3$ |
| farad | capacitance | F | |
| henry | inductance | H | |
| hertz | frequency | Hz | |
| joule | energy | J | 1 J = 0.2389 calories |
| kilogram per cubic meter | density | kg m$^{-3}$ | 1 kg m$^{-3}$ = 0.0624 lb. ft.$^{-3}$ |
| lumen | luminous flux | lm | |
| lux | illuminance | lx | |

*(continues)*

231

*(continued)*

| UNIT | QUANTITY | SYMBOL | CONVERSION |
|------|----------|--------|------------|
| meter per second | speed | m s$^{-1}$ | 1 m s$^{-1}$ = 3.281 ft s$^{-1}$ |
| meter per second squared | acceleration | m s$^{-2}$ | |
| mole per cubic meter | concentration | mol m$^{-3}$ | |
| newton | force | N | 1 N = 7.218 lb. force |
| ohm | electric resistance | Ω | |
| pascal | pressure | Pa | 1 Pa = 0.145 lb. in$^{-2}$ |
| radian per second | angular velocity | rad s$^{-1}$ | |
| radian per second squared | angular acceleration | rad s$^{-2}$ | |
| square meter | area | m$^2$ | 1 m$^2$ = 1.196 yards$^2$ |
| tesla | magnetic flux density | T | |
| volt | electromotive force | V | |
| watt | power | W | 1W = 3.412 Btu h$^{-1}$ |
| weber | magnetic flux | Wb | |

## Prefixes used with SI units

| PREFIX | SYMBOL | VALUE |
|--------|--------|-------|
| atto | a | × 10$^{-18}$ |
| femto | f | × 10$^{-15}$ |
| pico | p | × 10$^{-12}$ |
| nano | n | × 10$^{-9}$ |
| micro | μ | × 10$^{-6}$ |
| milli | m | × 10$^{-3}$ |
| centi | c | × 10$^{-2}$ |
| deci | d | × 10$^{-1}$ |
| deca | da | × 10 |
| hecto | h | × 10$^2$ |
| kilo | k | × 10$^3$ |
| mega | M | × 10$^6$ |

| PREFIX | SYMBOL | VALUE |
|--------|--------|-------|
| giga | G | $\times 10^9$ |
| tera | T | $\times 10^{12}$ |

Prefixes attached to SI units alter their value.

# SOIL CLASSIFICATION: ORDERS OF THE SOIL TAXONOMY

**Entisols**   Soils with weakly developed horizons, such as disturbed soils and soils developed over alluvial (river) deposits.

**Vertisols**   Soils with more than 30 percent clay that crack when dry.

**Inceptisols**   Soils with a composition that changes little with depth, such as young soils.

**Aridisols**   Soils with large amounts of salt, such as desert soils.

**Mollisols**   Soils with some horizons rich in organic matter.

**Spodosols**   Soils rich in organic matter, iron, and aluminum; in older classifications known as a podzol.

**Alfisols**   Basic soils in which surface constituents have moved to a lower level.

**Ultisols**   Acid soils in which surface constituents have moved to a lower level.

**Oxisols**   Soils rich in iron and aluminum oxides that have lost most of their nutrients through weathering; old soils often found in the humid Tropics.

**Histosols**   Soils rich in organic matter.

## Reference Soil Groups of the Food and Agriculture Organization of the United Nations (FAO)

**Histosols**   Soils with a peat layer more than 15.75 inches (40 cm) deep.

**Cryosols**   Soils with a permanently frozen layer within 39 inches (100 cm) of the surface.

**Anthrosols**   Soils that have been strongly affected by human activity.

**Leptosols**   Soils with hard rock within 10 inches (25 cm) of the surface, or more than 40 percent calcium carbonate within 10 inches (25 cm) of the surface, or less than 10 percent of fine earth to a depth of 30 inches (75 cm) or more.

**Vertisols**   Soil with a layer more than 20 inches (50 cm) deep containing more than 30 percent clay within 39 inches (100 cm) of the surface.

**Fluvisols**   Soils formed on river (alluvial) deposits with volcanic deposits within 10 inches (25 cm) of the surface and extending to a depth of more than 20 inches (50 cm).

**Solonchaks**   Soils with a salt-rich layer more than six inches (15 cm) thick at or just below the surface.

**Gleysols**   Soils with a sticky, bluish gray layer (gley) within 20 inches (50 cm) of the surface.

**Andosols**   Volcanic soils having a layer more than 12 inches (30 cm) deep containing more than 10 percent volcanic glass or other volcanic material within 10 inches (25 cm) of the surface.

**Podzols**   Pale soils with a layer containing organic material and/or iron and aluminum that has washed down from above.

**Plinthosols**   Soils with a layer more than six inches (15 cm) deep containing more than 25 percent iron and aluminum sesquioxides (oxides comprising two parts of the metal to three parts of oxygen) within 20 inches (50 cm) of the surface that hardens when exposed.

**Ferralsols**   Soils with a subsurface layer more than six inches (15 cm) deep with red mottling due to iron and aluminum.

**Solonetz**   Soils with a sodium- and clay-rich subsurface layer more than three inches (7.5 cm) deep.

**Planosols**   Soils that have had stagnant water within 40 inches (100 cm) of the surface for prolonged periods.

**Chernozems**   Soils with a dark-colored, well-structured, basic surface layer at least eight inches (20 cm) deep.

**Kastanozems**   Soils resembling chernozems, but with concentrations of calcium compounds within 40 inches (100 cm) of the surface.

**Phaeozems**   All other soils with a dark-colored, well structured, basic surface layer.

**Gypsisols**   Soils with a layer rich in gypsum (calcium sulfate) within 40 inches (100 cm) of the surface, or more than 15 percent gypsum in a layer more than 40 inches (100 cm) deep.

**Durisols**   Soils with a layer of cemented silica within 40 inches (100 cm) of the surface.

**Calcisols**   Soils with concentrations of calcium carbonate within 50 inches (125 cm) of the surface.

**Albeluvisols**   Soils with a subsurface layer rich in clay that has an irregular upper surface.

**Alisols**   Slightly acid soils containing high concentrations of aluminum and with a clay-rich layer within 40 inches (100 cm) of the surface.

**Nitisols**   Soils with a layer containing more than 30 percent clay more than 12 inches (30 cm) deep and no evidence of clay particles moving to lower levels within 40 inches (100 cm) of the surface.

**Acrisols**   Acid soils with a clay-rich subsurface layer.

**Luvisols**   Soils with a clay-rich subsurface layer containing clay particles that have moved down from above.

**Lixisols**   All other soils with a clay-rich layer within 40–80 inches (100–200 cm) of the surface.

**Umbrisols**   Soils with a thick, dark colored, acid surface layer.

**Cambisols**   Soils with an altered surface layer or one that is thick and dark colored, above a subsoil that is acid in the upper 40 inches (100 cm) and with a clay-rich or volcanic layer beginning 10–40 inches (25–100 cm) below the surface.

**Arenosols**   Weakly developed soils with a coarse texture.

**Regosols**   All other soils.

*Note:* A *basic* or alkaline soil is one containing more hydroxyl ions (OH⁻) than hydrogen ions (H⁺); an *acid* soil contains more H⁺ ions than OH⁻ ions. Acidity is measured on the pH scale, a logarithmic scale expressing the activity of H⁺ ions in solution, where pH 7.0 is a neutral reaction. A basic soil has a pH greater than 7.0; an acid soil has a pH lower than 7.0.

# GLOSSARY

**active margin**   a boundary between two tectonic plates (*see* PLATE TECTONICS) that are moving in relation to one another, producing earthquakes and volcanism

**adiabatic**   a change in temperature that involves no exchange of heat with an outside source

**adventitious**   arising from an unusual part of the plant. Roots that emerge from NODES are said to be adventitious

**air mass**   a large body of air, covering most of a continent or ocean and extending to the TROPOPAUSE, in which atmospheric conditions are fairly constant throughout

**alga**   an organism (a protist) that performs PHOTOSYNTHESIS; it may be single celled or multicelled. Seaweeds are algae

**alley cropping (corridor farming)**   a farming system in which annual crops are planted between rows of trees and the trees are regularly cropped to provide wood and food for livestock

**alpine meadow**   grassland that grows above the TREE LINE on mountainsides

**alpine savanna**   grassland that grows above the TREE LINE on tropical mountainsides, with vegetation related to that of SAVANNA

**angiosperm**   a flowering plant

**angular momentum**   a physical property of any body that is rotating about an axis. It is proportional to the mass of the body, its rate of rotation (called its angular velocity), and its radius of rotation

**angular velocity**   *see* ANGULAR MOMENTUM

**annual**   a plant that completes its life cycle in a single year

**anticyclone**   a region in which the atmospheric pressure is higher than it is in the surrounding air

**apomixis**   a form of plant reproduction that resembles sexual reproduction but does not involve fertilization and is therefore asexual. The progeny of apomixis are clones of their parent

**aquifer**   an underground body of permeable material (such as sand or gravel) lying above a layer of impermeable material (such as rock or clay) that is capable of storing water and through which the GROUNDWATER flows

**asthenosphere**   the upper part of the MANTLE, in which the rocks are slightly plastic and deform under pressure

**awn**   a hooked or barbed bristle at the tip of a grass GLUME

**axil**   the angle where a leaf joins the stem or a small branch joins a larger one

**Beltian body**   an organ at the tip of the leaves of some acacias that produces oils and proteins as food for ants

**biennial**   a plant that lives for two years, storing nutrient during its first year and producing flowers and seeds in the second

**biodiesel**   a fuel made from plant oils that can be used in diesel engines

**biofuel**   a fuel made from plants grown for the purpose or products derived from such plants

**biogas**   automobile fuel made from ETHANOL or a mixture of gasoline and ethanol

**biomass**   the total mass of all the living organisms present in a given area

**biome**   the largest biological community recognized, comprising of a type of vegetation (such as grassland) together with the other organisms associated with it, occupying a large geographical area

**blade**   the leaf of a grass plant

**bolas**   a South American hunting weapon, consisting of three cords joined together at one end and weighted at the other. When thrown, it tangles itself around the legs of the prey, causing the animal to fall

**bract**   a modified leaf that forms part of a flower

**brigalow**   *Acacia harpophylla,* an Australian shrub

**bunchgrass prairie**   *see* PALOUSE PRAIRIE

**bundle-sheath cells**   cells packed tightly around the leaf veins of $C_4$ PLANTS, where carbon enters the light-independent stage of PHOTOSYNTHESIS

**bushveld**   a region of dry, savanna-type vegetation in southern Africa

**$C_3$ plant**   a plant that uses a pathway of PHOTOSYNTHESIS in which the first product in the light-independent stage is 3-phosphoglycerate, a compound with three carbon atoms in each molecule

**$C_4$ plant**   a plant that uses a pathway of PHOTOSYNTHESIS in which the first product in the light-independent stage is oxaloacetate, a compound with four carbon atoms in each molecule

**campo cerrado** a type of SAVANNA grassland found in Brazil with scattered trees and shrubs and patches of woodland

**campo limpo** open SAVANNA grassland with no trees, found in Brazil

**campo sujo** a type of SAVANNA grassland, with trees, found in Brazil

**cap** a thin, impermeable layer on the surface of soil, produced by heavy rain falling on bare ground

**capillarity (capillary attraction)** the movement of water against gravity through a fine tube or narrow passageway

**capillary attraction** *see* CAPILLARITY

**capillary fringe** the region immediately above the WATER TABLE into which water rises by CAPILLARITY

**cerradão** woodland found in the SAVANNA regions of Brazil

**cerrado** SAVANNA grasslands found in Brazil

**chlorophyll** the pigment present in the leaves and sometimes stems of green plants that gives them their green color. Chlorophyll molecules trap light, thus supplying the energy for PHOTOSYNTHESIS

**chloroplast** the structure in plant cells that contains CHLORO-PHYLL and in which PHOTOSYNTHESIS takes place

**cloudburst** a brief but very heavy shower of rain that occurs when the currents of rising air in a storm cloud are suppressed and the cloud starts to dissipate, releasing all of its water

**consumer** an organism that obtains nourishment by ingesting other organisms

**continental drift** the movement of the continents in relation to one another across the Earth's surface

**convection** the transfer of heat by vertical movement within a fluid

**cordillera** a mountain range formed by the collision between an oceanic plate and a continental plate (*see* PLATE TECTONICS)

**Coriolis effect** the deflection due to the Earth's rotation experienced by bodies moving in relation to the Earth's surface; bodies are deflected to the right in the Northern Hemisphere and to the left in the Southern Hemisphere

**corridor farming** *see* ALLEY CROPPING

**coterie** a group of prairie dogs living together

**cotyledon** a seed leaf; the leaf that emerges from a germinating seed

**culm** the stem of a grass plant

**cyclone**	*see* DEPRESSION

**decomposer**	an organism that feeds on dead plant and animal material, thereby breaking down complex organic molecules into simpler ones

**deposition**	the changing of water vapor directly to ice, without passing through a liquid phase

**depression (cyclone)**	a region along a weather FRONT where the atmospheric pressure is lower than it is in the surrounding air

**detritivore**	an organism that feeds on DETRITUS

**detritus**	fragments of dead plant and animal material that form a layer on the surface of the ground

**dew-point temperature**	the temperature at which water vapor condenses to form dew or cloud droplets

**dicot (dicotyledon)**	a plant that produces seeds containing two COTYLEDONS

**dicotyledon**	*see* DICOT

**dry farming**	a farming method developed for semiarid conditions that conserves soil moisture

**dry-steppe**	STEPPE grassland in which the ground is dry most of the year

**ecological pyramid**	a diagram representing feeding relationships within an *ecosystem* as a series of bands, all the same thickness but varying in width, with PRODUCERS at the base and *consumers* stacked above them

**ecology**	the scientific study of the relationships among organisms inhabiting a specified area and between the organisms and the physical and chemical conditions in which they live

**ecosystem**	a clearly defined area or unit within which living organisms and their physical and chemical surroundings interact to form a stable system

**ectotherm**	an animal that maintains a fairly constant body temperature by behavioral means, such as basking in warm sunshine and seeking shade

**El Niño**	a weakening or reversal of the prevailing easterly winds over the tropical South Pacific Ocean that happens at intervals of two to seven years. This weakens the wind-driven surface ocean current, allowing warm water to accumulate off the South American coast and producing weather changes over a large area

**embryo**	a young plant contained within a plant seed, or a young animal contained within a fertilized egg or other reproductive structure (in humans an embryo is called a fetus after the first eight weeks of pregnancy)

**endotherm**   an animal that maintains a constant body core temperature by physiological means, such as by dilating or contracting blood vessels in the skin, shivering, and sweating

**ENSO**   the full cycle of El Niño and its opposite, La Niña, associated with the SOUTHERN OSCILLATION

**environmental lapse rate**   the rate, in degrees Fahrenheit or Celsius per 1,000 feet or per kilometer, at which the atmospheric temperature decreases with increasing altitude

**equinox**   March 20–21 and September 22–23, when the noonday Sun is directly overhead at the equator and day and night are of equal length everywhere in the world

**estancia**   a South American cattle ranch

**estivation**   a period of dormancy into which an animal enters to escape a period of hot or dry weather

**ethanol (ethyl alcohol)**   $CH_3CH_2OH$, the alcohol produced by the fermentation of sugar; it is the alcohol used in *biogas* as well as in alcoholic drinks

**ethyl alcohol**   *see* ETHANOL

**exotherm**   *see* POIKILOTHERM

**Ferrel cell**   the midlatitude part of the general circulation of the atmosphere lying between the HADLEY CELL and POLAR CELL. Air rises at the boundary between tropical and polar air, flows toward the equator at high altitude, subsides in the subtropics, and flows away from the equator at low level

**floret**   *see* INFLORESCENCE

**food chain**   a set of feeding relationships in which each in a sequence of organisms feeds on the preceding member

**food web**   a diagram that shows the inhabitants of an ECOSYSTEM linked by lines between species and the species on which they feed: that is, a series of FOOD CHAINS

**forb**   a herbaceous plant other than a grass

**forest limit**   *see* TREE LINE

**forest-steppe**   STEPPE grassland with scattered trees that borders the TAIGA

**front**   the boundary between two AIR MASSES

**funnel cloud**   a narrow, funnel-shaped cloud that forms beneath a storm cloud; if the funnel cloud touches the ground, it becomes a TORNADO

**gametangium**   the organ in fungi, mosses, ferns, and some ALGAE in which sex cells (GAMETES) are formed

**gamete**   a sex cell: that is, a spermatozoon or ovum

**gaucho**   one of the horsemen of the PAMPA, equivalent to the North American cowboy

**ger (yurt, yurta)**    the traditional dwelling of Mongolian nomads, consisting of a wooden frame usually covered with felt

**glacial**    a period when polar ice sheets advance; an ice age

**glume**    one of the two lowest BRACTS on a grass SPIKELET

**gluten**    a mixture of two proteins (gliadin and glutenin) found in wheat flour

**grassveld**    *see* VELD

**greenhouse effect**    the absorption and reradiation of long-wave radiation emitted by the Earth's surface by molecules of water vapor, carbon dioxide, ozone, and several other "greenhouse gases," warming the air

**groundwater**    underground water that flows through an AQUIFER

**gymnosperm**    a seed plant in which the OVULES are carried naked on the scales of a cone. Coniferous (cone-bearing) trees are the most abundant gymnosperms

**Hadley cell**    the tropical part of the general circulation of the atmosphere. Air rises over the equator, moves away from the equator at high altitude, subsides over the subtropics, and flows toward the equator at low altitude

**hail streak**    a strip of ground that is completely covered by fallen hailstones

**hefted**    description of a domestic animal raised in open country that will not move outside the boundaries of its owner's land

**hibernation**    a state of dormancy into which an animal enters to avoid a period of winter cold

**homeotherm**    an animal that maintains a constant body core temperature by either behavioral (an ECTOTHERM) or physiological (an ENDOTHERM) means

**hooked trades**    the change in direction of the TRADE WINDS between the equator and the INTERTROPICAL CONVERGENCE ZONE

**igneous rock**    a rock formed when molten MAGMA cools and solidifies

**inflorescence**    a mass of small but complete flowers (called florets) growing together and giving the appearance of a single flower. Sunflower and grass "flowers" are inflorescences

**interglacial**    a period of warmer weather between two GLACIALS

**internode**    the part of a plant stem between two NODES

**Intertropical Convergence Zone (ITCZ)**    the region where the TRADE WINDS from the Northern and Southern Hemisphere meet (converge)

**island-hopping**   migrating across an ocean by moving from island to island

**isostasy**   the theory that there is a constant mass of rocks above a certain level below the Earth's surface. If the volume of rock is greater in one place than in another, for instance, forming a mountain, then its density will be less dense than that of the thinner crust beneath

**ITCZ**   *see* INTERTROPICAL CONVERGENCE ZONE

**La Niña**   the opposite of EL NIÑO; a strengthening of the TRADE WINDS and east-to-west ocean currents producing sea surface temperatures that are warmer than usual in the western tropical South Pacific Ocean and cooler in the east

**lapse rate**   the rate at which the air temperature decreases (lapses) with increasing altitude. In unsaturated air the dry ADIABATIC lapse rate is 5.38°F per 1,000 feet (9.8°C/km); in saturated air the saturated adiabatic lapse rate varies but averages 2.75°F per 1,000 feet (5°C/km)

**latent heat**   the heat energy that is absorbed or released when a substance changes phase between solid and liquid, liquid and gas, or solid and gas. For water at 32°F (0°C) the latent heat of melting and freezing is 80 calories per gram (334 J/g); that of vaporization and condensation is 600 calories per gram (2,501 J/g); and that of SUBLIMATION and DEPOSITION is 680 calories per gram (2,835 J/g)

**laterite**   a rock rich in oxides and hydroxides, chiefly of iron and aluminum, found in lumps or a continuous layer in some tropical soils

**lek**   an area in which male birds display, competing to attract females for mating

**lemma**   the lower of the two BRACTS beneath each floret of a grass INFLORESCENCE

**ley**   temporary grassland, where pasture grass is grown as a crop and the ground is plowed and resown every few years

**lifting condensation level**   the altitude at which the air is at the DEW-POINT TEMPERATURE and water vapor begins to condense to form cloud; the lifting condensation level marks the cloud base

**ligule**   a membrane, in some grass species reduced to a few hairs, that covers the surface of a plant leaf

**lithosphere**   the uppermost part of the solid Earth, comprising the crust and upper MANTLE

**llanero**   one of the horsemen of the LLANOS, equivalent to the GAUCHO of the PAMPA

**llanos**    the SAVANNA grassland of Venezuela

**magma**    hot, molten rock from the base of the Earth's crust and the upper part of the MANTLE

**mallee**    grassland with dense eucalyptus thickets found in the south of Australia

**mantle**    that part of the Earth's interior lying between the outer edge of the inner core and the underside of the crust

**meadow-steppe**    STEPPE grassland lying to the south of the FOREST-STEPPE, where the climate is more moist

**meristem**    plant tissue composed of cells that are capable of dividing indefinitely

**mesa**    a wide, flat-topped hill

**mesocyclone**    a mass of air that is rotating inside a large storm cloud

**mesophyll**    the tissue lying just below the surface of a leaf, where PHOTOSYNTHESIS takes place

**metamorphic rock**    rock composed of minerals that crystallized when preexisting rock melted and cooled

**methanol (wood alcohol)**    $CH_2OH$, a colorless liquid produced from wood or from natural gas that can be used as a fuel in automobile engines

**microbivore**    an organism that feeds on microorganisms

**mitochondria (sing. mitochondrion)**    a body (organelle) present in large numbers in every fungal, plant, and animal cell, which is responsible for releasing energy by the process of RESPIRATION

**mitochondrial DNA (mtDNA)**    DNA (deoxyribonucleic acid) contained in MITOCHONDRIA. Only the nuclear DNA from the sperm enters an egg at fertilization. Consequently mtDNA is transmitted only from mothers to their offspring

**mitochondrion**    *see* MITOCHONDRIA

**monocot (monocotyledon)**    a plant that produces seeds containing only one COTYLEDON

**monocotyledon**    *see* MONOCOT

**monsoon**    a reversal in wind direction that occurs twice a year over much of the Tropics, producing two seasons with markedly different weather

**mtDNA**    *see* MITOCHONDRIAL DNA

**mulga**    *Acacia aneura,* a species of acacia that grows in one type of Australian grassland

**nectary**    a plant gland that secretes nectar

**node**    the point at which a leaf attaches to the plant stem

**occluded front**   *see* OCCLUSION

**occlusion (occluded front)**   the stage in the life cycle of a frontal weather system at which advancing cold air has pushed beneath warmer air and begun to lift the warm air clear of the surface

**ovule**   the structure in ANGIOSPERMS and GYMNOSPERMS that develops into the seed after fertilization

**palouse prairie (bunchgrass prairie)**   the type of vegetation found to the west of the Rocky Mountains from Colorado to Oregon and northward to British Columbia, and in part of California

**pampa**   the temperate grassland of South America

**Pangaea**   the SUPERCONTINENT that came into existence about 260 million years ago and began to break apart about 220 million years ago

**pantanal**   the world's largest continental area of wetland, situated in the CERRADO of Brazil

**Panthalassa**   the world ocean that surrounded PANGAEA

**pastoralism**   the way of life of people whose most important possessions are their livestock and who travel with their animals between areas of seasonal grazing

**perennial**   a plant that lives for more than two years

**permafrost**   permanently frozen ground. To become permafrost the ground must remain frozen throughout a minimum of two winters and the summer between

**permeability**   the capacity of a material to allow water to flow through it

**petiole**   the stalk that attaches a leaf to the stem of a plant

**pheromone**   a scent released by an animal as a signal to another animal, usually of the same species

**phloem**   tissue through which the products of photosynthesis and hormones are transported from the leaves to all parts of a VASCULAR PLANT

**photorespiration**   a reaction in which RUBISCO, the enzyme responsible for capturing carbon dioxide during PHOTOSYNTHESIS, instead captures oxygen, triggering a chain of reactions that release carbon dioxide but without releasing any energy

**photosynthesis**   the sequence of chemical reactions in which green plants and cyanobacteria use sunlight as a source of energy for the manufacture (synthesis) of sugars from hydrogen and carbon, obtained from water and carbon dioxide, respectively. The reactions can be summarized as

$$6CO_2 + 6H_2O + light \rightarrow C_6H_{12}O_6 + 6O_2 \uparrow$$

The upward arrow indicates that oxygen is released into the air; $C_6H_{12}O_6$ is glucose, a simple sugar

**plane of the ecliptic**   the imaginary disk with the Sun at its center and the Earth's orbital path around the Sun as its circumference

**plasmodesmata**   passages in the MESOPHYLL of plants through which passes the initial four-carbon compound in the $C_4$ pathway of PHOTOSYNTHESIS

**plate**   *see* PLATE TECTONICS

**plate tectonics**   the theory holding that the Earth's crust consists of a number of rigid sections, or plates, that move in relation to one another

**poikilotherm (exotherm)**   an animal that is unable to control its body CORE TEMPERATURE, which is therefore equal to the temperature of its surroundings

**polar molecule**   a molecule in which there is some separation of the charge on its atomic nuclei and electrons, giving the molecule a small positive charge on one side and a small negative charge on the other side. The two charges balance, so the molecule carries no net charge.

**porosity**   the percentage of the total volume of a material that consists of spaces between particles

**potential evaporation**   the amount of water that would evaporate if the supply of water were unlimited

**prairie**   the temperate grasslands of North America

**predator**   an organism that obtains energy by consuming, and usually killing, another organism

**pride**   the collective name for a group of lions

**producer**   an organism that synthesizes food from simple compounds. Green plants and certain bacteria are producers

**pronking**   jumping high into the air several times in succession. Some species of antelope and gazelle pronk when they observe a predator, probably to warn it that they have seen it and will escape, so it should abandon its pursuit

**puszta**   the Hungarian part of the STEPPE grassland

**rachilla**   the axis of the SPIKELET of a grass INFLORESCENCE

**relative humidity**   the amount of water vapor present in air at a particular temperature, expressed as the percentage of the water vapor needed to saturate the air at that temperature

**respiration** the sequence of chemical reactions in which carbon in sugar is oxidized with the release of energy; the opposite of PHOTOSYNTHESIS. The reactions can be summarized as

$$C_6H_{12}O_6 + 6O_2 \rightarrow 6CO_2 + 6H_2O + energy$$

$C_6H_{12}O_6$ is glucose, a simple sugar

**rhizome** a horizontal underground stem

**rubisco** the enzyme ribulose biphosphate carboxylase that catalyzes the reaction attaching molecules of carbon dioxide from the air to molecules of ribulose biphosphate at the start of the light-independent stage of PHOTOSYNTHESIS

**savanna** tropical grassland with varying densities of drought-resistant trees and shrubs

**seafloor spreading** the theory that the ocean floor is created at ridges where MANTLE material rises to the surface and the crustal rocks move away from the ridges on each side, causing the ocean basin to widen as the seafloor spreads

**sedimentary rock** rock formed from particles eroded from preexisting rock, often mixed with organic debris, that have settled onto a surface, usually on the seabed, where they have been compressed

**seed** the body, formed from a fertilized ovule, from which a young plant emerges

**sidereal day** the time the Earth takes to complete one rotation on its axis, measured in relation to the fixed stars; it is 4.09 minutes shorter than the rotational time measured with respect to the Sun (the solar day)

**soil erosion** the loss of soil particles through the action of wind and/or surface water

**soil horizon** a horizontal layer in a SOIL PROFILE that differs in its mineral or organic composition from the layers above and below it, and from which it can be clearly distinguished visually

**soil profile** a vertical section cut through a soil from the surface to the underlying rock

**soil solution** the liquid that moves through the soil and from which plants obtain nutrients; it is water into which mineral compounds have dissolved

**solar day** *see* SIDEREAL DAY

**solstice** one of the two dates each year when the noonday Sun is directly overhead at one or other of the Tropics and the difference in length between the hours of daylight and darkness is at its most extreme. The solstices occur on June 21–22 and December 22–23

**Southern Oscillation**   a change that occurs periodically in the distribution of surface atmospheric pressure over the equatorial South Pacific Ocean

**spikelet**   the basic unit of a grass INFLORESCENCE

**spore**   a reproductive unit, usually consisting of a single cell, that can develop into a new organism without fusing with another cell

**squall line**   a series of storms that merge to form a continuous line that advances at right angles to the line

**steppe**   the temperate grasslands of Eurasia

**stolon**   a stem that runs horizontally across the ground surface

**stoma (pl. stomata)**   a small opening, or pore, on the surface of a plant leaf through which the plant cells exchange gases with the outside air. Stomata can be opened or closed by the expansion or contraction of two guard cells surrounding each stoma

**stomata**   *see* STOMA

**stratosphere**   the region of the atmosphere that extends from the TROPOPAUSE to an altitude of about 31 miles (50 km)

**subduction**   the movement of one crustal plate beneath another, returning the crustal rock to the Earth's MANTLE

**sublimation**   the direct change of phase from solid to gas without passing through the liquid phase

**successional grassland**   grassland that is maintained by suppressing trees and shrubs, usually by means of burning or grazing

**supercontinent**   a landmass formed by the merging of previously separate continents as a result of CONTINENTAL DRIFT. PANGAEA was a supercontinent comprising all the present-day continents

**supercooled droplets**   water droplets that have cooled to below freezing temperature without solidifying

**taiga**   the conifer forest forming a belt across northern North America and Eurasia

**teleconnections**   climatic effects produced by events a long distance away, such as drought in Australia and northeastern China and wet weather in much of the United States caused by EL NIÑO

**tepee**   a temporary dwelling used by Native Americans and consisting of three or four long poles covered with bison skins to make a tent

**thermal equator**   the line around the Earth where the temperature is highest. It moves with the seasons, but its average location is at about 5°N

**tiller**   a shoot arising at ground level beside the main CULM of a grass plant

**timberline**   *see* TREE LINE

**tornado**   a rapidly spinning spiral of air that descends as a column from a large storm cloud

**torpor**   a condition certain animals enter to avoid extreme heat. They lose consciousness, their breathing and heartbeat slow, and their temperature rises

**township**   a number of steppe-marmot colonies linked by tunnels

**trade winds**   the winds that blow toward the equator in equatorial regions, from the northeast in the Northern Hemisphere and from the southeast in the Southern Hemisphere

**transhumance**   a livestock farming system in which animals spend the winter in the valleys and in spring herders drive them to upland pastures, where both animals and people remain until the end of summer

**transpiration**   the evaporation of water through leaf STOMATA when these are open for the exchange of gases

**tree line (timberline, forest limit)**   the elevation or latitude beyond which the climate is too severe for trees to grow

**trophic**   pertaining to food or feeding

**tropopause**   the boundary separating the TROPOSPHERE from the STRATOSPHERE. It occurs at an altitude of about 10 miles (16 km) over the equator, seven miles (11 km) in middle latitudes, and five miles (8 km) over the North and South Poles

**troposphere**   the layer of the atmosphere that extends from the surface to the TROPOPAUSE; it is the region where all weather phenomena occur

**upwelling**   a movement of water, in a lake or ocean, that carries cold water, rich in nutrients, from near the bottom to the surface. Upwelling is caused by wind

**vascular plant**   a plant possessing PHLOEM and XYLEM tissue through which water and nutrients are transported

**veld (grassveld)**   the temperate grassland of southern Africa

**water table**   the upper margin of the GROUNDWATER; soil is fully saturated below the water table but unsaturated above it

**weathering**   the breaking down of rocks by physical and chemical processes

**wind shear**    a change in the speed or direction of the wind with horizontal or vertical distance

**wood alcohol**    *see* METHANOL

**xylem**    plant tissue through which water entering at the roots is transported to all parts of the plant

**yurt**    *see* GER

**yurta**    *see* GER

# BIBLIOGRAPHY AND FURTHER READING

The African Conservation Foundation. "Profile on South Africa." Available online. URL: http://www.africanconservation.com/southafricaprofile.html. Accessed September 4, 2003.

Allaby, Michael. *Dangerous Weather: Floods*. Rev. ed. New York: Facts On File, 2003.

Australian National Botanic Gardens Education Service, Australian Government, Department of the Environment and Heritage. "Kangaroo Grass." Available online. URL: http://www.anbg.gov.au/aborig.s.e.aust/themeda-triandra.html. Accessed September 4, 2003.

Blue Planet Biomes. "Bermuda Grass." Available online. URL: http://www.blueplanetbiomes.org/bermuda_grass.htm. Accessed September 4, 2003.

———. "Ombu." Available online. URL: http://www.blueplanetbiomes.org/ombu.htm. Accessed August 29, 2003.

———. "The Pampas." Available online. URL: http://www.blueplanetbiomes.org/pampas.htm. Accessed August 29, 2003.

———. "Pampas Grass." Available online. URL: http://www.blueplanetbiomes.org/pampas_grass.htm. Accessed August 29, 2003.

Brewer, Richard. *The Science of Ecology*. 2d ed. Fort Worth: Saunders College Publishing, 1994.

Byrnes, Rita M., ed. "A Country Study: South Africa (Physical Setting)." Federal Research Division, Library of Congress, Available online. URL: http://leweb2loc.gov/cgi-bin/query/r?cstdy:@field (DOCID+200045). Last updated May 1996.

Chappell, Christopher B., and Jimmy Kagan. "Wildlife-Habitat Type Definitions. No. 10. Alpine Grassland and Shrublands." Interactive Biodiversity Information System, Available online. URL: http://www.nwhi.org/ibis/queries/wildhabs/WHDF_H10.asp. Accessed September 5, 2003.

Ciannamea, Nicolai. "Transhumance," Masseria Canestrello: The Gate of Apulia and Basilicata, Available online. URL: http://www.masseriacanestrello.it/english/pagine_web_eng/transhumance.htm. Accessed April 29, 2005.

Cobbett, William. *Rural Rides*. 1830. Reprint, Harmondsworth, U.K.: Penguin, 1967.

Collins, Russ. "The Transhumance." ProvenceBeyond (Beyond the French Riviera). Available online. URL: http://www.beyond. fr/themes/transhumance.html. Accessed September 5, 2003.

Conservation International. "Biodiversity Hotspots: Brazilian Cerrado." Available online. URL: http://www.biodiversityhotspots. org/xp/Hotspots/cerrado/?showpage=Biodiversity. Accessed September 2, 2003.

Department of the Environment and Heritage, Australian Government, Department of the Environment and Heritage, "Insight into Habitat Diversity and Threatened Species." Available online. URL: http://www.deh.gov.au/biodiversity/ threatened/publications/insight/index.html. Last updated December 7, 2004.

Discover Venezuela. "Los Llanos." Available online. URL: http:// www.discovervenezuela.com/losllanos/cfm. Accessed September 1, 2003.

Dudenhoefer, David. "On Once Ignored Lands Brazilian Farmers Find Money Grows on Trees." *Choices: The Human Development Magazine*. United Nations Development Program. Available online. URL: http://www.undp.org/dpa/choices/2003/june/brazil. html. Accessed September 2, 2003.

Ebeling, Walter. *The Fruited Plain: The Story of American Agriculture*. Berkeley: University of California Press, 1979.

Ford, Fred. "Brigalow Tropical Savanna (AA0702)," World Wildlife Fund. Available online. URL: http://www.worldwildlife.org/ wildworld/profiles/terrestrial/aa/aa0702_full.html. Accessed September 4, 2003.

———. "Mitchell Grass Downs (AA0707)," World Wildlife Fund. Available online. URL: http://www.worldwildlife.org/wildworld/ profiles/terrestrial/aa/aa0707_full.html. Accessed September 4, 2003.

The George Perkins Marsh Institute, Clark University, "George Perkins Marsh: Renaissance Vermonter." Available online. URL: http://www.clarku.edu/departments/marsh/georgemarsh.shtml. Accessed July 21, 2004.

Granger, Ed, and George Bredenkamp. "Grassland Biome: Alti Mountain Grassland," United Nations Environment Program/ GRID-Arendal. Available online. URL: http://www.ngo.grida. no/soesa/nsoer/Data/vegrsa/veg46.htm. Accessed September 5, 2003.

The Green Lane, Environment Canada, "Prairie Conservation Action Plan." Available online. URL: http://www.pnr-rpn. ec.gc.ca/nature/whp/df00s06.en.html. Last reviewed and updated April 14, 2004.

Hancock, Paul L., and Brian J. Skinner, eds. *The Oxford Companion to the Earth*. New York: Oxford University Press, 2000.

Hudson, Peter J., and Ottar N. Bjørnstad. "Vole Stranglers and Lemming Cycles." *Science* 31 (October 2003): 797–798.

Illinois Department of Natural Resources. "Prairies of illinois." Available online. URL: http://dnr.state.il.us/conservation/natural heritage/florafauna/document.htm. Accessed April 28, 2005.

Kohistani, Razwal. "Lesser Known Tribes of Indus Kohistan, NWFP, Pakistan." Available online. URL: http://www.geocities.com/razwal/prod05.htm. Last modified March 1, 2005.

Luhr, James F., ed. *Earth.* New York: Dorling Kindersley in association with The Smithsonian Institution, 2003.

Magin, Chris. "Sahelian Acacia Savanna (AT0713)." World Wildlife Fund. Available online. URL: http://www.worldwildlife.org/wildworld/profiles/terrestrial/at/at0713_full.html. Accessed September 3, 2003.

———. "West Sudanian Savanna (AT0722)." World Wildlife Fund. Available online. URL: http://www.worldwildlife.org/wildworld/profiles/terrestrial/at/at0722_full.html. Accessed September 3, 2003.

Marques, João José, "Cerrado Soils: An Introduction." Departamento de Ciência do Solo, Universidad Federal de Lavras. Available online. URL: http://www.dcs.ufla.br/cerrado/introd2.htm. Accessed April 29, 2005.

Marsh, G. P. *Man and Nature.* 1864. Annotated reprint, Cambridge, Mass.: Harvard University Press, 1965.

———. *The Earth as Modified by Human Action: Man and Nature.* 1874. Reprint, New York: Scribner, Armstrong, 1976.

Melamari, Lota. "Discover Serengeti." Tanzanian National Parks Official Site: Serengeti. Available online. URL: http://www.serengeti.org. Accessed April 29, 2005.

Moore, David M., ed. *Green Planet.* New York: Cambridge University Press, 1982.

Morrison, John. "Central Range Subalpine Grasslands (AA1002)." World Wildlife Fund. Available online. URL: http://www.worldwildlife.org/wildworld/profiles/terrestrial/aa/aa1002a.html. Accessed September 4, 2003.

National Weather Service Forecast Office, Louisville, Ky. "Structure and Dynamics of Supercell Thunderstorms." Available online. URL: http://www.crh.noaa.gov/lmk/soo/docu/supercell.htm. Accessed September 25, 2003.

Office of Technology Assessment. *Technologies to Maintain Biological Diversity.* Washington, D.C.: U.S. Government Printing Office, 1987.

Pérez, E. M., and L. Bulla. "Llanos (NT0709)," World Wildlife Fund. Available online. URL: http://www.worldwildlife.org/wildworld/profiles/terrestrial/nt/nt0709_full.html. Accessed September 1, 2003.

Peterken, George F. *Natural Woodland: Ecology and Conservation in Northern Temperate Regions.* Cambridge: Cambridge University Press, 1996.

Republic of Turkey Ministry of Culture and Tourism. "Transhumance in Turkey." Available online. URL: http://www.kulturturizm.gov.tr/portal/kultur_en.assp?belgeno=8874. Accessed September 5, 2003.

Secretariat of the Convention on Biological Diversity, United Nations Environment Program. "Convention on Biological Diversity." Available online. URL: http://www.biodiv.org. Updated June 10, 2004.

Sinclair, A. R. E., Simon Mduma, and Julian S. Brashares. "Patterns of Predation in a Diverse Predator–Prey System." *Nature* 425 (September 18, 2003): 288–290.

Thurston High School Ninth Graders. "Grassland." Thurston High School. Available online. URL: http://ths.sps.lane.edu/biomes/grassland3/grassland3.html. Accessed August 25, 2003.

Waldman, Carl. *Encyclopedia of Native American Tribes.* Rev. ed. New York: Facts On File, 1999.

Williams, Jack. "Supercells Are the Kings of Thunderstorms," *USA Today.* Available online. URL: http://www.usatoday.com/weather/wtsm2.htm. Posted April 4, 2005.

Wilmette Public Schools Fourth Grade Social Studies, "The Grassland." Wilmette Public Schools. Available online. URL: http://wilmette.nttc.org/central/resource/worldregions/grass.html. Last updated April 5, 2005.

Wilson, E. O. *The Diversity of Life.* Cambridge, Mass.: Belknap Press of Harvard University Press, 1992.

World Wildlife Fund Brasil. "Cerrado." Available online. URL: http://www.wwf.org.br/english/bioma/bioma.asp?item=13. Accessed September 2, 2003.

Note: *Italic* page numbers refer to illustrations.